29.95

ISBN 0-8373-0204-8

C-204 CAREER EXAMINATION SERIES

This is your PASSBOOK® for...

Deputy Sheriff

Test Preparation Study Guide

Questions & Answers

National Learning Corporation

212 Michael Drive, Syosset, New York 11791

(516) 921-8888
(800) 645-6337
FAX: (516) 921-8743
www.passbooks.com
sales @ passbooks.com
info @ passbooks.com

PRINTED IN THE UNITED STATES OF AMERICA

PASSBOOK®

NOTICE

This book is SOLELY intended for, is sold ONLY to, and its use is RESTRICTED to *individual*, bona fide applicants or candidates who qualify by virtue of having seriously filed applications for appropriate license, certificate, professional and/or promotional advancement, higher school matriculation, scholarship, or other legitimate requirements of educational and/or governmental authorities.

This book is NOT intended for use, class instruction, tutoring, training, duplication, copying, reprinting, excerption, or adaptation, etc., by:

(1) Other publishers

(2) Proprietors and/or Instructors of "Coaching" and/or Preparatory Courses

(3) Personnel and/or Training Divisions of commercial, industrial, and governmental organizations

(4) Schools, colleges, or universities and/or their departments and staffs, including teachers and other personnel

(5) Testing Agencies or Bureaus

(6) Study groups which seek by the purchase of a single volume to copy and/or duplicate and/or adapt this material for use by the group as a whole without having purchased individual volumes for each of the members of the group

(7) Et al.

Such persons would be in violation of appropriate Federal and State statutes.

PROVISION OF LICENSING AGREEMENTS. — Recognized educational commercial, industrial, and governmental institutions and organizations, and others legitimately engaged in educational pursuits, including training, testing, and measurement activities, may address a request for a licensing agreement to the copyright owners, who will determine whether, and under what conditions, including fees and charges, the materials in this book may be used by them. In other words, a licensing facility exists for the legitimate use of the material in this book on other than an individual basis. However, it is asseverated and affirmed here that the material in this book *CANNOT* be used without the receipt of the express permission of such a licensing agreement from the Publishers.

NATIONAL LEARNING CORPORATION
212 Michael Drive
Syosset, New York 11791

Inquiries re licensing agreements should be addressed to:
The President
National Learning Corporation
212 Michael Drive
Syosset, New York 11791

PASSBOOK SERIES®

THE *PASSBOOK SERIES®* has been created to prepare applicants and candidates for the ultimate academic battlefield – the examination room.

At some time in our lives, each and every one of us may be required to take an examination – for validation, matriculation, admission, qualification, registration, certification, or licensure.

Based on the assumption that every applicant or candidate has met the basic formal educational standards, has taken the required number of courses, and read the necessary texts, the *PASSBOOK SERIES®* furnishes the one special preparation which may assure passing with confidence, instead of failing with insecurity. Examination questions – together with answers – are furnished as the basic vehicle for study so that the mysteries of the examination and its compounding difficulties may be eliminated or diminished by a sure method.

This book is meant to help you pass your examination provided that you qualify and are serious in your objective.

The entire field is reviewed through the huge store of content information which is succinctly presented through a provocative and challenging approach – the question-and-answer method.

A climate of success is established by furnishing the correct answers at the end of each test.

You soon learn to recognize types of questions, forms of questions, and patterns of questioning. You may even begin to anticipate expected outcomes.

You perceive that many questions are repeated or adapted so that you can gain acute insights, which may enable you to score many sure points.

You learn how to confront new questions, or types of questions, and to attack them confidently and work out the correct answers.

You note objectives and emphases, and recognize pitfalls and dangers, so that you may make positive educational adjustments.

Moreover, you are kept fully informed in relation to new concepts, methods, practices, and directions in the field.

You discover that you are actually taking the examination all the time: you are preparing for the examination by “taking” an examination, not by reading extraneous and/or supererogatory textbooks.

In short, this PASSBOOK®, used directedly, should be an important factor in helping you to pass your test.

DEPUTY SHERIFF

DUTIES

This is a law enforcement position in the Sheriff's Office responsible for serving various summonses and complaints and carrying out court ordered Civil actions including, but not limited to, enforcing seizures, making civil arrests, evictions, observing clients to ensure compliance with court orders, pursuing offenders, and restraining and searching suspects.

Also may serves legal processes, transports prisoners and guard's prisoners in court. Makes periodic inspections of the jail. May work on special assignment as directed by superiors and works closely with federal, state, city and local police authorities in the exchange of information and the enforcement of law and order. May assist in the investigation of violations of law and the apprehension of criminals. Employees in this class are responsible for the efficient performance of routing patrol duties in a specified area of the county during a designated shift and on a temporary assignment basis to various other functions within the department including boat patrol, radar speed control and criminal investigations. Incumbents are required to carry firearms and apply modern scientific police methods and procedures to investigative and surveillance duties. In addition, incumbents perform civil enforcement duties and are responsible for the serving of civil process. The work is performed under general supervision of a higher ranking patrol officer with considerable independent responsibility allowed for exercise of sound judgment in normal work situations and emergencies. Does related work as required.

SCOPE OF THE EXAMINATION

The written test will cover knowledge, skills, and/or abilities in such areas as:

1. Reasoning clearly and making sound decisions related to law enforcement;
2. Following directions (maps);
3. Understanding and interpreting written material;
4. Preparing written material; and
5. Office record keeping

HOW TO TAKE A TEST

I. YOU MUST PASS AN EXAMINATION

A. WHAT EVERY CANDIDATE SHOULD KNOW

Examination applicants often ask us for help in preparing for the written test. What can I study in advance? What kinds of questions will be asked? How will the test be given? How will the papers be graded?

As an applicant for a civil service examination, you may be wondering about some of these things. Our purpose here is to suggest effective methods of advance study and to describe civil service examinations.

Your chances for success on this examination can be increased if you know how to prepare. Those "pre-examination jitters" can be reduced if you know what to expect. You can even experience an adventure in good citizenship if you know why civil service exams are given.

B. WHY ARE CIVIL SERVICE EXAMINATIONS GIVEN?

Civil service examinations are important to you in two ways. As a citizen, you want public jobs filled by employees who know how to do their work. As a job seeker, you want a fair chance to compete for that job on an equal footing with other candidates. The best-known means of accomplishing this two-fold goal is the competitive examination.

Exams are widely publicized throughout the nation. They may be administered for jobs in federal, state, city, municipal, town or village governments or agencies.

Any citizen may apply, with some limitations, such as the age or residence of applicants. Your experience and education may be reviewed to see whether you meet the requirements for the particular examination. When these requirements exist, they are reasonable and applied consistently to all applicants. Thus, a competitive examination may cause you some uneasiness now, but it is your privilege and safeguard.

C. HOW ARE CIVIL SERVICE EXAMS DEVELOPED?

Examinations are carefully written by trained technicians who are specialists in the field known as "psychological measurement," in consultation with recognized authorities in the field of work that the test will cover. These experts recommend the subject matter areas or skills to be tested; only those knowledges or skills important to your success on the job are included. The most reliable books and source materials available are used as references. Together, the experts and technicians judge the difficulty level of the questions.

Test technicians know how to phrase questions so that the problem is clearly stated. Their ethics do not permit "trick" or "catch" questions. Questions may have been tried out on sample groups, or subjected to statistical analysis, to determine their usefulness.

Written tests are often used in combination with performance tests, ratings of training and experience, and oral interviews. All of these measures combine to form the best-known means of finding the right person for the right job.

II. HOW TO PASS THE WRITTEN TEST

A. NATURE OF THE EXAMINATION

To prepare intelligently for civil service examinations, you should know how they differ from school examinations you have taken. In school you were assigned certain definite pages to read or subjects to cover. The examination questions were quite detailed and usually emphasized memory. Civil service exams, on the other hand, try to discover your present ability to perform the duties of a position, plus your potentiality to learn these duties. In other words, a civil service exam attempts to predict how successful you will be. Questions cover such a broad area that they cannot be as minute and detailed as school exam questions.

In the public service similar kinds of work, or positions, are grouped together in one "class." This process is known as *position-classification*. All the positions in a class are paid according to the salary range for that class. One class title covers all of these positions, and they are all tested by the same examination.

B. FOUR BASIC STEPS

1) Study the announcement

How, then, can you know what subjects to study? Our best answer is: "Learn as much as possible about the class of positions for which you've applied." The exam will test the knowledge, skills and abilities needed to do the work.

Your most valuable source of information about the position you want is the official exam announcement. This announcement lists the training and experience qualifications. Check these standards and apply only if you come reasonably close to meeting them.

The brief description of the position in the examination announcement offers some clues to the subjects which will be tested. Think about the job itself. Review the duties in your mind. Can you perform them, or are there some in which you are rusty? Fill in the blank spots in your preparation.

Many jurisdictions preview the written test in the exam announcement by including a section called "Knowledge and Abilities Required," "Scope of the Examination," or some similar heading. Here you will find out specifically what fields will be tested.

2) Review your own background

Once you learn in general what the position is all about, and what you need to know to do the work, ask yourself which subjects you already know fairly well and which need improvement. You may wonder whether to concentrate on improving your strong areas or on building some background in your fields of weakness. When the announcement has specified "some knowledge" or "considerable knowledge," or has used adjectives like "beginning principles of..." or "advanced ... methods," you can get a clue as to the number and difficulty of questions to be asked in any given field. More questions, and hence broader coverage, would be included for those subjects which are more important in the work. Now weigh your strengths and weaknesses against the job requirements and prepare accordingly.

3) Determine the level of the position

Another way to tell how intensively you should prepare is to understand the level of the job for which you are applying. Is it the entering level? In other words, is this the position in which beginners in a field of work are hired? Or is it an intermediate or advanced level? Sometimes this is indicated by such words as "Junior" or "Senior" in the class title. Other jurisdictions use Roman numerals to designate the level – Clerk I, Clerk II, for example. The word "Supervisor" sometimes appears in the title. If the level is not indicated by the title, check the description of duties. Will you be working under very close supervision, or will you have responsibility for independent decisions in this work?

4) Choose appropriate study materials

Now that you know the subjects to be examined and the relative amount of each subject to be covered, you can choose suitable study materials. For beginning level jobs, or even advanced ones, if you have a pronounced weakness in some aspect of your training, read a modern, standard textbook in that field. Be sure it is up to date and has general coverage. Such books are normally available at your library, and the librarian will be glad to help you locate one. For entry-level positions, questions of appropriate difficulty are chosen – neither highly advanced questions, nor those too simple. Such questions require careful thought but not advanced training.

If the position for which you are applying is technical or advanced, you will read more advanced, specialized material. If you are already familiar with the basic principles of your field, elementary textbooks would waste your time. Concentrate on advanced textbooks and technical periodicals. Think through the concepts and review difficult problems in your field.

These are all general sources. You can get more ideas on your own initiative, following these leads. For example, training manuals and publications of the government agency which employs workers in your field can be useful, particularly for technical and professional positions. A letter or visit to the government department involved may result in more specific study suggestions, and certainly will provide you with a more definite idea of the exact nature of the position you are seeking.

III. KINDS OF TESTS

Tests are used for purposes other than measuring knowledge and ability to perform specified duties. For some positions, it is equally important to test ability to make adjustments to new situations or to profit from training. In others, basic mental abilities not dependent on information are essential. Questions which test these things may not appear as pertinent to the duties of the position as those which test for knowledge and information. Yet they are often highly important parts of a fair examination. For very general questions, it is almost impossible to help you direct your study efforts. What we can do is to point out some of the more common of these general abilities needed in public service positions and describe some typical questions.

1) General information

Broad, general information has been found useful for predicting job success in some kinds of work. This is tested in a variety of ways, from vocabulary lists to questions about current events. Basic background in some field of work, such as sociology or economics, may be sampled in a group of questions. Often these are principles which have become familiar to most persons through exposure rather than through formal training. It is difficult to advise you how to study for these questions; being alert to the world around you is our best suggestion.

2) Verbal ability

An example of an ability needed in many positions is verbal or language ability. Verbal ability is, in brief, the ability to use and understand words. Vocabulary and grammar tests are typical measures of this ability. Reading comprehension or paragraph interpretation questions are common in many kinds of civil service tests. You are given a paragraph of written material and asked to find its central meaning.

3) Numerical ability

Number skills can be tested by the familiar arithmetic problem, by checking paired lists of numbers to see which are alike and which are different, or by interpreting charts and graphs. In the latter test, a graph may be printed in the test booklet which you are asked to use as the basis for answering questions.

4) Observation

A popular test for law-enforcement positions is the observation test. A picture is shown to you for several minutes, then taken away. Questions about the picture test your ability to observe both details and larger elements.

5) Following directions

In many positions in the public service, the employee must be able to carry out written instructions dependably and accurately. You may be given a chart with several columns, each column listing a variety of information. The questions require you to carry out directions involving the information given in the chart.

6) Skills and aptitudes

Performance tests effectively measure some manual skills and aptitudes. When the skill is one in which you are trained, such as typing or shorthand, you can practice. These tests are often very much like those given in business school or high school courses. For many of the other skills and aptitudes, however, no short-time preparation can be made. Skills and abilities natural to you or that you have developed throughout your lifetime are being tested.

Many of the general questions just described provide all the data needed to answer the questions and ask you to use your reasoning ability to find the answers. Your best preparation for these tests, as well as for tests of facts and ideas, is to be at your physical and mental best. You, no doubt, have your own methods of getting into an exam-taking mood and keeping "in shape." The next section lists some ideas on this subject.

IV. KINDS OF QUESTIONS

Only rarely is the "essay" question, which you answer in narrative form, used in civil service tests. Civil service tests are usually of the short-answer type. Full instructions for answering these questions will be given to you at the examination. But in case this is your first experience with short-answer questions and separate answer sheets, here is what you need to know:

1) Multiple-choice Questions

Most popular of the short-answer questions is the "multiple choice" or "best answer" question. It can be used, for example, to test for factual knowledge, ability to solve problems or judgment in meeting situations found at work.

A multiple-choice question is normally one of three types—

- It can begin with an incomplete statement followed by several possible endings. You are to find the one ending which *best* completes the statement, although some of the others may not be entirely wrong.
- It can also be a complete statement in the form of a question which is answered by choosing one of the statements listed.
- It can be in the form of a problem – again you select the best answer.

Here is an example of a multiple-choice question with a discussion which should give you some clues as to the method for choosing the right answer:

When an employee has a complaint about his assignment, the action which will *best* help him overcome his difficulty is to

A. discuss his difficulty with his coworkers
B. take the problem to the head of the organization
C. take the problem to the person who gave him the assignment
D. say nothing to anyone about his complaint

In answering this question, you should study each of the choices to find which is best. Consider choice "A" – Certainly an employee may discuss his complaint with fellow employees, but no change or improvement can result, and the complaint remains unresolved. Choice "B" is a poor choice since the head of the organization probably does not know what assignment you have been given, and taking your problem to him is known as "going over the head" of the supervisor. The supervisor, or person who made the assignment, is the person who can clarify it or correct any injustice. Choice "C" is, therefore, correct. To say nothing, as in choice "D," is unwise. Supervisors have and interest in knowing the problems employees are facing, and the employee is seeking a solution to his problem.

2) True/False Questions

The "true/false" or "right/wrong" form of question is sometimes used. Here a complete statement is given. Your job is to decide whether the statement is right or wrong.

SAMPLE: A person-to-person long-distance telephone call costs less than a station-to-station call to the same city.

This statement is wrong, or false, since person-to-person calls are more expensive.

This is not a complete list of all possible question forms, although most of the others are variations of these common types. You will always get complete directions for answering questions. Be sure you understand *how* to mark your answers – ask questions until you do.

V. RECORDING YOUR ANSWERS

For an examination with very few applicants, you may be told to record your answers in the test booklet itself. Separate answer sheets are much more common. If this separate answer sheet is to be scored by machine – and this is often the case – it is highly important that you mark your answers correctly in order to get credit.

An electric scoring machine is often used in civil service offices because of the speed with which papers can be scored. Machine-scored answer sheets must be marked with a pencil, which will be given to you. This pencil has a high graphite content which responds to the electric scoring machine. As a matter of fact, stray dots may register as answers, so do not let your pencil rest on the answer sheet while you are pondering the correct answer. Also, if your pencil lead breaks or is otherwise defective, ask for another.

Since the answer sheet will be dropped in a slot in the scoring machine, be careful not to bend the corners or get the paper crumpled.

The answer sheet normally has five vertical columns of numbers, with 30 numbers to a column. These numbers correspond to the question numbers in your test booklet. After each number, going across the page are four or five pairs of dotted lines. These short dotted lines have small letters or numbers above them. The first two pairs may also have a "T" or "F" above the letters. This indicates that the first two pairs only are to be used if the questions are of the true-false type. If the questions are multiple choice, disregard the "T" and "F" and pay attention only to the small letters or numbers.

Answer your questions in the manner of the sample that follows:

32. The largest city in the United States is
    - A. Washington, D.C.
    - B. New York City
    - C. Chicago
    - D. Detroit
    - E. San Francisco

1) Choose the answer you think is best. (New York City is the largest, so "B" is correct.)
2) Find the row of dotted lines numbered the same as the question you are answering. (Find row number 32)
3) Find the pair of dotted lines corresponding to the answer. (Find the pair of lines under the mark "B.")
4) Make a solid black mark between the dotted lines.

VI. BEFORE THE TEST

Common sense will help you find procedures to follow to get ready for an examination. Too many of us, however, overlook these sensible measures. Indeed, nervousness and fatigue have been found to be the most serious reasons why applicants fail to do their best on civil service tests. Here is a list of reminders:

- Begin your preparation early – Don't wait until the last minute to go scurrying around for books and materials or to find out what the position is all about.
- Prepare continuously – An hour a night for a week is better than an all-night cram session. This has been definitely established. What is more, a night a

week for a month will return better dividends than crowding your study into a shorter period of time.

- Locate the place of the exam – You have been sent a notice telling you when and where to report for the examination. If the location is in a different town or otherwise unfamiliar to you, it would be well to inquire the best route and learn something about the building.
- Relax the night before the test – Allow your mind to rest. Do not study at all that night. Plan some mild recreation or diversion; then go to bed early and get a good night's sleep.
- Get up early enough to make a leisurely trip to the place for the test – This way unforeseen events, traffic snarls, unfamiliar buildings, etc. will not upset you.
- Dress comfortably – A written test is not a fashion show. You will be known by number and not by name, so wear something comfortable.
- Leave excess paraphernalia at home – Shopping bags and odd bundles will get in your way. You need bring only the items mentioned in the official notice you received; usually everything you need is provided. Do not bring reference books to the exam. They will only confuse those last minutes and be taken away from you when in the test room.
- Arrive somewhat ahead of time – If because of transportation schedules you must get there very early, bring a newspaper or magazine to take your mind off yourself while waiting.
- Locate the examination room – When you have found the proper room, you will be directed to the seat or part of the room where you will sit. Sometimes you are given a sheet of instructions to read while you are waiting. Do not fill out any forms until you are told to do so; just read them and be prepared.
- Relax and prepare to listen to the instructions
- If you have any physical problem that may keep you from doing your best, be sure to tell the test administrator. If you are sick or in poor health, you really cannot do your best on the exam. You can come back and take the test some other time.

VII. AT THE TEST

The day of the test is here and you have the test booklet in your hand. The temptation to get going is very strong. Caution! There is more to success than knowing the right answers. You must know how to identify your papers and understand variations in the type of short-answer question used in this particular examination. Follow these suggestions for maximum results from your efforts:

1) Cooperate with the monitor

The test administrator has a duty to create a situation in which you can be as much at ease as possible. He will give instructions, tell you when to begin, check to see that you are marking your answer sheet correctly, and so on. He is not there to guard you, although he will see that your competitors do not take unfair advantage. He wants to help you do your best.

2) Listen to all instructions

Don't jump the gun! Wait until you understand all directions. In most civil service tests you get more time than you need to answer the questions. So don't be in a hurry.

Read each word of instructions until you clearly understand the meaning. Study the examples, listen to all announcements and follow directions. Ask questions if you do not understand what to do.

3) Identify your papers

Civil service exams are usually identified by number only. You will be assigned a number; you must not put your name on your test papers. Be sure to copy your number correctly. Since more than one exam may be given, copy your exact examination title.

4) Plan your time

Unless you are told that a test is a "speed" or "rate of work" test, speed itself is usually not important. Time enough to answer all the questions will be provided, but this does not mean that you have all day. An overall time limit has been set. Divide the total time (in minutes) by the number of questions to determine the approximate time you have for each question.

5) Do not linger over difficult questions

If you come across a difficult question, mark it with a paper clip (useful to have along) and come back to it when you have been through the booklet. One caution if you do this – be sure to skip a number on your answer sheet as well. Check often to be sure that you have not lost your place and that you are marking in the row numbered the same as the question you are answering.

6) Read the questions

Be sure you know what the question asks! Many capable people are unsuccessful because they failed to *read* the questions correctly.

7) Answer all questions

Unless you have been instructed that a penalty will be deducted for incorrect answers, it is better to guess than to omit a question.

8) Speed tests

It is often better NOT to guess on speed tests. It has been found that on timed tests people are tempted to spend the last few seconds before time is called in marking answers at random – without even reading them – in the hope of picking up a few extra points. To discourage this practice, the instructions may warn you that your score will be "corrected" for guessing. That is, a penalty will be applied. The incorrect answers will be deducted from the correct ones, or some other penalty formula will be used.

9) Review your answers

If you finish before time is called, go back to the questions you guessed or omitted to give them further thought. Review other answers if you have time.

10) Return your test materials

If you are ready to leave before others have finished or time is called, take ALL your materials to the monitor and leave quietly. Never take any test material with you. The monitor can discover whose papers are not complete, and taking a test booklet may be grounds for disqualification.

VIII. EXAMINATION TECHNIQUES

1) Read the general instructions carefully. These are usually printed on the first page of the exam booklet. As a rule, these instructions refer to the timing of the examination; the fact that you should not start work until the signal and must stop work at a signal, etc. If there are any *special* instructions, such as a choice of questions to be answered, make sure that you note this instruction carefully.

2) When you are ready to start work on the examination, that is as soon as the signal has been given, read the instructions to each question booklet, underline any key words or phrases, such as *least*, *best*, *outline*, *describe* and the like. In this way you will tend to answer as requested rather than discover on reviewing your paper that you *listed without describing*, that you selected the *worst* choice rather than the *best* choice, etc.

3) If the examination is of the objective or multiple-choice type – that is, each question will also give a series of possible answers: A, B, C or D, and you are called upon to select the best answer and write the letter next to that answer on your answer paper – it is advisable to start answering each question in turn. There may be anywhere from 50 to 100 such questions in the three or four hours allotted and you can see how much time would be taken if you read through all the questions before beginning to answer any. Furthermore, if you come across a question or group of questions which you know would be difficult to answer, it would undoubtedly affect your handling of all the other questions.

4) If the examination is of the essay type and contains but a few questions, it is a moot point as to whether you should read all the questions before starting to answer any one. Of course, if you are given a choice – say five out of seven and the like – then it is essential to read all the questions so you can eliminate the two that are most difficult. If, however, you are asked to answer all the questions, there may be danger in trying to answer the easiest one first because you may find that you will spend too much time on it. The best technique is to answer the first question, then proceed to the second, etc.

5) Time your answers. Before the exam begins, write down the time it started, then add the time allowed for the examination and write down the time it must be completed, then divide the time available somewhat as follows:
   - If 3-1/2 hours are allowed, that would be 210 minutes. If you have 80 objective-type questions, that would be an average of 2-1/2 minutes per question. Allow yourself no more than 2 minutes per question, or a total of 160 minutes, which will permit about 50 minutes to review.
   - If for the time allotment of 210 minutes there are 7 essay questions to answer, that would average about 30 minutes a question. Give yourself only 25 minutes per question so that you have about 35 minutes to review.

6) The most important instruction is to *read each question* and make sure you know what is wanted. The second most important instruction is to *time yourself properly* so that you answer every question. The third most

important instruction is to *answer every question*. Guess if you have to but include something for each question. Remember that you will receive no credit for a blank and will probably receive some credit if you write something in answer to an essay question. If you guess a letter – say "B" for a multiple-choice question – you may have guessed right. If you leave a blank as an answer to a multiple-choice question, the examiners may respect your feelings but it will not add a point to your score. Some exams may penalize you for wrong answers, so in such cases *only*, you may not want to guess unless you have some basis for your answer.

7) Suggestions

a. Objective-type questions

1. Examine the question booklet for proper sequence of pages and questions
2. Read all instructions carefully
3. Skip any question which seems too difficult; return to it after all other questions have been answered
4. Apportion your time properly; do not spend too much time on any single question or group of questions
5. Note and underline key words – *all, most, fewest, least, best, worst, same, opposite,* etc.
6. Pay particular attention to negatives
7. Note unusual option, e.g., unduly long, short, complex, different or similar in content to the body of the question
8. Observe the use of "hedging" words – *probably, may, most likely,* etc.
9. Make sure that your answer is put next to the same number as the question
10. Do not second-guess unless you have good reason to believe the second answer is definitely more correct
11. Cross out original answer if you decide another answer is more accurate; do not erase until you are ready to hand your paper in
12. Answer all questions; guess unless instructed otherwise
13. Leave time for review

b. Essay questions

1. Read each question carefully
2. Determine exactly what is wanted. Underline key words or phrases.
3. Decide on outline or paragraph answer
4. Include many different points and elements unless asked to develop any one or two points or elements
5. Show impartiality by giving pros and cons unless directed to select one side only
6. Make and write down any assumptions you find necessary to answer the questions
7. Watch your English, grammar, punctuation and choice of words
8. Time your answers; don't crowd material

8) Answering the essay question

Most essay questions can be answered by framing the specific response around several key words or ideas. Here are a few such key words or ideas:

M's: manpower, materials, methods, money, management

P's: purpose, program, policy, plan, procedure, practice, problems, pitfalls, personnel, public relations

a. Six basic steps in handling problems:
   1. Preliminary plan and background development
   2. Collect information, data and facts
   3. Analyze and interpret information, data and facts
   4. Analyze and develop solutions as well as make recommendations
   5. Prepare report and sell recommendations
   6. Install recommendations and follow up effectiveness

b. Pitfalls to avoid
   1. *Taking things for granted* – A statement of the situation does not necessarily imply that each of the elements is necessarily true; for example, a complaint may be invalid and biased so that all that can be taken for granted is that a complaint has been registered
   2. *Considering only one side of a situation* – Wherever possible, indicate several alternatives and then point out the reasons you selected the best one
   3. *Failing to indicate follow up* – Whenever your answer indicates action on your part, make certain that you will take proper follow-up action to see how successful your recommendations, procedures or actions turn out to be
   4. *Taking too long in answering any single question* – Remember to time your answers properly

IX. AFTER THE TEST

Scoring procedures differ in detail among civil service jurisdictions although the general principles are the same. Whether the papers are hand-scored or graded by machine we have described, they are nearly always graded by number. That is, the person who marks the paper knows only the number – never the name – of the applicant. Not until all the papers have been graded will they be matched with names. If other tests, such as training and experience or oral interview ratings have been given, scores will be combined. Different parts of the examination usually have different weights. For example, the written test might count 60 percent of the final grade, and a rating of training and experience 40 percent. In many jurisdictions, veterans will have a certain number of points added to their grades.

After the final grade has been determined, the names are placed in grade order and an eligible list is established. There are various methods for resolving ties between those who get the same final grade – probably the most common is to place first the name of the person whose application was received first. Job offers are made from the eligible list in the order the names appear on it. You will be notified of your grade and your rank as soon as all these computations have been made. This will be done as rapidly as possible.

People who are found to meet the requirements in the announcement are called "eligibles." Their names are put on a list of eligible candidates. An eligible's chances of getting a job depend on how high he stands on this list and how fast agencies are filling jobs from the list.

When a job is to be filled from a list of eligibles, the agency asks for the names of people on the list of eligibles for that job. When the civil service commission receives this request, it sends to the agency the names of the three people highest on this list. Or, if the job to be filled has specialized requirements, the office sends the agency the names of the top three persons who meet these requirements from the general list.

The appointing officer makes a choice from among the three people whose names were sent to him. If the selected person accepts the appointment, the names of the others are put back on the list to be considered for future openings.

That is the rule in hiring from all kinds of eligible lists, whether they are for typist, carpenter, chemist, or something else. For every vacancy, the appointing officer has his choice of any one of the top three eligibles on the list. This explains why the person whose name is on top of the list sometimes does not get an appointment when some of the persons lower on the list do. If the appointing officer chooses the second or third eligible, the No. 1 eligible does not get a job at once, but stays on the list until he is appointed or the list is terminated.

X. HOW TO PASS THE INTERVIEW TEST

The examination for which you applied requires an oral interview test. You have already taken the written test and you are now being called for the interview test – the final part of the formal examination.

You may think that it is not possible to prepare for an interview test and that there are no procedures to follow during an interview. Our purpose is to point out some things you can do in advance that will help you and some good rules to follow and pitfalls to avoid while you are being interviewed.

What is an interview supposed to test?

The written examination is designed to test the technical knowledge and competence of the candidate; the oral is designed to evaluate intangible qualities, not readily measured otherwise, and to establish a list showing the relative fitness of each candidate – as measured against his competitors – for the position sought. Scoring is not on the basis of "right" and "wrong," but on a sliding scale of values ranging from "not passable" to "outstanding." As a matter of fact, it is possible to achieve a relatively low score without a single "incorrect" answer because of evident weakness in the qualities being measured.

Occasionally, an examination may consist entirely of an oral test – either an individual or a group oral. In such cases, information is sought concerning the technical knowledges and abilities of the candidate, since there has been no written examination for this purpose. More commonly, however, an oral test is used to supplement a written examination.

Who conducts interviews?

The composition of oral boards varies among different jurisdictions. In nearly all, a representative of the personnel department serves as chairman. One of the members of the board may be a representative of the department in which the candidate would work. In some cases, "outside experts" are used, and, frequently, a businessman or some other representative of the general public is asked to serve. Labor and management or other special groups may be represented. The aim is to secure the services of experts in the appropriate field.

However the board is composed, it is a good idea (and not at all improper or unethical) to ascertain in advance of the interview who the members are and what groups they represent. When you are introduced to them, you will have some idea of their backgrounds and interests, and at least you will not stutter and stammer over their names.

What should be done before the interview?

While knowledge about the board members is useful and takes some of the surprise element out of the interview, there is other preparation which is more substantive. It *is* possible to prepare for an oral interview – in several ways:

1) Keep a copy of your application and review it carefully before the interview

This may be the only document before the oral board, and the starting point of the interview. Know what education and experience you have listed there, and the sequence and dates of all of it. Sometimes the board will ask you to review the highlights of your experience for them; you should not have to hem and haw doing it.

2) Study the class specification and the examination announcement

Usually, the oral board has one or both of these to guide them. The qualities, characteristics or knowledges required by the position sought are stated in these documents. They offer valuable clues as to the nature of the oral interview. For example, if the job involves supervisory responsibilities, the announcement will usually indicate that knowledge of modern supervisory methods and the qualifications of the candidate as a supervisor will be tested. If so, you can expect such questions, frequently in the form of a hypothetical situation which you are expected to solve. NEVER go into an oral without knowledge of the duties and responsibilities of the job you seek.

3) Think through each qualification required

Try to visualize the kind of questions you would ask if you were a board member. How well could you answer them? Try especially to appraise your own knowledge and background in each area, *measured against the job sought*, and identify any areas in which you are weak. Be critical and realistic – do not flatter yourself.

4) Do some general reading in areas in which you feel you may be weak

For example, if the job involves supervision and your past experience has NOT, some general reading in supervisory methods and practices, particularly in the field of human relations, might be useful. Do NOT study agency procedures or detailed manuals. The oral board will be testing your understanding and capacity, not your memory.

5) Get a good night's sleep and watch your general health and mental attitude

You will want a clear head at the interview. Take care of a cold or any other minor ailment, and of course, no hangovers.

What should be done on the day of the interview?

Now comes the day of the interview itself. Give yourself plenty of time to get there. Plan to arrive somewhat ahead of the scheduled time, particularly if your appointment is in the fore part of the day. If a previous candidate fails to appear, the board might be ready for you a bit early. By early afternoon an oral board is almost invariably behind schedule if there are many candidates, and you may have to wait.

Take along a book or magazine to read, or your application to review, but leave any extraneous material in the waiting room when you go in for your interview. In any event, relax and compose yourself.

The matter of dress is important. The board is forming impressions about you – from your experience, your manners, your attitude, and your appearance. Give your personal appearance careful attention. Dress your best, but not your flashiest. Choose conservative, appropriate clothing, and be sure it is immaculate. This is a business interview, and your appearance should indicate that you regard it as such. Besides, being well groomed and properly dressed will help boost your confidence.

Sooner or later, someone will call your name and escort you into the interview room. *This is it.* From here on you are on your own. It is too late for any more preparation. But remember, you asked for this opportunity to prove your fitness, and you are here because your request was granted.

What happens when you go in?

The usual sequence of events will be as follows: The clerk (who is often the board stenographer) will introduce you to the chairman of the oral board, who will introduce you to the other members of the board. Acknowledge the introductions before you sit down. Do not be surprised if you find a microphone facing you or a stenotypist sitting by. Oral interviews are usually recorded in the event of an appeal or other review.

Usually the chairman of the board will open the interview by reviewing the highlights of your education and work experience from your application – primarily for the benefit of the other members of the board, as well as to get the material into the record. Do not interrupt or comment unless there is an error or significant misinterpretation; if that is the case, do not hesitate. But do not quibble about insignificant matters. Also, he will usually ask you some question about your education, experience or your present job – partly to get you to start talking and to establish the interviewing "rapport." He may start the actual questioning, or turn it over to one of the other members. Frequently, each member undertakes the questioning on a particular area, one in which he is perhaps most competent, so you can expect each member to participate in the examination. Because time is limited, you may also expect some rather abrupt switches in the direction the questioning takes, so do not be upset by it. Normally, a board member will not pursue a single line of questioning unless he discovers a particular strength or weakness.

After each member has participated, the chairman will usually ask whether any member has any further questions, then will ask you if you have anything you wish to add. Unless you are expecting this question, it may floor you. Worse, it may start you off on an extended, extemporaneous speech. The board is not usually seeking more information. The question is principally to offer you a last opportunity to present further qualifications or to indicate that you have nothing to add. So, if you feel that a significant qualification or characteristic has been overlooked, it is proper to point it out in a sentence or so. Do not compliment the board on the thoroughness of their examination – they have been sketchy, and you know it. If you wish, merely say, "No thank you, I have nothing further to add." This is a point where you can "talk yourself out" of a good impression or fail to present an important bit of information. Remember, *you close the interview yourself.*

The chairman will then say, "That is all, Mr. ______, thank you." Do not be startled; the interview is over, and quicker than you think. Thank him, gather your belongings and take your leave. Save your sigh of relief for the other side of the door.

How to put your best foot forward

Throughout this entire process, you may feel that the board individually and collectively is trying to pierce your defenses, seek out your hidden weaknesses and embarrass and confuse you. Actually, this is not true. They are obliged to make an appraisal of your qualifications for the job you are seeking, and they want to see you in your best light. Remember, they must interview all candidates and a non-cooperative candidate may become a failure in spite of their best efforts to bring out his qualifications. Here are 15 suggestions that will help you:

1) Be natural – Keep your attitude confident, not cocky

If you are not confident that you can do the job, do not expect the board to be. Do not apologize for your weaknesses, try to bring out your strong points. The board is interested in a positive, not negative, presentation. Cockiness will antagonize any board member and make him wonder if you are covering up a weakness by a false show of strength.

2) Get comfortable, but don't lounge or sprawl

Sit erectly but not stiffly. A careless posture may lead the board to conclude that you are careless in other things, or at least that you are not impressed by the importance of the occasion. Either conclusion is natural, even if incorrect. Do not fuss with your clothing, a pencil or an ashtray. Your hands may occasionally be useful to emphasize a point; do not let them become a point of distraction.

3) Do not wisecrack or make small talk

This is a serious situation, and your attitude should show that you consider it as such. Further, the time of the board is limited – they do not want to waste it, and neither should you.

4) Do not exaggerate your experience or abilities

In the first place, from information in the application or other interviews and sources, the board may know more about you than you think. Secondly, you probably will not get away with it. An experienced board is rather adept at spotting such a situation, so do not take the chance.

5) If you know a board member, do not make a point of it, yet do not hide it

Certainly you are not fooling him, and probably not the other members of the board. Do not try to take advantage of your acquaintanceship – it will probably do you little good.

6) Do not dominate the interview

Let the board do that. They will give you the clues – do not assume that you have to do all the talking. Realize that the board has a number of questions to ask you, and do not try to take up all the interview time by showing off your extensive knowledge of the answer to the first one.

7) Be attentive

You only have 20 minutes or so, and you should keep your attention at its sharpest throughout. When a member is addressing a problem or question to you, give him your undivided attention. Address your reply principally to him, but do not exclude the other board members.

8) Do not interrupt

A board member may be stating a problem for you to analyze. He will ask you a question when the time comes. Let him state the problem, and wait for the question.

9) Make sure you understand the question

Do not try to answer until you are sure what the question is. If it is not clear, restate it in your own words or ask the board member to clarify it for you. However, do not haggle about minor elements.

10) Reply promptly but not hastily

A common entry on oral board rating sheets is "candidate responded readily," or "candidate hesitated in replies." Respond as promptly and quickly as you can, but do not jump to a hasty, ill-considered answer.

11) Do not be peremptory in your answers

A brief answer is proper – but do not fire your answer back. That is a losing game from your point of view. The board member can probably ask questions much faster than you can answer them.

12) Do not try to create the answer you think the board member wants

He is interested in what kind of mind you have and how it works – not in playing games. Furthermore, he can usually spot this practice and will actually grade you down on it.

13) Do not switch sides in your reply merely to agree with a board member

Frequently, a member will take a contrary position merely to draw you out and to see if you are willing and able to defend your point of view. Do not start a debate, yet do not surrender a good position. If a position is worth taking, it is worth defending.

14) Do not be afraid to admit an error in judgment if you are shown to be wrong

The board knows that you are forced to reply without any opportunity for careful consideration. Your answer may be demonstrably wrong. If so, admit it and get on with the interview.

15) Do not dwell at length on your present job

The opening question may relate to your present assignment. Answer the question but do not go into an extended discussion. You are being examined for a *new* job, not your present one. As a matter of fact, try to phrase ALL your answers in terms of the job for which you are being examined.

Basis of Rating

Probably you will forget most of these "do's" and "don'ts" when you walk into the oral interview room. Even remembering them all will not ensure you a passing grade. Perhaps you did not have the qualifications in the first place. But remembering them will help you to put your best foot forward, without treading on the toes of the board members.

Rumor and popular opinion to the contrary notwithstanding, an oral board wants you to make the best appearance possible. They know you are under pressure – but they also want to see how you respond to it as a guide to what your reaction would be under the pressures of the job you seek. They will be influenced by the degree of poise you display, the personal traits you show and the manner in which you respond.

EXAMINATION SECTION

EXAMINATION SECTION
TEST 1

DIRECTIONS: Each question or incomplete statement is followed by several suggested answers or completions. Select the one that BEST answers the question or completes the statement. *PRINT THE LETTER OF THE CORRECT ANSWER IN THE SPACE AT THE RIGHT.*

1. Physical and mental health are essential to the officer. According to this statement, the officer MUST be 1.____

   A. as wise as he is strong
   B. smarter than most people
   C. sound in mind and body
   D. stronger than the average criminal

2. Teamwork is the basis of successful law enforcement. The factor stressed by this statement is 2.____

   A. cooperation
   B. determination
   C. initiative
   D. pride

3. Legal procedure is a means, not an end. Its function is merely to accomplish the enforcement of legal rights. A litigant has no vested interest in the observance of the rules of procedure as such. All that he should be entitled to demand is that he be given an opportunity for a fair and impartial trial of his case. He should not be permitted to invoke the aid of technical rules merely to embarrass his adversary. 3.____
   According to this paragraph, it is MOST correct to state that

   A. observance of the rules of procedure guarantees a fair trial
   B. embarrassment of an adversary through technical rules does not make a fair trial
   C. a litigant is not interested in the observance of rules of procedure
   D. technical rules must not be used in a trial

4. One theory states that all criminal behavior is taught by a process of communication within small intimate groups. An individual engages in criminal behavior if the number of criminal patterns which he has acquired exceed the number of non-criminal patterns. 4.____
   This statement indicates that criminal behavior is

   A. learned
   B. instinctive
   C. hereditary
   D. reprehensible

5. The law enforcement staff of today requires training and mental qualities of a high order. The poorly or partially prepared staff member lowers the standard of work, retards his own earning power, and fails in a career meant to provide a livelihood and social improvement. 5.____
   According to this statement,

   A. an inefficient member of a law enforcement staff will still earn a good livelihood
   B. law enforcement officers move in good social circles
   C. many people fail in law enforcement careers
   D. persons of training and ability are essential to a law enforcement staff

6. In any state, no crime can occur unless there is a written law forbidding the act or the omission in question, and even though an act may not be exactly in harmony with public policy, such act is not a crime unless it is expressly forbidden by legislative enactment. According to the above statement, 6.___

   A. a crime is committed with reference to a particular law
   B. acts not in harmony with public policy should be forbidden by law
   C. non-criminal activity will promote public welfare
   D. legislative enactments frequently forbid actions in harmony with public policy

7. The unrestricted sale of firearms is one of the main causes of our shameful crime record. According to this statement, one of the causes of our crime record is 7.___

   A. development of firepower
   B. ease of securing weapons
   C. increased skill in using guns
   D. scientific perfection of firearms

8. Every person must be informed of the reason for his arrest unless he is arrested in the actual commission of a crime. Sufficient force to effect the arrest may be used, but the courts frown on brutal methods.
   According to this statement, a person does NOT have to be informed of the reason for his arrest if 8.___

   A. brutal force was not used in effecting it
   B. the courts will later turn the defendant loose
   C. the person arrested knows force will be used if necessary
   D. the reason for it is clearly evident from the circumstances

9. An important duty of an officer is to keep order in the court.
   On the basis of this statement, it is PROBABLY true that 9.___

   A. it is more important for an officer to be strong than it is for him to be smart
   B. people involved in court trials are noisy if not kept in check
   C. not every duty of an officer is important
   D. the maintenance of order is important for the proper conduct of court business

10. Ideally, a correctional system should include several types of institutions to provide different degrees of custody.
    On the basis of this statement, one could MOST reasonably say that 10.___

    A. as the number of institutions in a correctional system increases, the efficiency of the system increases
    B. the difference in degree of custody for the inmate depends on the types of institutions in a correctional system
    C. the greater the variety of institutions, the stricter the degree of custody that can be maintained
    D. the same type of correctional institution is not desirable for the custody of all prisoners

11. The enforced idleness of a large percentage of adult men and women in our prisons is one of the direct causes of the tensions which burst forth in riot and disorder. On the basis of this statement, a good reason why inmates should perform daily work of some kind is that

11.____

A. better morale and discipline can be maintained when inmates are kept busy
B. daily work is an effective way of punishing inmates for the crimes they have committed
C. law-abiding citizens must work, therefore, labor should also be required of inmates
D. products of inmates' labor will in part pay the cost of their maintenance

12. With industry invading rural areas, the use of the automobile, and the speed of modern communications and transportation, the problems of neglect and delinquency are no longer peculiar to cities but an established feature of everyday life. This statement implies MOST directly that

12.____

A. delinquents are moving from cities to rural areas
B. delinquency and neglect are found in rural areas
C. delinquency is not as much of a problem in rural areas as in cities
D. rural areas now surpass cities in industry

13. Young men from minority groups, if unable to find employment, become discouraged and hopeless because of their economic position and may finally resort to any means of supplying their wants. The MOST reasonable of the following conclusions that may be drawn from this statement only is that

13.____

A. discouragement sometimes leads to crime
B. in general, young men from minority groups are criminals
C. unemployment turns young men from crime
D. young men from minority groups are seldom employed

14. To prevent crime, we must deal with the possible criminal long before he reaches the prison. Our aim should be not merely to reform the law breakers but to strike at the roots of crime: neglectful parents, bad companions, unsatisfactory homes, selfishness, disregard for the rights of others, and bad social conditions. The above statement recommends

14.____

A. abolition of prisons
B. better reformatories
C. compulsory education
D. general social reform

15. There is evidence which shows that comic books which glorify the criminal and criminal acts have a distinct influence in producing young criminals. According to this statement,

15.____

A. comic books affect the development of criminal careers
B. comic books specialize in reporting criminal acts
C. young criminals read comic books exclusively
D. young criminals should not be permitted to read comic books

16. Suppose a study shows that juvenile delinquents are equal in intelligence but three school grades behind juvenile non-delinquents. On the basis of this information only, it is MOST reasonable to say that   16._

    A. a delinquent usually progresses to the educational limit set by his intelligence
    B. educational achievement depends on intelligence only
    C. educational achievement is closely associated with delinquency
    D. lack of intelligence is closely associated with delinquency

17. There is no proof today that the experience of a prison sentence makes a better citizen of an adult. On the contrary, there seems some evidence that the experience is an unwholesome one that frequently confirms the criminality of the inmate. From the above paragraph only, it may be BEST concluded that   17._

    A. prison sentences tend to punish rather than rehabilitate
    B. all criminals should be given prison sentences
    C. we should abandon our penal institutions
    D. penal institutions are effective in rehabilitating criminals

18. Some courts are referred to as *criminal* courts while others are known as *civil* courts. This distinction in name is MOST probably based on the   18._

    A. historical origin of the court
    B. link between the court and the police
    C. manner in which the judges are chosen
    D. type of cases tried there

19. Many children who are exposed to contacts and experiences of a delinquent nature become educated and trained in crime in the course of participating in the daily life of the neighborhood. From this statement only, we may reasonably conclude that   19._

    A. delinquency passes from parent to child
    B. neighborhood influences are usually bad
    C. schools are training grounds for delinquents
    D. none of the above conclusions is reasonable

20. Old age insurance, for whose benefits a quarter of a million city employees may elect to become eligible, is one feature of the Social Security Act that is wholly administered by the Federal government. On the basis of this paragraph only, it may MOST reasonably be inferred that   20._

    A. a quarter of a million city employees are drawing old age insurance
    B. a quarter of a million city employees have elected to become eligible for old age insurance
    C. the city has no part in administering Social Security old age insurance
    D. only the Federal government administers the Social Security Act

21. An officer's revolver is a defensive, and not offensive, weapon. On the basis of this statement only, an officer should BEST draw his revolver to   21._

    A. fire at an unarmed burglar
    B. force a suspect to confess
    C. frighten a juvenile delinquent
    D. protect his own life

22. Prevention of crime is of greater value to the community than the punishment of crime. If this statement is accepted as true, GREATEST emphasis should be placed on 22.____

A. malingering
B. medication
C. imprisonment
D. rehabilitation

23. The criminal is rarely or never reformed. Acceptance of this statement as true would mean that GREATEST emphasis should be placed on 23.____

A. imprisonment
B. parole
C. probation
D. malingering

24. The MOST accurate of the following statements about persons convicted of crimes is that 24.____

A. their criminal behavior is almost invariably the result of low intelligence
B. they are almost invariably legally insane
C. they are more likely to come from underprivileged groups than from other groups
D. they have certain facial characteristics which distinguish them from non-criminals

25. Suppose a study shows that the I.Q. (Intelligence Quotient) of prison inmates is 95 as opposed to an I.Q. of 100 for a numerically equivalent civilian group. A claim, on the basis of this study, that criminals have a lower I.Q. than non-criminals would be 25.____

A. *improper;* prison inmates are criminals who have been caught
B. *proper;* the study was numerically well done
C. *improper;* the sample was inadequate
D. *proper;* even misdemeanors are sometimes penalized by prison sentences

Questions 26-45.

DIRECTIONS: Select the letter of the word or expression that MOST NEARLY expresses the meaning of the capitalized word in the group.

26. ABDUCT 26.____

A. lead B. kidnap C. sudden D. worthless

27. BIAS 27.____

A. ability B. envy C. prejudice D. privilege

28. COERCE 28.____

A. cancel B. force C. rescind D. rugged

29. CONDONE 29.____

A. combine B. pardon C. revive D. spice

30. CONSISTENCY 30.____

A. bravery B. readiness C. strain D. uniformity

31. CREDENCE
    A. belief B. devotion C. resemblance D. tempo
    31.___

32. CURRENT
    A. backward B. brave C. prevailing D. wary
    32.___

33. CUSTODY
    A. advisement B. belligerence
    C. guardianship D. suspicion
    33.___

34. DEBILITY
    A. deceitfulness B. decency
    C. strength D. weakness
    34.___

35. DEPLETE
    A. beg B. empty C. excuse D. fold
    35.___

36. ENUMERATE
    A. name one by one B. disappear
    C. get rid of D. pretend
    36.___

37. FEIGN
    A. allow B. incur C. pretend D. weaken
    37.___

38. INSTIGATE
    A. analyze B. coordinate C. oppose D. provoke
    38.___

39. LIABLE
    A. careless B. growing C. mistaken D. responsible
    39.___

40. PONDER
    A. attack B. heavy C. meditate D. solicit
    40.___

41. PUGILIST
    A. farmer B. politician
    C. prize fighter D. stage actor
    41.___

42. QUELL
    A. explode B. inform C. shake D. suppress
    42.___

43. RECIPROCAL
    A. mutual B. organized C. redundant D. thoughtful
    43.___

44. RUSE
    A. burn B. impolite C. rot D. trick
    44.___

45. STEALTHY 45.____

A. crazed B. flowing C. sly D. wicked

Questions 46-50.

DIRECTIONS: Each of the sentences numbered 46 to 50 may be classified under one of the following four categories:

A faulty because of incorrect grammar
B faulty because of incorrect punctuation
C faulty because of incorrect capitalization or incorrect spelling
D correct

Examine each sentence carefully to determine under which of the above four options it is best classified. Then, in the corresponding space at the right, write the letter preceding the option which is the BEST of the four suggested above. Each faulty sentence contains but one type of error. Consider a sentence to be correct if it contains none of the types of errors mentioned, even though there may be other correct ways of expressing the same thought.

46 They told both he and I that the prisoner had escaped. 46.____

47. Any superior officer, who, disregards the just complaints of his subordinates, is remiss in the performance of his duty. 47.____

48. Only those members of the national organization who resided in the Middle west attended the conference in Chicago. 48.____

49. We told him to give the investigation assignment to whoever was available. 49.____

50. Please do not disappoint and embarass us by not appearing in court. 50.____

KEY (CORRECT ANSWERS)

1. C	11. A	21. D	31. A	41. C
2. A	12. B	22. D	32. C	42. D
3. B	13. A	23. A	33. C	43. A
4. A	14. D	24. C	34. D	44. D
5. D	15. A	25. A	35. B	45. C
6. A	16. C	26. B	36. A	46. A
7. B	17. A	27. C	37. C	47. B
8. D	18. D	28. B	38. D	48. C
9. D	19. D	29. B	39. D	49. D
10. D	20. C	30. D	40. C	50. C

TEST 2

DIRECTIONS: Each question or incomplete statement is followed by several suggested answers or completions. Select the one that BEST answers the question or completes the statement. *PRINT THE LETTER OF THE CORRECT ANSWER IN THE SPACE AT THE RIGHT.*

1 Suppose a man falls from a two-story high scaffold and is unconscious. You should 1._

A. call for medical assistance and avoid moving the man
B. get someone to help you move him indoors to a bed
C. have someone help you walk him around until he revives
D. hold his head up and pour a stimulant down his throat

2. For proper first aid treatment, a person who has fainted should be 2._

A. doused with cold water and then warmly covered
B. given artificial respiration until he is revived
C. laid down with his head lower than the rest of his body
D. slapped on the face until he is revived

3. If you are called on to give first aid to a person who is suffering from shock, you should 3._

A. apply cold towels
B. give him a stimulant
C. keep him awake
D. wrap him warmly

4. Artificial respiration would NOT be proper first aid for a person suffering from 4._

A. drowning
B. electric shock
C. external bleeding
D. suffocation

5. Suppose you are called on to give first aid to several victims of an accident. FIRST attention should be given to the one who is 5._

A. bleeding severely
B. groaning loudly
C. unconscious
D. vomiting

6. If an officer's weekly salary is increased from $400.00 to $450.00, then the percent of increase is ______ percent. 6._

A. 10 B. 11 1/9 C. 12 1/2 D. 20

7. Suppose that one-half the officers in a department have served for more than ten years, and one-third have served for more than 15 years. 7._
Then, the fraction of officers who have served between ten and fifteen years is

A. 1/3 B. 1/5 C. 1/6 D. 1/12

8. In a city prison, there are four floors on which prisoners are housed. The top floor houses one-quarter of the inmates, the bottom floor houses one-sixth of the inmates, one-third are housed on the second floor. The rest of the inmates are housed on the third floor. If there are 90 inmates housed on the third floor, the total number of inmates housed on all four floors together is 8._

A. 270 B. 360 C. 450 D. 540

9. Suppose that ten percent of those who commit serious crimes are convicted and that fifteen percent of those convicted are sentenced for more than 3 years. The percentage of those committing serious crimes who are sentenced for more than 3 years is ______ percent. 9.____

A. 15 B. 1.5 C. .15 D. .015

10. Assume that there are 1,100 employees in a city agency. Of these, 15 percent are officers, 80 percent of whom are attorneys; of the attorneys, two-fifths have been with the agency over five years. Then the number of officers who are attorneys and have over five years' experience with the agency is MOST NEARLY 10.____

A. 45 B. 53 C. 132 D. 165

11. An employee who has 500 cartons of supplies to pack can pack them at the rate of 50 an hour. After this employee has worked for half an hour, he is jointed by another employee who can pack 45 cartons an hour. Assuming that both employees can maintain their respective rates of speed, the total number of hours required to pack all the cartons is 11.____

A. 4 1/2 B. 5 C. 5 1/2 D. 6 1/2

12. Thirty-six officers can complete an assignment in 22 days. Assuming that all officers work at the same rate of speed, the number of officers that would be needed to complete this assignment in 12 days is 12.____

A. 42 B. 54 C. 66 D. 72

Questions 13-15.

DIRECTIONS: Questions 13 through 15, inclusive, are to be answered on the basis of the table below. Data for certain categories have been omitted from the You are to calculate the missing numbers if needed to answer the questions.

	2007	2008	Numerical Increase
Correction Officers	1,226	1,347	
Court Officers		529	34
Deputy Sheriffs	38	40	
Supervisors			
	2,180	2,414	

13. The number in the *Supervisors* group in 2007 was MOST NEARLY 13.____

A. 500 B. 475 C. 450 D. 425

14. The LARGEST percentage increase from 2007 to 2008 was in the group of 14.____

A. Correction officers
B. Court officers
C. Deputy sheriffs
D. Supervisors

15. In 2008, the ratio of the number of Correction Officers to the total of the other three categories of employees was MOST NEARLY 15.____

A. 1:1 B. 2:1 C. 3:1 D. 4:1

16. A directed verdict is made by a court when 16.____

    A. the facts are not disputed
    B. the defendant's motion for a directed verdict has been denied
    C. there is no question of law involved
    D. neither party has moved for a directed verdict

17. Papers on appeal of a criminal case do NOT include one of the following: 17.____

    A. Summons
    B. Minutes of trial
    C. Complaint
    D. Intermediate motion papers

18. A pleading titled *Smith vs. Jones, et al.* indicates 18.____

    A. two plaintiffs
    B. two defendants
    C. more than two defendants
    D. unknown defendants

19. A District Attorney makes a *prima facie* case when 19.____

    A. there is proof of guilt beyond a reasonable doubt
    B. the evidence is sufficient to convict in the absence of rebutting evidence
    C. the prosecution presents more evidence than the defense
    D. the defendant fails to take the stand

20. A person is NOT qualified to act as a trial juror in a criminal action if he or she 20.____

    A. has been convicted previously of a misdemeanor
    B. is under 18 years of age
    C. has scruples against the death penalty
    D. does not own property of a value at least $500

21. A court clerk who falsifies a court record commits a(n) 21.____

    A. misdemeanor
    B. offense
    C. felony
    D. no crime, but automatically forfeits his tenure

22. Insolent and contemptuous behavior to a judge during a court of record proceeding is punishable as 22.____

    A. civil contempt
    B. criminal contempt
    C. disorderly conduct
    D. a disorderly person

23. Offering a bribe to a court clerk would not constitute a crime UNLESS the 23.____

    A. court clerk accepted the bribe
    B. bribe consisted of money
    C. bribe was given with intent to influence the court clerk in his official functions
    D. court was actually in session

24. A defendant comes to trial in the same court in which he had previously been defendant in a similar case. 24.____
The court officer should

    A. tell him, *Knew we'd be seeing you again*
    B. tell newspaper reporters what he knows of the previous action

C. treat him the same as he would any other defendant
D. warn the judge that the man had previously been a defendant

25. Suppose in conversation with you, an attorney strongly criticizes a ruling of the judge, and you believe the attorney to be correct.
You should

A. assure him you feel the same way
B. tell him the judge knows the law
C. tell him to ask for an exception
D. refuse to discuss the matter

25.____

26. Suppose a doorman refuses to admit you to an apartment house in which you are attempting to serve a process on a tenant.
Of the following, the BEST action for you to take is to

A. bribe the doorman to admit you
B. discard the process since it cannot be served
C. gain entrance by force
D. report the matter to your superior

26.____

27. False arrest is an offense for which the deputy sheriff may be held liable.
Therefore, before making an arrest, the deputy sheriff should

A. be sure a witness is present
B. be sure it is legal
C. seek assistance from a patrolman
D. deputize a private citizen

27.____

28. An arrested person should not be transported upon a public conveyance such as a streetcar, subway, or bus, except in an extreme emergency.
The reason for this regulation is MOST probably the

A. danger of escape
B. embarrassment to the prisoner
C. expense involved
D. possible delays

28.____

29. Except in rare emergencies, a deputy should not attempt to make an arrest without a partner.
The BEST reason for this is that the partner may be needed to

A. arbitrate the matter
B. lend prestige to the sheriff's office
C. overcome resistance
D. provide company for the deputy

29.____

30. At the end of each month, the deputy sheriff must submit to his superior officer an activity report covering the status of his assignments and the extent of his activities in the service of process during the month.
It is MOST important that such report be

A. accurate
B. brief
C. grammatically correct
D. lengthy

30.____

31. Deputies are required to hold seized chattels for three days after service of the replevin papers. This means three full 24-hour days, exclusive of the day of service, and the property should not be turned over earlier than 12:01 A.M. on the fourth day. When one day of the period falls on a Sunday or a public holiday, that day is excluded and an additional day must be added to make up the three. 31._

According to this statement only, if service of replevin papers is made on Thursday, June 23rd, the property should be turned over on

A. Sunday, June 26th
B. Monday, June 27th
C. Tuesday, June 28th
D. Wednesday, June 29th

32. Certain property is declared by law to be exempt from seizure to satisfy a debt because it is of importance to the comfort of the family, although of small money On the basis of this law, which of the following would you MOST expect to be exempt from seizure? 32._

A. Broadloom rug
B. Dining table
C. Marble statuette
D. Modern painting

33. As a general rule, a deputy sheriff is justified in refusing to seize an article which differs from the description in the replevin papers, unless the difference is clearly unimportant in the light of other identifying facts. According to this statement, which of the following would a deputy sheriff BEST be justified in seizing where there is a difference from the description in the papers? 33._

A(n)

A. automobile corresponding in make, year, model, and engine number, but differing in color
B. sofa corresponding in upholstery material, color, width, and height, but differing in length
C. television set corresponding in year, model, and size of screen, but differing in number of tubes required
D. typewriter corresponding in year, model, size of type, and color, but differing in name of manufacturer

34. The legal aspect of the sheriff's duties is emphasized by his unique personal liability, not only for his own acts and omissions, but also for those of any deputy or employee in his office. 34._

According to the foregoing quotation, it would be MOST correct to state that the sheriff

A. and his employees have unique legal duties to perform
B. is held responsible for actions taken by his subordinates
C. is liable for the acts of his employees only under unique circumstances
D. must personally serve many legal papers

35. Which one of the following descriptions of a defendant would help MOST in identifying him? 35._

A. Age - 31 years; weight - 168 pounds
B. At time of escape was wearing gray hat, dark overcoat
C. Deep scar running from left ear to chin
D. Height - 5 feet, 9 inches; complexion - sallow

36. Which of the following could a deputy sheriff BEST accept as proof of a man's identity? 36.____

A. A personal letter
B. Automobile driver's license
C. Automobile registration certificate
D. Social security card

37. It was formerly the practice to require someone who knew the defendant by sight to accompany the deputy sheriff. It has been learned through experience that the value of such identification is over-rated. 37.____
From this paragraph only, it may be BEST inferred that

A. circumstantial evidence is not reliable
B. identifications are sometimes inaccurate
C. people are usually for the underdog
D. testimony is often contradictory

38. The depositions must set forth the facts tending to establish that an illegal act was committed and that the defendant is guilty. 38.____
According to this statement only, the one of the following which need NOT be included in a deposition is evidence that establishes the

A. fact that an illegal act was committed
B. fact that defendant committed the illegal act
C. guilt of the defendant
D. method of commission of the illegal act

39. Each deputy sheriff should understand how his own work helps to accomplish the purpose of the entire agency. 39.____
This statement means MOST NEARLY that the deputy sheriff should understand the

A. efficiency of a small agency
B. importance of his own job
C. necessity for initiative
D. value of a large organization

40. When X is accused of having cheated Y of a sum of money and Y is proven to have been deprived of the money, there is an additional requirement for a verdict against X. 40.____
The additional requirement is to prove that

A. the money was stolen from Y
B. X had the money after Y had it
C. X had the money before Y had it
D. X cheated Y of the money

41. To gain a verdict against X in a trial, it was necessary to show that he could have been at Y Street at 5 P.M. 41.____
It was proven that he was seen at Z Street at 4:45 P.M. The question that MUST be answered to show whether X is guilty is:

A. How long does it take to get from Z Street to Y Street?
B. In what sort of neighborhood is Z Street located?
C. Was X acting suspiciously on the day in question?
D. Who was with X when he was seen at Z Street at 4:45 P.M.?

42. The deputy sheriff must give the defendant reasonable time to secure the bail fixed in the process before confining him to jail. 42.___
The CHIEF purpose of bail is to

A. permit personnel to act as bondsmen
B. permit the defendant his liberty while assuring his presence at the trial
C. raise additional money for the general fund of the city treasury
D. relieve the city of the necessity of bringing the defendant before a judge

43. When a jury is selected, the attorney for each side has a right to refuse to accept a certain number of prospective jurors without giving any reason therefor. 43.___
The reason for this is MAINLY that

A. attorneys can exclude persons likely to be biased even though no prejudice is admitted
B. persons who will suffer economically by being summoned for jury duty can be excused forthwith
C. relatives of the litigants can be excused, thus insuring a fair trial for each side
D. there will be a greater number of people from which the jury can be selected, thus insuring better quality

44. Suppose a deputy sheriff, feeling that the verdict against a judgment debtor was unfair, permits him to escape. 44.___
On the basis of this information only, it is safe to assume that the

A. judge passing sentence was unduly harsh
B. judgment debtor had possession of a large sum of money
C. deputy sheriff was recently appointed
D. deputy sheriff used poor judgment

45. A deputy sheriff shall not receive a gift from any defendant or other person on the defendant's behalf. 45.___
The BEST explanation for this departmental rule is that

A. acceptance of a gift has no significance
B. favors may be expected in return
C. gifts are only an expression of good will
D. litigants cannot usually afford gifts

46. All concerned are MOST likely to recognize the deputy sheriff's authority and cooperate with him if he conveys by his manner a complete confidence that they will do so. According to this statement only, a deputy sheriff should display 46.___

A. arrogance B. agitation C. assurance D. excitement

47. Since he is a city employee, a deputy sheriff who refuses to waive immunity from prosecution when called on to testify in court automatically terminates his employment. 47.___
From this statement only, it may be BEST inferred that

A. a deputy sheriff is a city employee
B. all city employees are deputy sheriffs
C. city employees may be fired only for malfeasance
D. deputy sheriffs who waive immunity may not be prosecuted

48. In one case, a mistrial was declared because the indictment used the pronoun *he* instead of *she*. 48.____
The MOST useful information a deputy sheriff can derive from this statement is that

A. accuracy is important
B. mistrial is a legal term
C. one must always use good grammar
D. to misrepresent is felonious

49. It is desirable that a deputy sheriff acquire a knowledge of the procedures of the division to which he is assigned MAINLY because such knowledge will help him 49.____

A. become familiar with anti-social behavior
B. discharge his duties properly
C. gain insight into causes of crime
D. in any personal legal proceeding

50. It is a frequent misconception that deputy sheriffs can be recruited from those registers established for the recruitment of police officers or firefighters. While it is true that many common qualifications are found in all of these, specific standards for a sheriff's work are indicated, varying with the size, geographical location and policies of the office. 50.____
According to this paragraph only, it may BEST be inferred that

A. a successful deputy sheriff must have some qualifications not required of a policeman or fireman
B. qualifications which make a successful patrolman will also make a successful fireman
C. the same qualifications are required of a deputy sheriff regardless of the office to which he is assigned
D. the successful deputy sheriff is required to be both more intelligent and stronger than a fireman

---

KEY (CORRECT ANSWERS

1. A	11. C	21. C	31. C	41. A
2. C	12. C	22. B	32. B	42. B
3. D	13. D	23. C	33. A	43. A
4. C	14. D	24. C	34. B	44. D
5. A	15. A	25. D	35. C	45. B
6. C	16. A	26. D	36. B	46. C
7. C	17. D	27. B	37. B	47. A
8. B	18. C	28. A	38. D	48. A
9. B	19. B	29. C	39. B	49. B
10. B	20. B	30. A	40. D	50. A

SOLUTIONS TO PROBLEMS

6 CORRECT ANSWER: C

$$\frac{50}{400} = \frac{1}{8} = 12\frac{1}{2}\%$$

7. CORRECT ANSWER: C

$1/2 + 1/3 = 3/6 + 2/6 = 5/6$

$\therefore 1 - 5/6 = 1/6$

8. CORRECT ANSWER: B

$1/4 + 1/6 + 1/3 = 3/12 + 2/12 + 4/12 = 9/12 = 3/4$

$\therefore$ 1 - 3/4 = 1/4 (rest of inmates housed on the third floor) Since 90 = 1/4, therefore, 4/4 (or 1) = 360.

9. CORRECT ANSWER: B

.10 x .15 = .0150 = 1.5%

10. CORRECT ANSWER: B

Step (1)

```
 1100
 ×.15
 5500
1100
165.00 (peace officers)
```

Step (2)

```
   165
  ×.80
132.00 (attorneys)
```

Step (3) 132 x 2/5 = 264/5 = 52.8 (peace officers who are attorneys and have over five years' experience with the agency)

11. CORRECT ANSWER: C

Since the first employee worked for 1/2 hour, he packed 25 cartons (50 ÷ 2). This leaves 475 cartons to be packed. This first employee packs at the rate of 50 an hour. The second employee, who joins him after 1/2 hour, packs at the rate of 45 an hour. 50 + 45 = 95 (rate of both employees together)

$\therefore$ 475 ÷ 95 = 5 hours (time it takes both employees together) 5 hours + 1/2 hour = 5 1/2 hours

12. CORRECT ANSWER: C

$x : 36 = 22:12$

$12 \times x = 36 \times 22$

$12x = 792$

$x = 66$

EXAMINATION SECTION
TEST 1

DIRECTIONS: Each question or incomplete statement is followed by several suggested answers or completions. Select the one that BEST answers the question or completes the statement. *PRINT THE LETTER OF THE CORRECT ANSWER IN THE SPACE AT THE RIGHT.*

1. An order of civil arrest is signed by the Supreme Court, New York County, on September 24, 1998. On September 28, 1998, a deputy sheriff duly arrests the defendant on Queens Blvd. in the County of Queens. If the defendant is not released on bail, the defendant will thereafter be brought for a hearing in Supreme Court 1.___
   A. New York County
   B. Queens County
   C. of any county in New York City
   D. of any county in New York State

2. In the preceding Question 1, the hearing must be held NO LATER THAN _____, 1998. 2.___
   A. September 28
   B. September 29
   C. September 30
   D. October 10

3. In the preceding Question 1, the sheriff's office must notify the plaintiff or his attorney about the hearing NOT LATER THAN _____ the hearing. 3.___
   A. twenty-four hours before
   B. forty-eight hours before
   C. thirty-six hours before
   D. the morning of

4. John Doe has been held in contempt for his refusal to call off an illegal strike against his employer. Doe has been arrested and is lodged in the civil jail. Doe may be kept in jail 4.___
   A. not more than three months
   B. not more than six months
   C. until he posts bail
   D. until he calls off the strike

5. In the preceding Question 4, assume that upon being arrested Doe has a change of heart and agrees to call off the strike. The deputy's BEST course of action would be to 5.___
   A. accompany Doe to an appropriate place to insure that Doe keeps his word
   B. release Doe immediately
   C. contact the attorney for the employer and seek his instructions
   D. accept cash bail from Doe and not arrest him

6. A warrant of arrest has been properly issued to insure the presence of John Roe as a witness at a departmental trial in a city agency. The warrant is issued on June 1. The trial is scheduled for June 4. The MOST appropriate day to make the arrest would be 6.____
   A. as soon as possible after June 1
   B. on June 4, if possible
   C. on June 3, if possible
   D. when it is most convenient for the sheriff's office

7. Upon receipt of an order of civil arrest, the deputy sheriff checked the office file and found that there was a prior order of arrest which had never been executed. Of the following, the one which would NOT be an appropriate course of action for the deputy is to 7.____
   A. execute the earlier order of arrest
   B. execute the later order of arrest
   C. execute the earlier order and file a detainer for the later one with the warden of the jail
   D. call counsel for the plaintiff in that action to ascertain the status of the earlier order

8. In executing an order of civil arrest, the LEAST desirable place to make the arrest is 8.____
   A. the defendant's place of business
   B. in a public place
   C. on the street outside the defendant's home
   D. the defendant's home

9. An order of civil arrest has been issued for an orthodox Jew. On which of the following days is he immune from arrest? 9.____
   A. Only on Saturday
   B. Only on Sunday
   C. On both Saturday and Sunday
   D. Neither on Saturday nor on Sunday

10. Of the following persons, the one who is NOT immune from civil arrest is a(n) 10.____
   A. ordained clergyman
   B. maid who works at the French Ambassador's home
   C. fireman on duty
   D. marine on active duty

11. An order for the civil arrest of John P. Doe is delivered to the sheriff's office. A photograph of Mr. Doe accompanies the papers. Upon arriving at the home of Mr. Doe, the deputy sheriff finds that there are two men living together: John P. Doe and John Q. Doe. The photograph is that of John Q. Doe. Which of the following is the LEAST appropriate course of action for the deputy to follow? 11.____
   A. Arrest John Q. Doe
   B. Take no immediate arrest, but call the attorney for the plaintiff for instructions

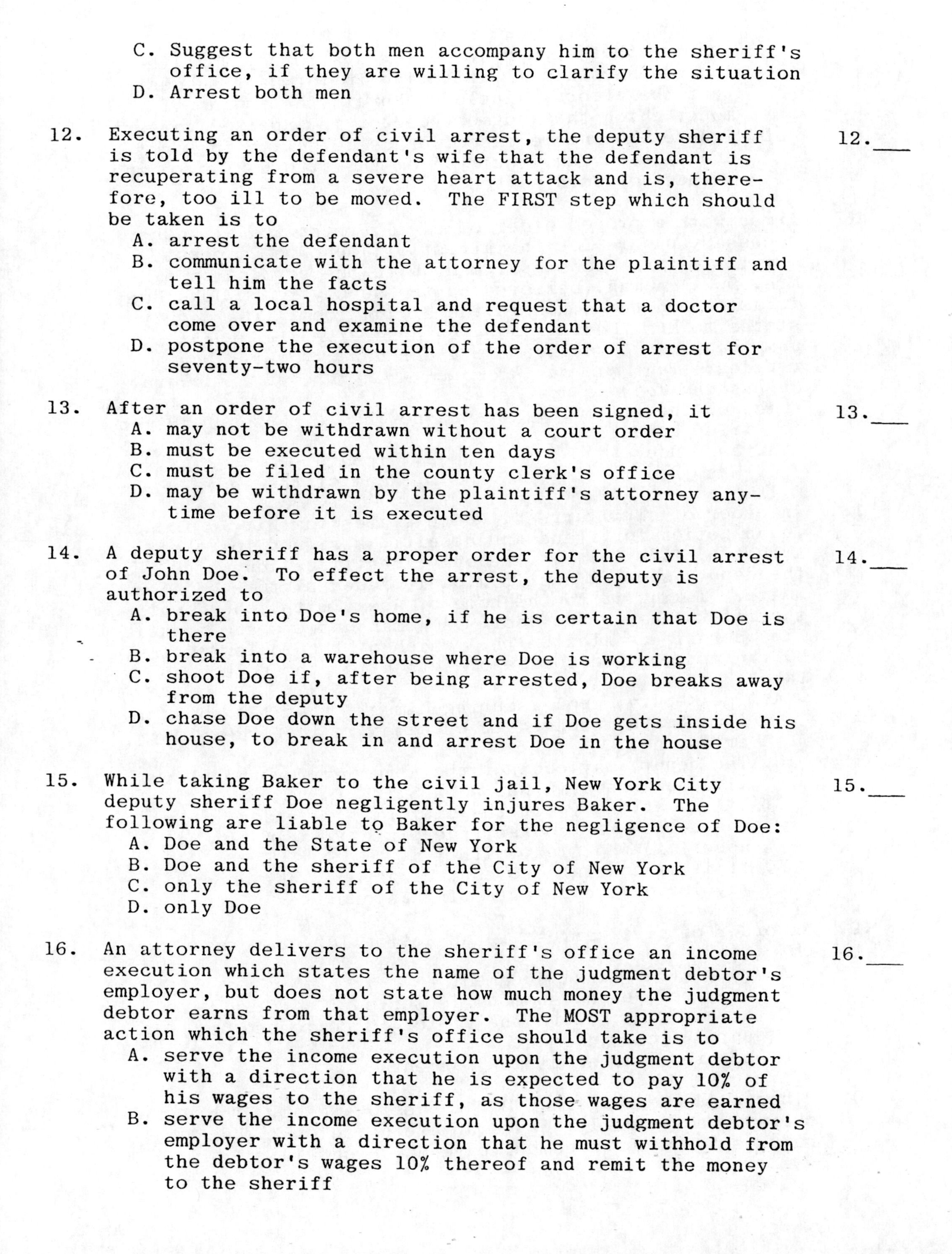

C. Suggest that both men accompany him to the sheriff's office, if they are willing to clarify the situation
D. Arrest both men

12. Executing an order of civil arrest, the deputy sheriff is told by the defendant's wife that the defendant is recuperating from a severe heart attack and is, therefore, too ill to be moved. The FIRST step which should be taken is to 12.___
A. arrest the defendant
B. communicate with the attorney for the plaintiff and tell him the facts
C. call a local hospital and request that a doctor come over and examine the defendant
D. postpone the execution of the order of arrest for seventy-two hours

13. After an order of civil arrest has been signed, it 13.___
A. may not be withdrawn without a court order
B. must be executed within ten days
C. must be filed in the county clerk's office
D. may be withdrawn by the plaintiff's attorney anytime before it is executed

14. A deputy sheriff has a proper order for the civil arrest of John Doe. To effect the arrest, the deputy is authorized to 14.___
A. break into Doe's home, if he is certain that Doe is there
B. break into a warehouse where Doe is working
C. shoot Doe if, after being arrested, Doe breaks away from the deputy
D. chase Doe down the street and if Doe gets inside his house, to break in and arrest Doe in the house

15. While taking Baker to the civil jail, New York City deputy sheriff Doe negligently injures Baker. The following are liable to Baker for the negligence of Doe: 15.___
A. Doe and the State of New York
B. Doe and the sheriff of the City of New York
C. only the sheriff of the City of New York
D. only Doe

16. An attorney delivers to the sheriff's office an income execution which states the name of the judgment debtor's employer, but does not state how much money the judgment debtor earns from that employer. The MOST appropriate action which the sheriff's office should take is to 16.___
A. serve the income execution upon the judgment debtor with a direction that he is expected to pay 10% of his wages to the sheriff, as those wages are earned
B. serve the income execution upon the judgment debtor's employer with a direction that he must withhold from the debtor's wages 10% thereof and remit the money to the sheriff

C. apprise the judgment creditor's attorney that the income execution is defective in form and suggest that the attorney include therein the amount of money which the judgment debtor is expected to earn
D. ignore the income execution as defective in form and wait for an inquiry from the attorney as to why it has not been served

17. Armed with a proper order of civil arrest and all other necessary papers for the arrest of John Doe, a deputy sheriff enters Doe's apartment with the permission of Mrs. Doe. A man, believed by the deputy to be John Doe, is asleep on the couch in the living room. The deputy states to Mrs. Doe: *I have an order for the arrest of your husband. Consider him under arrest.* Mrs. Doe replies: *That man on the couch is my brother, Richard. My husband John is not here.*
Which of the following persons now has a cause of action for false arrest?
A. John Doe
B. Richard
C. Mrs. Doe
D. None of the above

17.___

18. An order of civil arrest, which states that it is issued in an action for fraud and deceit, is signed for the arrest of *Alex Smith*. The only identification which the deputy sheriff has is a badly faded picture of Alex Smith. Taking it to the home of Alex Smith, the deputy sheriff knocks on the door. A woman answers and identifies herself as Alex Smith. Which of the following is NOT an appropriate course of action for the deputy to take?
A. The deputy, upon assuring himself that the woman is Alex Smith intended to be named in the order, may arrest her.
B. The deputy may contact the attorney for the plaintiff to ascertain who Alex Smith is.
C. If the attorney for the plaintiff is unavailable, the deputy may contact the plaintiff himself to ascertain who Alex Smith is.
D. If it is too late to contact anyone, the deputy may leave without arresting anyone.

18.___

19. An order of civil arrest in an action for conversion may be signed
A. only after final judgment
B. only before the summons is served
C. at any time before the action is commenced and up until final judgment
D. before or after final judgment

19.___

20. P has a judgment against D. X owes D a debt. The deputy sheriff has properly served an execution on X, but X refuses to pay. To compel payment, P should

20.___

A. make a motion in the original action to compel payment
B. make a motion in the original action to punish X for contempt
C. commence a special proceeding to compel payment of the debt
D. commence a special proceeding to punish X for contempt

21. Even though the defendant is known to be in New York, the one of the following which need NOT be personally served upon him is
A. an order preliminarily enjoining the defendant
B. an order temporarily restraining the defendant
C. a subpoena duces tecum commanding defenant to deliver books
D. a summons

21.___

22. In an action to recover possession of an automobile, plaintiff, before commencing the action, has properly directed the sheriff by requisition to seize the chattel and restore immediate possession to the plaintiff. Under the C.P.L.R., the summons must be served
A. within thirty days after the requisition is delivered to the sheriff or else the sheriff may not seize the chattel
B. when the sheriff seizes the chattel from the defendant
C. within thirty days after the sheriff seizes the chattel
D. within three days after the sheriff seizes the chattel

22.___

23. The provisional remedy of civil arrest is available in an action for
A. trespass to a chattel
B. ejectment
C. specific performance of a contract to convey land located outside New York
D. specific performance of a contract to convey land located in New York

23.___

24. In which of the following provisional remedies, granted before a summons is served, must jurisdiction be acquired over the defendant or his property within a certain time limit or else the provisional remedy becomes void?
Attachment
A. and arrest
B. and lis pendens (notice of pendency)
C. , arrest, and receivership
D. , injunction, and lis pendens (notice of pendency)

24.___

25. In an action for damages based upon fraud, a defendant who has been arrested 25.___
A. may be released upon bail only in the discretion of the court
B. may be released upon bail only after he has served three days in jail
C. may have the order of arrest vacated as unauthorized in an action for fraud
D. has an absolute right to post bail for his release

KEY (CORRECT ANSWERS)

1. B
2. C
3. A
4. D
5. C

6. B
7. B
8. D
9. C
10. A

11. D
12. B
13. D
14. B
15. B

16. C
17. D
18. A
19. C
20. C

21. A
22. B
23. C
24. B
25. D

TEST 2

DIRECTIONS: Each question or incomplete statement is followed by several suggested answers or completions. Select the one that BEST answers the question or completes the statement. *PRINT THE LETTER OF THE CORRECT ANSWER IN THE SPACE AT THE RIGHT.*

1. The sheriff has properly delivered an income execution to D's employer. The employer has refused to honor the execution. The plaintiff's lawyer should now serve 1.____
   A. motion papers on the employer to punish him for contempt
   B. a notice of petition and a petition to obtain a judgment against the employer
   C. motion papers on the employer to obtain an order directing payment
   D. a subpoena upon the employer restraining him from paying D

2. An order of civil arrest has been signed against Doe in an action for fraud. The action has not yet been commenced. The summons must be served 2.____
   A. within 48 hours after Doe is arrested
   B. within 30 days after the arrest order is signed or the arrest order will become void
   C. at the time the deputy sheriff arrests Doe
   D. at a time not specified by any of the foregoing

3. The date on which a summons is prepared in a civil action 3.____
   A. is the date upon which the statute of limitations stops running
   B. is the date from which the defendant measures his time in which to appear
   C. must be typed on the face of the summons
   D. has no legal significance

4. An attorney has delivered an execution to the sheriff's office. A levy may thereafter be made under this execution within sixty days 4.____
   A. or else the execution becomes void and cannot be extended
   B. unless the period is extended (by a maximum of one sixty-day increment) in writing by the plaintiff's attorney
   C. unless the period is extended by court order
   D. unless the period is extended by successive sixty-day periods in writing by the plaintiff's attorney

5. John Doe works as a bank messenger for the Acme Bank in Manhattan. Doe lives in Nassau County. Peters has obtained a judgment against Doe in the Supreme Court, Queens County. Peters now delivers an income execution to the sheriff's office UNLESS 5.___
   A. Peters has already tried unsuccessfully to execute against personal property owned by Doe, the income execution is unauthorized
   B. Peters has already tried unsuccessfully to execute against real property owned by Doe, the income execution is unauthorized
   C. Doe earns in excess of thirty dollars per week, his salary is exempt from an income execution
   D. Doe earns in excess of eighty-five dollars per week, his salary is exempt from an income execution

6. In the preceding Question 5, the appropriate sheriff's office for Peters to deliver the income execution to would be located in 6.___
   A. Nassau County
   B. New York County
   C. either Nassau or New York County
   D. any county of the state

7. In the preceding Question 6, assuming the propriety of the income execution, the sheriff should INITIALLY serve it upon 7.___
   A. an official of the Acme Bank
   B. John Doe
   C. an official of the Acme Bank or John Doe, in the sheriff's discretion
   D. both John Doe and an official of the Acme Bank

Questions 8-13.

DIRECTIONS: In answering Questions 8 through 13, assume the following set of facts.

Abel commences an action against Dunn in the Supreme Court, Erie County, on January 10, 1998. Baker commences his action against Dunn in Supreme Court, Orange County, on January 20, 1998.

On January 30, 1998, Charles, who also intends to sue Dunn, obtains an order of attachment from the Supreme Court, Bronx County. The same day, levying under this order, a deputy sheriff (1) leaves a copy of the order of attachment and all necessary papers with Dunn's employer; and (2) leaves a copy of the order of attachment and all necessary papers with the person managing *Blackacre*, Dunn's palatial summer estate in Jefferson County.

On February 10, 1998, Dunn, who is a resident of Queens County, was properly served with a summons at his home in Charles' action.

On November 2, 2000, the jury in Baker's action returned a verdict in Baker's favor. On November 10, 2000, the jury in Charles' action returned a verdict in Charles' favor. On November 20, 2000, the jury in Abel's action returned a verdict in Abel's favor.

On December 1, 2000, Charles entered and docketed his judgment in the office of the clerk of Bronx County, and on the same afternoon docketed it by transcript in Queens County. On December 10, 2000, Abel entered and docketed his judgment in the office of the clerk of Erie County. On December 21, 2000, Baker entered and docketed his judgment in the office of the clerk of Orange County.

8. Who has first lien on Blackacre? 8.___
   A. Abel
   B. Baker
   C. Charles
   D. None of the above

9. With respect to Dunn's employer, Charles 9.___
   A. obtained a lien on January 30, 1998 on 10% of all income which Dunn would thereafter earn from his employer
   B. obtained no lien of any kind on the income which Dunn would earn from his employer
   C. would have obtained a lien on 10% of Dunn's income if the deputy had delivered the order of attachment to Dunn instead of to the employer
   D. has first lien on Dunn's income, but the lien becomes effective only on December 1, 2000

10. With respect to executing upon Charles' judgment of December 1, 2000, Charles' judgment may be satisfied 10.___
   A. by levying upon a car owned by Dunn and garaged in Manhattan
   B. only out of the sale of Blackacre
   C. only out of the income Dunn earns from his employer
   D. only out of the sale of Blackacre and the income Dunn earns

11. Without any further procedural steps, Abel may immediately deliver an execution to the sheriff of 11.___
   A. Queens County only
   B. Jefferson County only
   C. neither Queens County nor Jefferson County
   D. both Queens County and Jefferson County

12. Assume further that Abel dockets his judgment on August 1, 2001 in Jefferson County. Baker does the same on August 15, 2001, and Charles does it on September 1, 2001. If Charles then delivers an execution to the sheriff of Jefferson County on January 10, 2002 and if the sheriff notifies Abel and Baker who deliver similar executions to him on January 20, 2002, the proceeds of the sale of Blackacre will 12.___

A. be prorated equally among Abel, Baker, and Charles
B. go to Charles first, then to Abel; the balance to Baker
C. go to Charles first; the balance to be prorated between Abel and Baker
D. go to none of the above

13. If Dunn had sold Blackacre on October 1, 2000 to Y, a bona fide purchaser for value ignorant of the pending litigations, _____ could reach Blackacre on execution. 13.___
A. Abel
B. Baker
C. both Abel and Baker
D. neither Abel nor Baker

Questions 14-15.

DIRECTIONS: In Questions 14 and 15, select the BEST option.

14. Richard Roe lives and works in Manhattan, earning $300 a week in a brokerage house. Three judgments are entered against Roe by different plaintiffs, named A, B, and C. B delivers an income execution to the sheriff's office in New York County; then A does the same thing. A week later, C, who has a civil court judgment, delivers an income execution to a New York City marshal. In the circumstances, 14.___
A. if all three executions are thereafter served, A, B, and C will each be entitled to ten percent of Roe's salary
B. if C's income execution is the first one served upon Roe, C will have priority over A and B
C. B has priority over A and C
D. A has priority over B and C

15. In the preceding Question 14, assume that C, who has the civil court judgment, is the first to deliver the execution to a marshal and that B next delivers his execution to the sheriff, and, finally, that A delivers his execution to the sheriff. In the circumstances, 15.___
A. C has priority over A and B
B. the priority will depend upon which execution is thereafter served upon Roe
C. the priority will depend upon which execution is thereafter served upon the brokerage house
D. B has priority

16. An attorney delivers a property execution to the sheriff's office with a direction that it be immediately returned unsatisfied since the attorney has already ascertained that the judgment debtor has no property. The BEST course of action for the sheriff is to 16.___
A. comply with the attorney's request
B. mail the execution to the judgment debtor's home

C. mail the execution to the judgment debtor's place of business
D. make a bona fide attempt to locate the judgment debtor and demand that he pay the judgment

17. John Doe, a judgment debtor, has personal property stored in a warehouse owned by X. X has issued to Doe a negotiable warehouse receipt for the property. A PROPER way to levy upon this property is
A. to go to the warehouse and seize the property
B. to seize the warehouse receipt from Doe
C. to go to the warehouse and leave the execution with X
D. none of the above

17.___

18. Pursuant to an order of attachment, a deputy sheriff has levied upon a Rolls-Royce automobile which, the plaintiff says, belongs to the defendant. Defendant denies that the automobile is his. The automobile has been stored in X's warehouse. Of the following courses of action, the one which would NOT be appropriate is to
A. publish a notice in the New York Law Journal that the automobile is in storage and inviting the true owner to come forward
B. get the plaintiff and X to agree that plaintiff will be solely responsible for the storage charges
C. get the plaintiff's lawyer and X to agree that the lawyer will be solely responsible for the storage charges
D. get an agreement from the plaintiff's lawyer that he will indemnify the sheriff in the event the sheriff is held responsible for the storage charges

18.___

19. Assume that in the preceding Question 18, the attorney agrees to advance the foreseeable storage charges. The recommended period of storage for which advance payment should be exacted is
A. no more than three months
B. no more than six months
C. at least six months
D. at least a year

19.___

20. An order of attachment has been issued against John Doe, a tailor who earns $500.00 a week in his own shop. A levy may be made by
A. closing up the tailor shop over the objection of Doe
B. seizing a number of customers' suits found on a rack in the tailor shop
C. taking Doe's wedding ring
D. physically removing a portable sewing machine from the tailor shop

20.___

21. Of the following, the property which is generally exempt from levy of execution is
A. a Picasso painting that has been in the defendant's family for fifty years
B. a television set

21.___

C. property on the defendant's person
D. the defendant's home, worth $50,000

22. A and B, two individuals, are partners in a finance company known as Ace Finance. A judgment has been entered against B for his negligence in driving his family automobile on a pleasure trip to Miami. This judgment may be executed by levying upon
A. B's desk in the office of Ace Finance
B. B's interest in the partnership
C. a bank account maintained in the name of Ace Finance
D. B's Timex watch, worth $25.00

22.___

23. A deputy sheriff, who has been levying under an order of attachment against John Doe, reads in a trade journal that Doe has filed a petition for bankruptcy. Of the following courses of action, the one which would NOT be appropriate is for the deputy to
A. continue to levy upon Doe's assets as they are found
B. call his superiors and notify them of the bankruptcy
C. notify the plaintiff's attorney of the bankruptcy
D. seek to determine whether the John Doe he read about is the same John Doe who is the defendant

23.___

24. Seeking to make a levy under an order of attachment, a deputy sheriff finds the defendant in possession of a 1998 Cadillac automobile, which the defendant asserts belongs to his brother. The defendant, however, has no registration for the automobile, asserting that the registration is with his brother. Of the following courses of action, the one which would NOT be appropriate is to
A. drive with the defendant to his brother's house to check the registration
B. obtain the consent of the plaintiff to let the defendant keep the automobile
C. levy upon the automobile, if no immediate proof of ownership is available
D. desist from levying on the auto if no immediate proof of ownership is available

24.___

25. In the preceding Question 24, assume that it is proven that the automobile belongs to the defendant, but there is a security interest filed by the Ace Finance Company. Then the automobile may
A. not be levied on
B. be levied upon and the purchaser at the eventual execution sale will obtain a clear and free title
C. be levied upon and the purchaser at the eventual execution sale will obtain a title which is subject to the filed security interest of the Ace Finance Company
D. be levied upon but the Ace Finance Company may not buy it at eventual execution sale

25.___

KEY (CORRECT ANSWERS)

1. B
2. C
3. D
4. D
5. D

6. A
7. B
8. D
9. B
10. A

11. D
12. D
13. D
14. C
15. A

16. D
17. B
18. A
19. C
20. D

21. C
22. B
23. A
24. D
25. C

TEST 3

DIRECTIONS: Each question or incomplete statement is followed by several suggested answers or completions. Select the one that BEST answers the question or completes the statement. *PRINT THE LETTER OF THE CORRECT ANSWER IN THE SPACE AT THE RIGHT.*

1. An execution against Doe has been delivered to the sheriff's office. Doe is found to possess a pawn ticket for a rare Stradivarius violin worth $2,500.00, which he pledged for $50.00. 1.____
   A. The court may permit the execution sale of the violin, even though it remains in the custody of the pawnbroker.
   B. The violin may not be sold upon execution unless it is first taken from the pawnbroker.
   C. If Doe is a professional violinist, the violin may NOT be sold upon execution.
   D. The violin may be sold upon execution only if the pawn ticket can be seized to prevent its negotiation.

2. A judgment has been obtained against John Doe, the president of a corporation. Although an income execution was properly served upon Doe, he has refused to pay any of his salary to the sheriff. A deputy has now been sent to serve the income execution upon the corporation. In the circumstances, 2.____
   A. the deputy must serve the execution upon John Doe as president of the corporation
   B. although the deputy may serve any officer of the corporation, the better practice is to serve John Doe as president
   C. if possible, the deputy should serve some other officer of the corporation
   D. preferred practice is simply to mail the income execution to the corporation

3. Peters obtains a judgment against Doe on June 1, 2000. On June 10, Peters learns that Doe, who has been in financial difficulties, intends to make an assignment for the benefit of creditors. On June 11, Peters delivers an execution to the sheriff. On June 15, Doe makes the assignment, in writing, to X for the benefit of all of Doe's creditors. In the circumstances, the 3.____
   A. sheriff may not levy under Peters' execution
   B. sheriff may levy under Peters' execution and sell Doe's property, but must hold the proceeds for the benefit of all Doe's creditors
   C. sheriff may levy under Peters' execution and sell the property for the benefit of Peters
   D. assignment for the benefit of creditors is void since no court approval was obtained for it

4. Before the commencement of an action by Peters against Doe, Doe transfers substantial amounts of stocks and bonds to his wife. This is done as a gift, though it is apparent that Doe did it to defeat any judgment which Peters might obtain. Doe continues to control the stocks and bonds. Peters has now obtained a judgment against Doe and has delivered an execution to the sheriff. In the circumstances,
   A. the stocks and bonds may not be levied upon
   B. the stocks and bonds may be levied upon, but only after a court has declared the transfer to Doe's wife to be fraudulent
   C. if the deputy is convinced that the transfer was fraudulent, he should on his own authority proceed to levy on the stocks and bonds
   D. if the deputy believes that the transfer was fraudulent, the better practice is to refer the question to his superior who may authorize the levy if there is convincing evidence that the transfer was fraudulent

4.____

5. An order of attachment has been signed in an action against Doe. Plaintiff's attorney notifies a deputy sheriff that Smith owes Doe $5,000 which Smith has borrowed from Doe. In the circumstances,
   A. Smith's debt may be levied upon by serving a copy of the order of attachment upon Smith
   B. Smith's debt to Doe may not be levied upon
   C. if Smith's debt is not presently due but is certain to become due within six months, it may not be levied upon
   D. Smith's debt may be levied upon ONLY if there is a negotiable instrument representing the debt

5.____

6. An order of attachment has been signed in an action against Doe. Investigation discloses that a friend of Doe named George has two automobiles belonging to Doe. On June 1, 2000, a deputy sheriff delivers a copy of the order of attachment to George. In the circumstances,
   A. no valid levy was made on June 1, 2000 because no automobile was physically seized
   B. no valid levy was made on June 1, 2000 unless a special order of the court was obtained to dispense the deputy sheriff from physically seizing the automobiles
   C. a valid levy was made on June 1, 2000 when the order of attachment and sheriff's Form S-30 were left with George
   D. a valid levy was made on June 1, 2000 and nothing further need be done to reduce the automobiles to possession until the lawsuit is over

6.____

7. In the preceding Question 6, assume that a proper levy was made on June 1, 2000. Assume further that another of Doe's automobiles is delivered to George thereafter. In the circumstances, the third automobile 7.____
   A. is subject to the levy of June 1, 2000 if the automobile comes into George's possession on or before November 1, 2000, even though George delivered the first two automobiles to the sheriff on July 1, 2000
   B. cannot be subjected to levy unless there is a new service of the order of attachment upon George
   C. is subject to the levy of June 1, 2000 if it comes into George's possession within 120 days after June 1, 2000
   D. is subject to the levy of June 1, 2000 if it comes into George's possession within 90 days after June 1, 2000, and George still has undisputed possession of the first two automobiles

8. Doe is the life beneficiary, along with his three brothers, of a trust set up by his father. Doe receives $500.00 per month from the trust. The Acme Bank is serving as trustee. Peters has a judgment against Doe. The PROPER way in which to levy upon Doe's interest in the trust is to 8.____
   A. serve the appropriate papers upon Doe's three brothers
   B. serve the appropriate papers upon the Acme Bank
   C. serve the appropriate papers upon one of Doe's brothers
   D. file the papers with the State Department of Trusts

9. In the preceding Question 8, 9.____
   A. Doe has no interest in the trust which may be levied upon
   B. Doe's entire interest in the trust may be levied upon
   C. 10% of the income earned by Doe from the trust is exempt from levy
   D. 90% of the income earned by Doe from the trust is exempt from levy

10. An order of attachment has been signed in an action against Doe. Investigation reveals that Doe owns 500 shares of IBM stock. The stock certificates are in a safe deposit box in the Acme Bank. The stock may be levied upon by serving the appropriate papers upon 10.____
   A. Doe, although the stock certificates are in a safe deposit box in the Acme Bank
   B. the president of IBM Corporation
   C. the Acme Bank which has the certificates and then taking possession of the certificates
   D. the Secretary of State in Albany

11. An order of attachment has been signed in an action against Doe. A friend of Doe's is known to possess much valuable property belonging to Doe. The order of attachment and the other appropriate papers are served upon the friend on June 1, 2000. The friend must then serve upon the sheriff's office a statement of the property he possesses within _____ days.   11.___
    A. 10   B. 15   C. 30   D. 90

12. In the preceding Question 11, the sheriff's office will send the statement to   12.___
    A. the court where the action is pending
    B. the defendant
    C. the plaintiff's attorney
    D. other judgment creditors of Doe

13. In the preceding Question 11, which of the following would NOT be an appropriate course of action to follow in the 90-day period after June 1, 2000?   13.___
    The
    A. sheriff may seize all of Doe's property in the friend's possession
    B. plaintiff may obtain an order extending the 90-day period
    C. plaintiff may commence a special proceeding to compel the friend to deliver the property to the sheriff
    D. sheriff may commence a special proceeding to compel the friend to deliver the property to the sheriff

14. In which of the following cases may a deputy sheriff make a constructive seizure of property simply by leaving the appropriate papers with the person in possession of the property?   14.___
    When he is levying
    A. upon personal property capable of delivery, under a writ of execution
    B. upon personal property capable of delivery, under an order of attachment
    C. under a proper requisition to replevy
    D. under a writ of execution for the delivery of possession of a chattel

15. A deputy sheriff has been sent to a warehouse to actually seize property in execution of a judgment. Upon entering the warehouse, he is shown an office with a glass door inside of which is located the property the deputy wants. To make a PROPER levy, the deputy   15.___
    A. need only peer through the glass door
    B. does not have to enter the office but need only say: *That property is now subject to a levy*
    C. must enter the office and touch the property
    D. must enter the office, view the property, and have it under his immediate ability to control

16. Assuming that the deputy sheriff is certain that the defendant has property, in which of the following cases may the deputy break and enter in order to seize the property? 16.___
    A. When the property is in the defendant's home
    B. When the property is in the defendant's locker at work
    C. When the property is in a hotel room where the defendant has been living
    D. In none of the above cases

17. After an order of attachment is signed against Doe, a deputy sheriff learns that Doe's automobile is in Joe's Garage for repairs. Although the deputy presents the necessary attachment papers, Joe's Garage is reluctant to release the automobile until its repair bill is paid. Which of the following courses of action would be LEAST appropriate? 17.___
    The
    A. sheriff may seize and remove the car over the objection of Joe's Garage
    B. sheriff may persuade the plaintiff to pay the garage bill
    C. deputy may persuade the garage to surrender the automobile by advising the garage owner that his rights will be fully protected
    D. deputy may persuade the plaintiff's attorney to permit a constructive seizure of the car in the hope that the case may be settled within 90 days thereafter

18. After levying on a valuable book collection upon execution of a judgment against Doe, the sheriff is notified by an attorney that the collection belongs to the attorney's client, and not to the defendant. The book collection has not yet been sold in execution of the judgment. The PROPER course of action to be pursued by the attorney is to 18.___
    A. start an action for an injunction to enjoin the execution sale
    B. start an action against Doe to replevy the book collection
    C. start a special proceeding to determine his client's rights to the book collection
    D. issue a precept to the sheriff directing the return of the book collection to his client

19. An order of attachment has been signed in an action against Doe. The only asset which Doe has is an apartment house in Brooklyn. The PROPER way to levy upon the house is to 19.___
    A. serve the order of attachment upon Doe
    B. serve the order of attachment upon the person who manages the house

C. serve the order of attachment upon any tenant, if the manager of the house cannot be found
D. file a notice of attachment with the county clerk in Kings County

20. On September 1, 1993, Peters entered and docketed in Kings County a judgment against Doe. An execution was returned unsatisfied since Doe had no assets in Kings. In January 2001, Peters learns that Doe had inherited a house worth $60,000 in Kings upon the death of his father in 1999. Peters immediately sends an execution to the sheriff. Of the following, the MOST accurate statement is that the

20.___

A. house may not be levied on and sold because Peters has no lien thereon
B. sheriff may now proceed to sell the house
C. sheriff must file with the clerk of Kings County a notice describing the judgment, the execution, and the house
D. buyer at the execution sale will take whatever title and interest Doe had as of January 2001

21. John Doe bought a house for $50,000 by paying $20,000 in cash and by executing a bond and mortgage to the Acme Bank for $30,000. Eight years later, John Doe fell upon hard times and could not pay the mortgage. Acme Bank sued Doe on the bond and got a money judgment for $25,000, the amount then due on the bond and mortgage. Which of the following properties CANNOT be sold in execution of Acme's judgment?

21.___

A. Doe's house
B. Doe's interest in a joint bank account held with his wife
C. Doe's automobile which he uses to get to and from work
D. Doe's interest in a boat which he jointly owns with his brother

22. The Ace Finance Company intends to bring an action to replevy an automobile which it had sold to John Doe but upon which Doe had failed to make the necessary payments. On December 1, 2000, counsel for the finance company, without a court order, sends a requisition and the other appropriate papers to the sheriff's office directing the sheriff to seize the automobile before the action is commenced. The APPROPRIATE course of action for the sheriff's office to follow is to

22.___

A. seize the car, but only if it can be found on a public street
B. seize the car, no matter where it is found, if it can be done without breaking and entering
C. seize the car, no matter where it is found, even if the sheriff has to break and enter to get the car
D. apprise counsel for the finance company that a court order is required to authorize the seizure of the car

23. A properly issued requisition in a replevin case requires the sheriff to seize a Philco television set with a serial number Q-4289J. Upon arriving at the defendant's home, an RCA television, with serial number Q-69452, is the only one found. Which of the following courses of action would be the LEAST appropriate? To

    A. ascertain from the defendant whether he ever bought a television from the plaintiff and, if it appears that the RCA television is the only set he ever bought from the plaintiff, to seize it
    B. call the plaintiff's attorney and ask for a clarification
    C. seize the RCA television because that is the only one found on the premises
    D. leave the defendant's home and return the requisition to the plaintiff's attorney with an explanation as to why it was not executed

23.___

24. Defendant purchased a dishwasher from plaintiff and then installed it in his apartment in such a fashion that it became a fixture. It would require major carpentry to remove the dishwasher and to repair the area where the dishwasher had been installed. In an action of replevin, the sheriff is served with a properly issued requisition for the dishwasher. Upon arrival at defendant's home, a deputy discovers that the dishwasher has been installed as described. Which of the following courses of action would be MOST appropriate?

    A. The deputy may pull out the dishwasher and leave the defendant to repair the damage.
    B. Without checking with the plaintiff, the deputy may pull out the dishwasher and leave the plaintiff to pay the damage.
    C. The deputy may seal the dishwasher and direct the defendant to hold on to it *for the account of the plaintiff*.
    D. Refrain from seizure of the dishwasher since replevin does not lie for fixtures.

24.___

25. Plaintiff has commenced an action to replevy certain rare wood from the defendant. Pursuant to a properly issued requisition for the wood, a deputy sheriff arrives at defendant's home only to find that the defendant has used the wood to make a magnificent piano. Which of the following statements is TRUE?

    A. Plaintiff is NOT entitled to replevy the piano.
    B. Plaintiff may replevy the piano, but the deputy should not seize it pursuant to the requisition unless it is specifically described as a piano.
    C. The deputy should seize the piano, although the requisition mentions only wood.
    D. Wood is not the proper subject of a replevin action.

25.___

KEY (CORRECT ANSWERS)

1. A
2. C
3. C
4. D
5. A

6. C
7. D
8. B
9. D
10. C

11. A
12. C
13. D
14. B
15. D

16. B
17. A
18. C
19. D
20. B

21. A
22. D
23. C
24. D
25. B

TEST 4

DIRECTIONS: Each question or incomplete statement is followed by several suggested answers or completions. Select the one that BEST answers the question or completes the statement. *PRINT THE LETTER OF THE CORRECT ANSWER IN THE SPACE AT THE RIGHT.*

1. After the defendant has appeared in a replevin action, a proper set of papers is delivered to the sheriff requiring the seizure of the chattel. Unless the court orders otherwise, a set of all the papers must be served upon the 1.____
   A. defendant in the same manner as a summons
   B. defendant's attorney
   C. defendant's attorney, only if the attorney is in possession of the chattel being replevied
   D. defendant's attorney, only if the defendant is in possession of the chattel

2. Pursuant to a proper set of papers, a deputy sheriff seizes a chattel in a replevin action. The seizure occurs at 2:00 P.M. on Monday, December 14, 1999. Before he can deliver the chattel to the plaintiff, the sheriff must wait until _____, 1999. 2.____
   A. Friday, December 18
   B. Thursday, December 17
   C. Wednesday, December 16
   D. Tuesday, December 15

3. Pursuant to a proper order of attachment, defendant's automobile is levied upon while it is in a parking lot. The parking lot owner has been served with the correct papers. Which of the following statements is TRUE? 3.____
   A. The automobile must be removed from the parking lot within 60 days.
   B. The automobile may be left in the parking lot despite the objections of the parking lot owner, so long as the plaintiff agrees to pay the necessary expenses.
   C. With the consent of the parking lot owner, the car may be left in the parking lot and the plaintiff will pay the parking lot owner's fee.
   D. The automobile may NOT be left in the parking lot longer than it takes to find another place to store it.

4. When real property is to be sold in execution of a judgment, notice of the sale must be posted in at least three places at least _____ days prior to the sale. 4.____
   A. 60
   B. 80
   C. 46
   D. 56

5. When personal property is to be sold in execution of a judgment, notice of the sale must be posted in at least three places at least _____ days prior to the sale. 5.____
   A. 6
   B. 9
   C. 30
   D. 90

6. The sheriff intends to sell a parcel of land in execution of a money judgment against its owner. Which of the following is CORRECT? 6.___
The sheriff
   A. may negotiate a private sale to a customer to whom the land has peculiar value, so long as the sheriff receives a better price than a public auction would have yielded
   B. must sell only at a public auction
   C. may sell at either a public auction or a private negotiation, so long as he acts in good faith
   D. may sell at either a public auction or a private negotiation, so long as he has the permission of the plaintiff

Questions 7-12.

DIRECTIONS: In answering Questions 7 through 12, assume the following facts.

Judgments were entered and docketed against a defendant named X in the places and at the times indicated:

June 1, 2000: P-1 v. X in New York County
June 10, 2000: P-2 v. X in Bronx County
June 19, 2000: P-3 v. X in Queens County
June 30, 2000: P-4 v. X in New York County

X owns a Cadillac automobile which he keeps in Putnam County and a bank account with C-M Bank in Kings County. On June 25, 2000, X bought a parcel of land known as Blackacre, located in New York County, from Y, giving Y $60,000 in cash and executing a purchase money bond and mortgage to Y for $140,000.

Further assume, for question 7 only, that a restraining notice is served on X on behalf of P-4 on September 1, 2000; that an execution is delivered to the sheriff in Putnam County on behalf of P-2 on September 10, 2000; that an execution is delivered to the sheriff in Queens County on behalf of P-1 on September 15, 2000; that the sheriff in Queens County has now levied on the Cadillac which was moved from Putnam County to Queens County on September 12, 2000.

7. Who is entitled to the proceeds of the sale of the Cadillac? 7.___
   A. P-4 may obtain an order directing the sheriff in Queens to turn over the proceeds to him
   B. P-2 may obtain an order directing the sheriff in Queens to turn over the proceeds to him
   C. P-1 may obtain an order directing the sheriff in Queens to turn over the proceeds to him
   D. P-4, P-2, and P-1 share in proportion to their judgments

Further assume, for question 8 only, that a restraining notice and information subpoena are served on C-M Bank on behalf of P-4 on September 1, 2000; that a special proceeding is commenced on September 7, 2000 by P-3 to obtain a delivery order against C-M Bank; that P-2 delivers an execution to the sheriff in Kings County on September 10, 2000; that P-3 obtains and files his delivery order on September 21, 2000; and that the sheriff levies on the account on September 30, 2000.

8. Who is entitled to the account? 8.____
   A. P-4, P-3, and P-2 share in proportion to their judgments
   B. P-3
   C. P-2
   D. P-4

Further assume, for question 9 only, that Y obtains a judgment of foreclosure on September 1, 2000; that P-3 and P-4 deliver executions to the sheriff in New York County on September 15, 2000; that P-1 delivers an execution to the sheriff in New York County on September 30, 2000; and that the land is properly sold thereafter.

9. Who is entitled to priority in the proceeds? 9.____
   A. Y
   B. P-3 and P-4 share in proportion to their judgments
   C. Y, P-3, and P-4 share in proportion to their judgments
   D. P-1

Further assume, for question 10 only, that P-2 delivers an execution to the sheriff in New York County on September 1, 2000; that P-3 delivers an execution to the same sheriff on September 4, 2000; that P-4 delivers an execution to the same sheriff on September 10, 2000; and that Blackacre is properly sold thereafter.

10. Who is entitled to priority in the proceeds? 10.____
   A. P-4
   B. P-3
   C. P-1
   D. P-1, P-2, and P-3 share in proportion to their judgments

11. In the preceding Question 10, the execution buyer takes 11.____
   A. title to Blackacre, free and clear of all encumbrances
   B. subject only to P-1's interest
   C. Blackacre subject only to Y's mortgage interest
   D. subject to P-1's and Y's interest

Further assume, for question 12 only, that P-4 delivers an execution to the sheriff in New York County on September 1, 2000; that P-2 delivers an execution to the same sheriff on September 10, 2000; that P-3 delivers an execution to the same sheriff on September 15, 2000; that P-1 delivers an execution to the same sheriff on September 18, 2000; and that Blackacre is properly sold thereafter.

12. Who is entitled to priority in the proceeds? 12.___
    A. P-1, P-2, and P-3 share in the proceeds in proportion to their judgments
    B. P-4 is entitled to priority in the proceeds.
    C. P-1 is entitled to priority in the proceeds.
    D. P-1 and P-4 share the proceeds in proportion to their judgments.

13. Doe, a citizen and resident of the State of Maine, voluntarily agrees to testify in an action by A against B, pending in Supreme Court, New York County. A summons has been left with the sheriff by Peters for service on Doe. The sheriff now learns from Peters that Doe is in the Supreme Court building awaiting his turn to testify. A deputy sheriff serves Doe with the summons while Doe is standing around in the hallway of the courthouse. Doe has moved to set aside the service of the summons. The court should 13.___
    A. set aside service of process on the ground that Doe was immune from service
    B. set aside service on the ground that process may not be served in a courthouse
    C. set aside service on the ground that, there being no unusual circumstances in the case, the sheriff's office should not have become involved in serving a summons
    D. deny the motion

14. On June 1, 1999, a deputy sheriff makes a proper levy upon an automobile owned by Doe, a defendant in an action wherein an order of attachment has been signed. On July 1, 1999, the deputy makes a proper levy upon Doe's bank account. On October 15, 1999, Doe files a petition in bankruptcy. The trustee in bankruptcy is appointed on November 10, 1999. The bankruptcy court may properly compel the sheriff to turn over to the trustee 14.___
    A. the automobile
    B. the bank account
    C. both the automobile and the bank account
    D. neither the automobile nor the bank account

15. Real property has been sold to X in execution of a judgment in favor of the plaintiff. Which of the following statements is TRUE?
The defendant may 15.___
    A. redeem his property at any time by paying to X the same amount that X paid for the property plus interest
    B. redeem his property within one year after the sale by paying to X the same amount that X paid for the property plus interest
    C. redeem his property within one year after the sale by paying the full judgment to the plaintiff
    D. not redeem his property after the sheriff has delivered a sheriff's deed to X

16. With the statute of limitations due to expire on June 1, 1999, an attorney for the plaintiff delivers a summons on May 15, 1999 to the sheriff's office for service upon the defendant. The statute of limitations will NOT be a defense if the summons is served within _____ days after _____, 1999. 16.____

A. 60; May 15
B. 60; June 1
C. 90; May 15
D. 90; June 1

17. A deputy sheriff must serve a Supreme Court summons upon John Doe. Doe, a resident of New York, has carefully avoided being served. The deputy has learned that Doe is in a hotel room in Manhattan. The deputy goes to the hotel, calls from the lobby, and states that he is a former colleague of Doe's and would like to invite Doe for a drink. Doe comes down to the bar, where the deputy serves him. Doe now moves to set aside the service of process. 17.____
The court should

A. *grant* the motion since the deputy was guilty of deception
B. *grant* the motion since the deputy never actually touched Doe with the summons
C. *grant* the motion since the deputy did not serve a complaint with the summons
D. *deny* the motion since the service was valid

18. In the preceding Question 17, assume that John Doe was a citizen and resident of New Jersey who was in New York for a vacation. All other facts are the same. 18.____
The court should

A. *grant* the motion since the deputy was guilty of deception
B. *grant* the motion since, as a nonresident, Doe was immune from service
C. *deny* the motion since the service was valid
D. *deny* the motion since a nonresident may be served anywhere in the state, anytime, including Sunday

19. In the preceding Question 18, assume that Doe was spotted on the street racing to his home. The deputy arrives at the home and is admitted peacefully by Doe's wife. Once in the house, the deputy goes from room to room, without express permission, locates Doe, and serves him. 19.____
Of the following, the MOST accurate statement is that the

A. service is void since the deputy committed an illegal search and seizure
B. deputy could have broken into the house if he had been refused admittance
C. service is valid
D. deputy has a legal privilege to effectuate service and is never liable for trespass

20. A deputy sheriff is sent to the headquarters of Acme, Inc. to serve the corporation with a summons. Upon arriving there at 12:30 P.M., he is told by a building employee that everybody in the Acme office is out to lunch. The building employee volunteers to accept the summons and to redeliver it to the President of Acme when the latter returns from lunch.
Of the following, the MOST accurate statement is that the
    A. service is void even if the building employee does redeliver the summons to the President of Acme, Inc.
    B. service is valid if the building employee does redeliver the summons to the President of Acme, Inc.
    C. service upon the building employee was itself a valid service upon Acme, Inc.
    D. deputy should have demanded access to the office of Acme, Inc. where he should have posted the summons in a conspicuous place

20.___

21. Service upon a partnership may be made by serving the summons on
    A. the managing agent of the partnership
    B. the director of the firm's legal department
    C. any partner at all
    D. only the partner who is designated by the firm to accept process

21.___

22. Before making substituted (nail and mail) service, the rule-of-thumb followed in the sheriff's office is that a deputy must have tried to make personal delivery of the summons at LEAST _____ times.
    A. 5   B. 4   C. 3   D. 2

22.___

23. Defendant John Doe lives in Queens and works for the Ace Company in Manhattan. After numerous unsuccessful attempts to deliver the summons personally to Doe, a deputy sheriff has been told by the plaintiff's attorney to try some other form of service.
Of the following, the MOST accurate statement is that
    A. the deputy may mail a copy of the summons to Doe's home in Queens and may leave another copy at the same place with Doe's wife
    B. the deputy may mail a copy of the summons to Doe at the office of Ace Company and may leave another copy on Doe's desk at the Ace Company
    C. the deputy may mail a copy of the summons to Doe at the office of the Ace Company and may affix another copy to the office door of the Ace Company
    D. none of the above methods of service is valid

23.___

24. Poundage, in attachment cases, is allowed
    A. only if the sheriff actually reduces the property to physical custody
    B. on the value of the property levied upon, even though the property has never been reduced to physical custody
    C. at the rate of 3% on the first $10,000
    D. at the rate of 5% on the first $10,000

24.___

25. When the city issues an execution to the sheriff's office, 25.___
   A. the city must pay desk fees in advance
   B. a deputy should collect the desk fees from the defendant
   C. the city will pay the desk fees after the execution has been satisfied
   D. the desk fees may be used to reimburse a deputy sheriff for his use of his personal automobile on sheriff's business

---

KEY (CORRECT ANSWERS)

1. B
2. A
3. C
4. D
5. A

6. B
7. B
8. B
9. A
10. A

11. C
12. C
13. A
14. B
15. D

16. B
17. D
18. C
19. C
20. A

21. C
22. C
23. A
24. B
25. B

EXAMINATION SECTION
TEST 1

DIRECTIONS: Each question or incomplete statement is followed by several suggested answers or completions. Select the one that BEST answers the question or completes the statement. *PRINT THE LETTER OF THE CORRECT ANSWER IN THE SPACE AT THE RIGHT.*

1. The delivery of an arrested person to his sureties, upon their giving security for his appearance at the time and place designated to submit to the jurisdiction and judgment of the court, is known as 1.____

   A. bail
   B. habeas corpus
   C. parole
   D. probation

2. Jones was charged with the murder of Smith. Brown, Jones' landlord, testified at the trial that Jones had in his home a well-equipped laboratory which contained all the necessary chemicals for producing the poison which an autopsy showed caused Smith's death. Brown's testimony constitutes what is called ______ evidence. 2.____

   A. corroborative
   B. opinion
   C. hearsay
   D. circumstantial

3. In addressing a class of recruits, a police lieutenant remarked: "Carelessness and failure are twins." 3.____
   The one of the following that *most nearly* expresses his meaning is

   A. negligence seldom accompanies success
   B. incomplete work is careless work
   C. conscientious work is never attended by failure
   D. a conscientious person never makes mistakes

4. In taking a statement from a person who has been shot by an assailant and is not expected to live, police are instructed to ask the person: "Do you believe you are about to die?" 4.____
   Of the following, the MOST probable reason for this question is

   A. the theory that a person about to die will tell the truth
   B. to determine if the victim is conscious and capable of making a statement
   C. to put the victim mentally at ease and more willing to talk
   D. that the statement could not be used in court if his mind was distraught by the fear of impending death

5. If, while you are on duty at a busy intersection, a pedestrian asks you for directions to a particular place, the BEST course of conduct is to 5.____

   A. ignore the question and continue directing operations
   B. tell the pedestrian to ask a patrolman on foot patrol
   C. answer the question in a brief, courteous manner
   D. leave your post only long enough to give clear and adequate directions

6. In lecturing on the law of arrest, a lieutenant remarked: "To go beyond is as bad as to fall short." 6.____
   The one of the following which *most nearly* expresses his meaning is

A. never undertake the impossible
B. extremes are not desirable
C. look before you leap
D. too much success is dangerous

7. Suppose you are an officer assigned to a patrol precinct. While you are in the vicinity of a school, your attention is called to a man who is selling small packages to school children. You are told that this man distributes similar packages to these same children daily and that he is suspected of dealing in narcotics.
Of the following, the BEST action for you to take is to 7.___

A. pretend to be an addict and attempt to purchase narcotics from him
B. observe the man's action yourself for several days in order to obtain grounds for arrest
C. stop and question one or more of the children after they have transacted business with the man
D. stop and question the man as he leaves the children

8. In the event of a poison gas attack, civil defense authorities advise civilians to 8.___

A. open doors and windows and go to upper floors
B. close doors and windows and go to upper floors
C. open doors and windows and go to the basement
D. close doors and windows and go to the basement

9. The procedure whereby a defendant is brought before a magistrate, informed of the charge against him and asked how he pleads thereto, is called 9.___

A. arraignment
B. indictment
C. presentment
D. inquisition

10. A written accusation of a crime presented by a grand jury is called a(n) 10.___

A. commitment
B. arraignment
C. indictment
D. demurrer

11. The one of the following statements made by a prisoner that is *correctly* called an alibi is: 11.___

A. "He struck me first."
B. "I didn't intend to hurt him."
C. "I was miles away from there at the time."
D. "I don't remember what happened."

12. A person who, after the commission of a crime, conceals the offender with the intent that the latter may escape from arrest and trial, is called a(n) 12.___

A. accessory
B. accomplice
C. confederate
D. associate

13. A sworn statement of fact is called a(n) 13.___

A. affidavit
B. oath
C. acknowledgment
D. subpoena

14. The right of trial by jury in the courts of the state is *primarily* safeguarded by a provision of 14.____

    A. the United States Constitution
    B. the constitution of the state
    C. a state statute
    D. a Federal statute

15. The task of protecting the President and his family is entrusted *primarily* to the 15.____

    A. Federal Bureau of Investigation
    B. United States Secret Service
    C. Central Intelligence Agency
    D. District of Columbia Police Department

16. The co-ordinating organization for the various Federal agencies engaged in intelligence activities is the 16.____

    A. Federal Bureau of Investigation
    B. Federal Security Agency
    C. Mutual Security Agency
    D. Central Intelligence Agency

17. A drug addict whose arm shows many scars from the injection of a hypodermic needle is MOST apt to be addicted to 17.____

    A. heroin B. cocaine C. opium D. marijuana

18. All of the following drugs are derived from opium EXCEPT 18.____

    A. cocaine B. heroin C. morphine D. codeine

19. In addition to cases of submersion, artificial respiration is a recommended first aid procedure for 19.____

    A. sunstroke
    B. chemical poisoning
    C. electrical shock
    D. apoplexy

20. An injury to a muscle or tendon brought about by severe exertion and resulting in pain and stiffness is called a 20.____

    A. strain B. sprain C. bruise D. fracture

21. Of the following kinds of wounds, the one in which there is the LEAST danger of infection is a(n) ______ wound. 21.____

    A. abrasive B. punctured C. lacerated D. incised

22. When a person is found injured on the street, it is *generally* advisable, pending arrival of a physician,
    to help prevent fainting or shock by keeping the patient 22.____

    A. in a sitting position
    B. lying down with the head level
    C. lying down with the head raised
    D. standing on his feet

23. When an injured person appears to be suffering from shock, of the following, it is MOST essential to 23.___

A. loosen his clothing
B. keep him warm
C. administer a stimulant
D. place him in a prone position

24. In the sentence, "Malice was immanent in all his remarks," the word "immanent" means *most nearly* 24.___

A. elevated
B. inherent
C. threatening
D. foreign

25. In the sentence, "The extant copies of the document were found in the safe," the word "extant" means *most nearly* 25.___

A. existing
B. original
C. forged
D. duplicate

26. In the sentence, "The recruit was more complaisant after the captain spoke to him," the word "complaisant" means *most nearly* 26.___

A. calm
B. affable
C. irritable
D. confident

27. In the sentence, "The man was captured under highly creditable circumstances," the word "creditable" means *most nearly* 27.___

A. doubtful
B. believable
C. praiseworthy
D. unexpected

28. In the sentence, "His superior officers were more sagacious than he," the word "sagacious" means *most nearly* 28.___

A. shrewd
B. obtuse
C. absurd
D. verbose

29. In the sentence, "He spoke with impunity," the word "impunity" means *most nearly* 29.___

A. rashness
B. caution
C. without fear
D. immunity

30. In the sentence, "The new patrolman displayed unusual temerity during the emergency," the word "temerity" means *most nearly* 30.___

A. fear
B. rashness
C. calmness
D. anxiety

31. In the sentence, "The portions of food were parsimoniously served," the word "parsimoniously" means *most nearly* 31.___

A. stingily
B. piously
C. elaborately
D. generously

32. In the sentence, "Generally the speaker's remarks were sententious," the word "sententious" means *most nearly* 32.____

A. verbose
B. witty
C. argumentative
D. pithy

33. In the sentence, "The prisoner was fractious when brought to the station house," the word "fractious" means *most nearly* 33.____

A. penitent
B. talkative
C. irascible
D. broken-hearted

34. In the sentence, "The judge was implacable when the attorney pleaded for leniency," the word 'implacable" means *most nearly* 34.____

A. inexorable
B. disinterested
C. inattentive
D. indifferent

35. In the sentence, "The court ordered the mendacious statements stricken from the record," the word "mendacious" means *most nearly* 35.____

A. begging
B. lying
C. threatening
D. lengthy

36. In the sentence, "The district attorney spoke in a strident voice," the word "strident" means *most nearly* 36.____

A. loud
B. harsh-sounding
C. sing-song
D. low

37. In the sentence, "The speaker had a predilection for long sentences," the word "predilection" means *most nearly* 37.____

A. aversion
B. talent
C. propensity
D. diffidence

38. In the sentence, "The candidate wants to file his application for preference before it is too late," the word "before" is used as a(n) 38.____

A. preposition
B. subordinating conjunction
C. pronoun
D. adverb

39. The one of the following sentences which is grammatically *preferable* to the others is: 39.____

A. Our engineers will go over your blueprints so that you may have no problems in construction.
B. For a long time he had been arguing that we, not he, are to blame for the confusion.
C. I worked on this automobile for two houys and still cannot find out what is wrong with it.
D. Accustomed to all kinds of hardships, fatigue seldom bothers veteran policemen.

40. The plural of

40.___

A. turkey is turkies
B. cargo is cargoes
C. bankruptcy is bankruptcys
D. son-in-law is son-inlaws

41. The abbreviation "viz." means *most nearly*

41.___

A. namely
B. for example
C. the following
D. see

42. In the sentence, "A man in a light-grey suit waited thirty-five minutes in the ante-room for the all-important document," the word *improperly* hyphenated is

42.___

A. lightgrey
B. thirty-five
C. ante-room
D. all-important

43. The MOST accurate of the following sentences is:

43.___

A. The commissioner, as well as his deputy and various bureau heads, were present.
B. A new organization of employers and employees have been formed.
C. One or the other of these men have been selected.
D. The number of pages in the book is enough to discourage a reader.

44. The MOST accurate of the following sentences is:

44.___

A. Between you and me, I think he is the better man.
B. He was believed to be me.
C. Is it us that you wish to see?
D. The winners are him and her.

45. In the sentence, "The committee favored submiting the amendment to the electorate," the MISSPELLED word is

45.___

A. committee
B. submiting
C. amendment
D. electorate

46. In the sentence, "He maliciously demurred to an ajournment of the proceedings," the MISSPELLED word is

46.___

A. maliciously
B. demurred
C. ajournment
D. proceedings

47. In the sentence, "His innocence at that time is irrelevant in view of his more recent villianous demeanor," the MISSPELLED word is

47.___

A. innocence
B. irrelevant
C. villanous
D. demeanor

48. In the sentence, "The mischievous boys aggrevated the annoyance of their neighbor," the MISSPELLED word is

48.___

A. mischievous
B. aggrevated
C. annoyance
D. neighbor

49. In the sentence, "While his perseverence was commendable, his judgment was debatable," the MISSPELLED word is 49.____

A. perseverence B. commendable
C. judgment D. debatable

50. In the sentence, "He was hoping the appeal would facilitate In the sentence, "He was hoping the appeal would facilitate his aquittal," the MISSPELLED word is 50.____

A. hoping B. appeal
C. facilitate D. aquittal

51. In the sentence, "It would be preferable for them to persue separate courses," the MISSPELLED word is 51.____

A. preferable B. persue
C. separate D. courses

52. In the sentence, "The litigant was complimented on his persistance and achievement," the MISSPELLED word is 52.____

A. litigant B. complimented
C. persistance D. achievement

53. In the sentence, "Ocassionally there are discrepancies in the descriptions of miscellaneous items," the MISSPELLED word is 53.____

A. ocassionally B. discrepancies
C. descriptions D. miscellaneous

54. In the sentence, "The councilmanic seargent-at-arms enforced the prohibition," the MISSPELLED word is 54.____

A. councilmanic B. seargent-at-arms
C. enforced D. prohibition

55. In the sentence, "The teacher had an ingenious device for mantaining attendance," the MISSPELLED word is 55.____

A. ingenious B. device
C. mantaining D. attendance

QUESTIONS 56-63.

Questions 56-63 are based on the following excerpt from a recorded annual report of the police department. This material should be read first and then referred to in answering these questions, which are to be answered *solely* on the basis of the material herein contained.

LEGAL BUREAU

One of the more important functions of this bureau is to analyze and furnish the department with pertinent information concerning Federal and State statutes and Local Laws which affect the department, law enforcement or crime prevention. In addition, all measures introduced in the State Legislature and the City Council which may affect this department are carefully reviewed by members of the Legal Bureau and, where necessary, opinions and recommendations thereon are prepared.

Another important function of this office is the prosecution of cases in the Magistrate's Courts. This is accomplished by assignment of attorneys who are members of the Legal Bureau to appear in those cases which are deemed to raise issues of importance to the department or questions of law which require technical presentation to facilitate proper determination; and also in those cases where request is made for such appearances by a magistrate, some other official of the city, or a member of the force. Attorneys are regularly assigned to prosecute all cases in the Women's Court.

Proposed legislation was prepared and sponsored for introduction in the State Legislature and, at this writing, one of these proposals has already been enacted into law and five others are presently on the Governor's desk awaiting executive action. The new law prohibits the sale or possession of a hypodermic syringe or needle by an unauthorized person. The bureau's proposals awaiting executive action pertain to an amendment to the Code of Criminal Procedure prohibiting desk officers from taking bail in gambling cases or in cases mentioned in Section 552, Code of Criminal Procedure; including confidence men and swindlers as jostlers in the Penal Law; prohibiting the sale of switch-blade knives of any size to children under 16 and bills extending the licensing period of gunsmiths.

The Legal Bureau has regularly cooperated with the Corporation Counsel and the" District Attorneys in respect to matters affecting this department, and has continued to advise and represent the Police Athletic League, the Police Sports Association, the Police Relief Fund and the Police Pension Fund.

The following is a statistical report of the activities of the bureau during the current year as compared with the previous year:

	Current Year	Previous Year
Memoranda of law prepared	68	83
Legal matters forwarded to Corporation Counsel	122	144
Letters requesting legal information	756	807
Letters requesting departmental records	139	111
Matters for publication	17	26
Court appearances of members of bureau	4,678	4,621
Conferences	94	103
Lectures at Police Academy	30	33
Reports on proposed legislation	194	255
Deciphering of codes	79	27
Expert testimony	31	16
Notices to court witnesses	55	81
Briefs prepared	22	18
Court papers prepared	258	--

56. One of the functions of the Legal Bureau is to

56.____

A. review and make recommendations on proposed Federal laws affecting law enforcement
B. prepare opinions on all measures introduced in the State Legislature and the City Council
C. furnish the Police Department with pertinent information concerning all new Federal and State laws
D. analyze all laws affecting the work of the Police Department

57. The one of the following that is NOT a function of the Legal Bureau is 57.____
    A. law enforcement and crime prevention
    B. prosecution of all cases in Women's Court
    C. advise and represent the Police Sports Association
    D. lecturing at the Police Academy

58. Members of the Legal Bureau frequently appear in Magistrate's Court for the purpose of 58.____
    A. defending members of the Police Force
    B. raising issues of importance to the Police Department
    C. prosecuting all offenders arrested by members of the Force
    D. facilitating proper determination of questions of law requiring technical presentation

59. The Legal Bureau sponsored a bill that would 59.____
    A. extend the licenses of gunsmiths
    B. prohibit the sale of switch-blade knives to children of any size
    C. place confidence men and swindlers in the same category as jostlers in the Penal Law
    D. prohibit desk officers from admitting gamblers, confidence men and swindlers to bail

60. From the report, it is NOT reasonable to infer that 60.____
    A. fewer bills affecting the Police Department were introduced in the current year
    B. the preparation of court papers was a new activity assumed in the current year
    C. the Code of Criminal Procedure authorizes desk officers to accept bail in certain cases
    D. the penalty for jostling and swindling is the same

61. According to the statistical report, the activity showing the GREATEST percentage of *decrease* in the current year as compared to the previous year was 61.____
    A. matters for publication
    B. reports on proposed legislation
    C. notices to court witnesses
    D. memoranda of law prepared

62. According to the statistical report, the activity showing the GREATEST percentage of *increase* in the current year as compared with the previous year was 62.____
    A. court appearances of members of the bureau
    B. giving expert testimony
    C. deciphering of codes
    D. letters requesting departmental records

63. According to the report, the percentage of bills prepared and sponsored by the Legal Bureau which were passed by the State Legislature and sent to the Governor for approval was *approximately* 63.____
    A. 3.1% B. 2.6% C. .5%
    D. not capable of determination from the data given

64. A squad of patrolmen assigned to enforce a new parking regulation in a particular area issued tag summonses on a particular day as follows: four patrolmen issued 16 summonses each; three issued 19 each; one issued 22; seven issued 25 each; eleven issued 28 each; ten issued 30 each; two issued 36 each; one issued 41; and three issued 45 each. The *average* number of summonses issued by a member of this squad was *most nearly* 64._

A. 6.2 B. 17.2 C. 21.0 D. 27.9

65. A water storage tank is 75 feet long and 30 feet wide and has a depth of 6 1/2 feet. Each cubic foot of the tank holds 9 1/2 gallons. The TOTAL capacity of the tank is _______ gallons. 65._

A. 73,125 1/2
B. 131, 625
C. 138, 937 1/2
D. 146, 250

66. The price of admission to a PAL entertainment were $.25 each for adults and $.10 for children; the turnstile at the entrance showed that 358 persons entered and the gate receipts were $62.65. The number of children who attended was 66._

A. 170 B. 175 C. 179 D. 183

67. A patrol car travels six times as fast as a bicycle. 67._
If the patrol car goes 168 miles in two hours less time than the bicycle requires to go 42 miles, their respective rates of speed are _______ miles per hour.

A. 36 and 6
B. 42 and 7
C. 63 and 10 1/2
D. 126 and 21

68. The radiator of an automobile already contains six quarts of a 10% solution of alcohol. In order to make a mixture of 20% alcohol, it will be necessary to add _______ quarts of alcohol. 68._

A. 3/4 B. 1 3/4 C. 2 1/2 D. 3

69. A man received an inheritance of $8,000 and wanted to invest it so that it would produce an annual income sufficient to pay his rent of $40 a month. In order to do this he will have to receive interest or dividends at the rate of _______% per annum. 69._

A. 3 B. 4 C. 5 3/4 D. 6

70. If the price of a bus ticket varies *directly* as the mileage involved, and a ticket to travel 135 miles costs $2.97, a ticket for a 30 mile trip will cost 70._

A. $1.52 B. $1.34 C. $.66 D. $.22

71. A man owed a debt of $580. After a first payment of $10, he agreed to pay the balance by monthly payments in which each payment after this first would be $2 more than that of the preceding month. If no interest charge is made, he will have to make, including the first payment, a total of _______ monthly payments. 71._

A. 16 B. 20 C. 24 D. 28

72. The written test of a civil service examination has a weight of 30, the oral test a weight of 20, experience a weight of 20 and the physical test a weight of 30. A candidate received ratings of 76 on the written test, 84 on the oral, and 80 for experience. In order to attain an average of 85 on the examination, his rating on the physical test must be 72.____

A. 86 B. 90 C. 94 D. 98

73. A family has an income of $320 per month. It spends 22% of this amount for rent, 36% for food, 16% for clothing and 12% for additional household expenses. After meeting these expenses, 50% of the balance is deposited in the bank. The amount deposited *monthly* is 73.____

A. $22.40 B. $36.60 C. $44.80 D. $52.00

74. Upon retirement last July, a patrolman bought a farm of 64 acres for $1,800 per acre. He made a down payment of $61,200 and agreed to pay the balance in installments of $750 a month commencing on August 1, 2008. Disregarding interest, he will make his LAST payment in 74.____

A. July 2014
B. August 2016
C. January 2018
D. April 2021

75. 40% of those who commit a particular crime are subsequently arrested and convicted. 75% of those convicted receive sentences of 10 years or more. Assuming that those arrested for the first time serve less than 10 years, the percentage of those committing this crime who receive sentences of ten years or more is *most nearly* 75.____

A. 20% B. 30% C. 40% D. 50%

KEY (CORRECT ANSWERS)

1. A	16. D	31. A	46. C	61. A
2. D	17. A	32. D	47. C	62. C
3. A	18. A	33. C	48. B	63. D
4. A	19. C	34. A	49. A	64. D
5. C	20. A	35. B	50. D	65. C
6. B	21. D	36. B	51. B	66. C
7. C	22. B	37. C	52. C	67. B
8. B	23. B	38. B	53. A	68. A
9. A	24. B	39. A	54. B	69. D
10. C	25. A	40. B	55. C	70. C
11. C	26. B	41. A	56. D	71. B
12. A	27. C	42. C	57. A	72. D
13. A	28. A	43. D	58. D	73. A
14. B	29. D	44. A	59. C	74. A
15. B	30. B	45. B	60. D	75. B

EXAMINATION SECTION
TEST 1

DIRECTIONS: Each question or incomplete statement is followed by several suggested answers or completions. Select the one that BEST answers the question or completes the statement. *PRINT THE LETTER OF THE CORRECT ANSWER IN THE SPACE AT THE RIGHT.*

Questions 1-6.

DIRECTIONS: Questions 1 through 6 are to be answered on the basis of the following list of items permitted in cells.

ITEMS PERMITTED IN CELLS	
comb	mop
spoon	towel
cup	letters
envelopes	pen
broom	soap
washcloth	money
writing paper	chair
books	dustpan
toothpaste	brushes
toothbrush	pencil

The questions consist of sets of pictures of four objects labeled A, B, C, and D. Choose the one object that is NOT in the above list of items permitted and mark its letter in the space at the right. Disregard any information you may have about what is or is not permitted in any institution. Base your answers SOLELY on the above list. Mark only one answer for each question.

1. 1.____

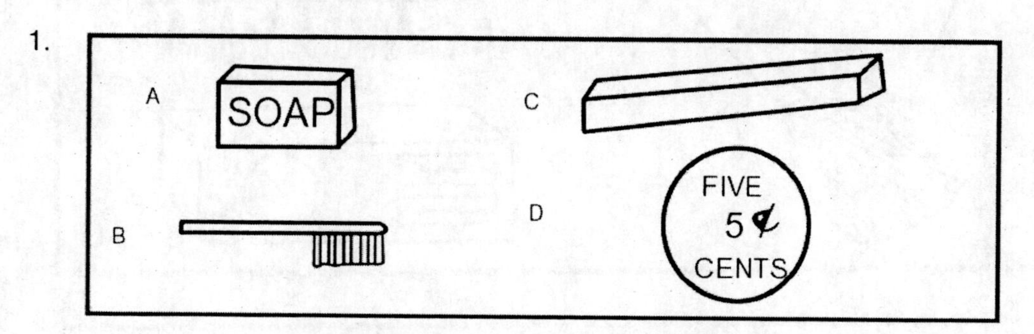

2. 2.____

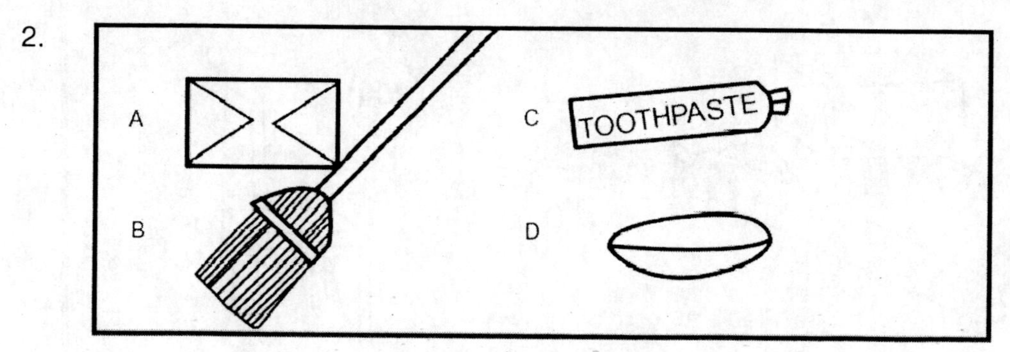

3.___

4.___

5.___

6.___

Questions 7-11.

DIRECTIONS: Questions 7 through 11 are to be answered on the basis of the following list showing the name and number of each of nine inmates.

1 - Johnson	4 - Thompson	7 - Gordon
2 - Smith	5 - Frank	8 - Porter
3 - Edwards	6 - Murray	9 - Lopez

Each question consists of 3 sets of numbers and letters.
Each set should consist of the numbers of three inmates and the first letter of each of their names. The letters should be in the same order as the numbers. In at least two of the three choices, there will be an error.

In the space at the right, mark only that choice in which the letters correspond with the numbers and are in the same order. If all three sets are wrong, mark Choice D in the space at the right.

SAMPLE QUESTION: A. 386 EPM
B. 542 FST
C. 474 LGT

Since 3 corresponds to E for Edwards, 8 corresponds to P for Porter, and 6 corresponds to M for Murray, Choice A is correct and should be entered in the answer space. Choice B is wrong because letters T and S have been reversed. Choice C is wrong because the first number, which is 4, does NOT correspond with the first letter of Choice C, which is L. It should have been T. If Choice A were also wrong, then D would have been the correct answer.

7. A. 382 EGS   B. 461 TMJ   C. 875 PLF   7.____

8. A. 549 FLT   B. 692 MJS   C. 758 GSP   8.____

9. A. 936 LEM   B. 253 FSE   C. 147 JTL   9.____

10. A. 569 PML   B. 716 GJP   C. 842 PTS   10.____

11. A. 356 FEM   B. 198 JPL   C. 637 MEG   11.____

Questions 12-16.

DIRECTIONS: Questions 12 through 16 are to be answered on the basis of the following passage.

Mental disorders are found in a fairly large number of the inmates in correctional institutions. There are no exact figures as to the number of inmates who are mentally disturbed—partly because it is hard to draw a precise line between "mental disturbance" and "normality"—but experts find that somewhere between 15% and 25% of inmates are suffering from disorders that are obvious enough to show up in routine psychiatric examinations. Society has not yet really come to grips with the problem of what to do with mentally disturbed offenders. There is not enough money available to set up treatment programs for all the people identified as mentally disturbed; and there would probably not be enough qualified psychiatric personnel available to run such programs even if they could be set up. Most mentally disturbed offenders are therefore left to serve out their time in correctional institutions, and the burden of dealing with them falls on correction officers. This means that a correction officer must be sensitive enough to human behavior to know when he is dealing with a person who is not mentally normal, and that the officer must be imaginative enough to be able to sense how an abnormal individual might react under certain circumstances.

12. According to the above passage, mentally disturbed inmates in correctional institutions 12.___

    A. are usually transferred to mental hospitals when their condition is noticed
    B. cannot be told from other inmates because tests cannot distinguish between insane people and normal people
    C. may constitute as much as 25% of the total inmate population
    D. should be regarded as no different from all the other inmates

13. The above passage says that today the job of handling mentally disturbed inmates is MAINLY up to 13.___

    A. psychiatric personnel
    B. other inmates
    C. correction officers
    D. administrative officials

14. Of the following, which is a reason given in the above passage for society's failure to provide adequate treatment programs for mentally disturbed inmates? 14.___

    A. Law-abiding citizens should not have to pay for fancy treatment programs for citizens.
    B. A person who breaks the law should not expect society to give him special help.
    C. It is impossible to tell whether an inmate is mentally disturbed.
    D. There are not enough trained people to provide the kind of treatment needed.

15. The expression *abnormal individual,* as used in the last sentence of the above passage, refers to an individual who is 15.___

    A. of average intelligence
    B. of superior intelligence
    C. completely normal
    D. mentally disturbed

16. The reader of the above passage would MOST likely agree that 16.___

    A. correction officers should not expect mentally disturbed persons to behave the same way a normal person would behave
    B. correction officers should not report infractions
    C. of the rules committed by mentally disturbed persons
    D. mentally disturbed persons who break the law should be treated exactly the same way as anyone else
    E. mentally disturbed persons who have broken the law should not be imprisoned

Questions 17-23.

DIRECTIONS: Questions 17 through 23 are to be answered on the basis of the roster of inmates, the instructions, the table, and the sample question given below.

Twelve inmates of a correctional institution are divided into three permanent groups in their workshop. They must be present and accounted for in these groups at the beginning of each workday. During the day, the inmates check out of their groups for various activities.

They check back in again when those activities have been completed. Assume that the day is divided into three activity periods.

ROSTER OF INMATES

GROUP X	Ted	Frank	George	Harry
GROUP Y	Jack	Ken	Larry	Mel
GROUP Z	Phil	Bob	Sam	Vic

The following table shows the movements of these inmates from their groups during the day. Assume that all were present and accounted for at the beginning of Period I.

		GROUP X	GROUP Y	GROUP Z
Period I	Check-outs	Ted, Frank	Ken, Larry	Phil
Period II	Check- ins	Frank	Ken, Larry	Phil
	Check-outs	George	Jack, Mel	Bob, Sam, Vic
Period III	Check-ins	George	Mel, Jack	Sam, Bob, Vic
	Check-outs	Frank, Harry	Ken	Vic

SAMPLE QUESTION: At the end of Period II, the inmates remaining in Group X were

A. Ted, Frank, Harry
B. Frank, Harry
C. Ted, George
D. Frank, Harry, George

During Period I, Ted and Frank were checked out from Group X. During Period II, Frank was checked back in, and George was checked out. Therefore, the members of the group remaining out are Ted and George. The two other members of the group, Frank and Harry, should be present. The correct answer is B.

17. At the end of Period I, the TOTAL number of inmates remaining in their own permanent groups was 17.____

A. 8 B. 7 C. 6 D. 5

18. At the end of Period I, the inmates remaining in Group Z were 18.____

A. George and Harry
B. Jack and Mel
C. Bob, Sam, and Vic
D. Phil

19. At the end of Period II, the inmates remaining in Group Y were 19.____

A. Ken and Larry
B. Jack, Ken, and Mel
C. Jack and Ken
D. Ken, Mel, and Larry

20. At the end of Period II, the TOTAL number of inmates remaining in their own permanent groups was 20.____

A. 8 B. 7 C. 6 D. 5

21. At the end of Period II, the inmates who were NOT present in Group Z were 21.____

A. Phil, Bob, and Sam
B. Sam, Bob, and Vic
C. Sam, Vic, and Phil
D. Vic, Phil, and Bob

22. At the end of Period III, the inmates remaining in Group Y were 22._

 A. Ted, Frank, and George B. Jack, Mel, and Ken
 C. Jack, Larry, and Mel D. Frank and Harry

23. At the end of Period III, the TOTAL number of inmates NOT present in their own permanent groups was 23._

 A. 4 B. 5 C. 6 D. 7

24. Of the 100 inmates in a certain cellblock, one-half were assigned to clean-up work, and one-fifth were assigned to work in the laundry.
How many inmates were NOT assigned for clean-up work or laundry work? 24._

 A. 30 B. 40 C. 50 D. 60

25. A certain cellblock has a maximum capacity of 250 inmates. On March 26, there were 200 inmates housed in the cellblock. 12 inmates were added on that day, and 17 inmates were added on the following day. No inmates left on either day.
How many more inmates could this cellblock have accommodated on the second day? 25._

 A. 11 B. 16 C. 21 D. 28

KEY (CORRECT ANSWERS)

1. C
2. D
3. A
4. B
5. D

6. A
7. B
8. D
9. A
10. C

11. C
12. C
13. C
14. D
15. D

16. A
17. B
18. C
19. A
20. D

21. B
22. C
23. B
24. A
25. C

TEST 2

DIRECTIONS: Each question or incomplete statement is followed by several suggested answers or completions. Select the one that BEST answers the question or completes the statement. *PRINT THE LETTER OF THE CORRECT ANSWER IN THE SPACE AT THE RIGHT.*

Questions 1-5.

DIRECTIONS: Questions 1 through 5 are to be answered SOLELY on the basis of the Report of Offense that appears below.

REPORT OF OFFENSE			
		Report No.	*26743*
		Date of Report	*10-12*
Inmate	*Joseph Brown*		
Age	*27*	Number	*61274*
Sentence	*90 days*	Assignment	*KU-187*
Place of Offense	*R.P.W. 4-1*	Date of Offense	*10/11*
Offense	*Assaulting inmate*		
Details	*During 9:00 p.m. cellblock clean-up, inmate John Jones asked for pail being used by Brown. Brown refused. Correction officer requested that Brown comply. Brown then threw pail at Jones with intent to injure him and said he would "get" Jones. Jones not hurt.*		
Force Used by Officer	*None*		
Name of Reporting Officer	*R. Rodriguez*	No.	*C-2056*
Name of Superior Officer	*P. Ferguson*		

1. The person who made out this report is 1.____

   A. Joseph Brown
   B. John Jones
   C. R. Rodriguez
   D. P. Ferguson

2. Disregarding the details, the specific offense reported was 2.____

   A. insulting a fellow inmate
   B. assaulting a fellow inmate
   C. injuring a fellow inmate
   D. disobeying a correction officer

3. The number of the inmate who committed the offense is 3.____

   A. 26743
   B. 61274
   C. KU-187
   D. C-2056

4. The offense took place on 4.____

   A. October 11
   B. June 12
   C. December
   D. November 13

5. The place where the offense occurred is identified in the report as 5.____

   A. Brown's cell
   B. Jones' cell
   C. KU-187
   D. R.P.W., 4-1

6. Add $51.79, $29.39, and $8.98. The CORRECT answer is 6.___

A. $78.97 B. $88.96 C. $89.06 D. $90.16

7. Add $72.07 and $31.54, then subtract $25.75. The CORRECT answer is 7.___

A. $77.86 B. $82.14 C. $88.96 D. $129.36

8. Start with $82.47, then subtract $25.50, $4.75, and 35¢. The CORRECT answer is 8.___

A. $30.60 B. $51.87 C. $52.22 D. $65.25

9. Add $19.35 and $37.75, then subtract $9.90 and $19.80. The CORRECT answer is 9.___

A. $27.40 B. $37.00 C. $37.30 D. $47.20

10. Multiply $38.85 by 2; then subtract $27.90. The CORRECT answer is 10.___

A. $21.90 B. $48.70 C. $49.80 D. $50.70

11. Add $53.66, $9.27, and $18.75, then divide by 2. The CORRECT answer is 11.___

A. $35.84 B. $40.34 C. $40.84 D. $41.34

12. Out of 192 inmates in a certain cellblock, 96 are to go on a work detail and another 32 are to report to a vocational class. All the rest are to remain in the cellblock. How many inmates should be left on the cellblock? 12.___

A. 48 B. 64 C. 86 D. 128

13. Assume that you, as a correction officer, are responsible for seeing that the right number of utensils are counted out for a meal. You need enough utensils for 620 men. One fork and one spoon are needed for each man. In addition, one ladle is needed for each group of 20 men. How many utensils will be needed altogether? 13.___

A. 1240 B. 1271 C. 1550 D. 1860

14. Assume that you, as a correction officer, are supervising the inmates who are assigned to a dishwashing detail. There is a direct relationship between the amount of time it takes to do all the dishwashing and the number of inmates who are washing dishes. When two inmates are washing dishes, the job takes six hours. If there are four inmates washing dishes, how long should the job take? _______ hour(s). 14.___

A. 1 B. 2 C. 3 D. 4

15. Assume that you, as a correction officer, are in charge of supervising the laundry sorting and counting. You expect that on a certain day there will be nearly 7,000 items to be sorted and counted.
If one inmate can sort and count 500 items in an hour, how many inmates are needed to sort all 7,000 items in one hour?

15.____

A. 2 B. 5 C. 7 D. 14

16. A carpentry course is being given for inmates who want to learn a skill. The course will be taught in several different groups. Each group should contain at least 12 but not more than 16 men. The smaller the group, the better, as long as there are at least 12 men per group. If 66 inmates are going to take the course, they should be divided into

16.____

A. 4 groups of 16 men
B. 4 groups of 13 men and 1 group of 14 men
C. 3 groups of 13 men and 2 groups of 14 men
D. 6 groups of 11 men

Questions 17-21.

DIRECTIONS: Questions 17 through 21 are to be answered on the basis of the Fact Situation and the Report of Inmate Injury form below. The questions ask how the report form should be filled in, based on the information given in the Fact Situation.

FACT SITUATION

Peter Miller is a correction officer assigned to duty in Cellblock A. His superior officer is John Doakes. Miller was on duty at 1:30 P.M. on March 21, 2004, when he heard a scream for help from Cell 12. He hurried to Cell 12 and found inmate Richard Rogers stamping out a flaming book of matches. Inmate John Jones was screaming. It seems that Jones had accidentally set fire to the entire book of matches while lighting a cigarette, and he had burned his left hand. Smoking was permitted at this hour. Miller reported the incident by phone, and Jones was escorted to the dispensary where his hand was treated at 2:00 P.M. by Dr. Albert Lorillo. Dr. Lorillo determined that Jones could return to his cellblock, but that he should be released from work for four days. The doctor scheduled a re-examination for March 22. A routine investigation of the incident was made by James Lopez. Jones confirmed to this officer that the above statement of the situation was correct.

REPORT OF INMATE INJURY

(1) Name of Inmate ______ (2) Assignment ______
(3) Number ______ (4) Location ______
(5) Nature of Injury ______ (6) Date ______
(7) Details (how, when, where injury was incurred) ______

(8) Received medical attention: Date ______ Time ______
(9) Treatment ______
(10) Disposition (check one or more):
___ (10-1) Return to housing area ___ (10-2) Return to duty
___ (10-3) Work release ___ ___ days ___ (10-4) Re-examine in ___ days

(11) Employing reporting injury ______
(12) Employee's supervisor or superior officer ______
(13) Medical officer treating injury ______
(14) Investigating officer ______
(15) Head of institution ______

17. Which of the following should be entered in Item 1? 17.___

A. Peter Miller
B. John Doakes
C. Richard Rogers
D. John Jones

18. Which of the following should be entered in Item 11? 18.___

A. Peter Miller
B. James Lopez
C. Richard Rogers
D. John Jones

19. Which of the following should be entered in Item 8? 19.___

A. 2/21/04, 1:30 P.M.
B. 2/21/04, 2:00 P.M.
C. 3/21/04, 1:30 P.M.
D. 3/21/04, 2:00 P.M.

20. For Item 10, which of the following should be checked? 20.___

A. Only 10-4
B. 10-1 and 10-4
C. 10-1, 10-3, and 10-4
D. 10-2, 10-3, and 10-4

21. Of the following items, which one CANNOT be filled in on the basis of the information given in the Fact Situation? 21.___
Item ______.

A. 12
B. 13
C. 14
D. 15

Questions 22-25.

DIRECTIONS: Questions 22 through 25 are to be answered on the basis of the chart which appears on the following page. The chart shows an 8-hour schedule for 4 groups of inmates. The numbers across the top of the chart stand for hours of the day: the hour beginning at 8:00, the hour beginning at 9:00, and so forth. The exact number of men in each group is given at the lefthand side of the chart. An hour when the men in a particular group are scheduled to be OUT of their cellblock is marked with an X.

	8	9	10	11	12	1	2	3
GROUP Q 44 men	X		X			X		
GROUP R 60 men	X		X	X		X	X	
GROUP S 24 men	X				X			
GROUP T 28 men	X		X		X			

22. How many of the men were in their cellblock from 11:00 to 12:00? 22.____

    A. 60 B. 96 C. 104 D. 156

23. At 10:45, how many of the men were NOT in their cellblock? 23.____

    A. 24 B. 60 C. 96 D. 132

24. At 12:30, what proportion of the men were NOT in their cellblock? 24.____

    A. 1/4 B. 1/3 C. 1/2 D. 2/3

25. During the period covered in the chart, what percentage of the time did the men in Group S spend in their cellblock? 25.____

    A. 60% B. 65% C. 70% D. 75%

KEY (CORRECT ANSWERS)

1. C
2. B
3. B
4. A
5. D

6. D
7. A
8. B
9. A
10. C

11. C
12. B
13. B
14. C
15. D

16. B
17. D
18. A
19. D
20. C

21. D
22. B
23. D
24. B
25. D

EXAMINATION SECTION
TEST 1

DIRECTIONS: Each question or incomplete statement is followed by several suggested answers or completions. Select the one that BEST answers the question or completes the statement. *PRINT THE LETTER OF THE CORRECT ANSWER IN THE SPACE AT THE RIGHT.*

Questions 1-25.

DIRECTIONS: Questions 1 through 25 describe situations which might occur in a correctional institution. The institution houses its inmates in cells divided into groups called cellblocks. In answering the questions, assume that you are a correction officer.

1. *Correction officers are often required to search inmates and the various areas of the correctional institution for any items which may be considered dangerous or which are not permitted. In making a routine search, officers should not neglect to examine an item just because it is usually regarded as a permitted item. For instance, some innocent-looking object can be converted into a weapon by sharpening one of its parts or replacing a part with a sharpened or pointed blade.* 1.____

   Which of the following objects could MOST easily be converted into a weapon in this way? A

   A. ballpoint pen
   B. pad of paper
   C. crayon
   D. handkerchief

2. *Only authorized employees are permitted to handle keys. Under no circumstances should an inmate be permitted to use door keys. When not in use, all keys are to be deposited with the security officer.* 2.____

   Which one of the following actions does NOT violate these regulations?

   A. A correction officer has given a trusted inmate the key to a supply room and sends the inmate to bring back a specific item from that room.
   B. A priest comes to make authorized visits to inmates. The correction officer is very busy, so he gives the priest the keys needed to reach certain groups of cells.
   C. An inmate has a pass to go to the library. A cellblock officer examines the pass, then unlocks the door and lets the inmate through.
   D. At the end of the day, a correction officer puts his keys in the pocket of his street clothes and takes them home with him.

3. *Decisions about handcuffing or restraining inmates are often up to the correction officers involved. However, an officer is legally responsible for exercising good judgment and for taking necessary precautions to prevent harm both to the inmate involved and to others.* 3.____

   In which one of the following situations is handcuffing or other physical restraint MOST likely to be needed?

A. An inmate seems to have lost control of his senses and is banging his fists repeatedly against the bars of his cell.
B. During the past two weeks, an inmate has deliberately tried to start three fights with other inmates.
C. An inmate claims to be sick and refuses to leave his cell for a scheduled meal.
D. During the night, an inmate begins to shout and sing, disturbing the sleep of other inmates.

4. *Some utensils that are ordinarily used in a kitchen can also serve as dangerous weapons – for instance, vegetable parers, meat saws, skewers, and icepicks. These should be classified as extremely hazardous.* 4.___

The MOST sensible way of solving the problems caused by the use of these utensils in a correctional institution is to

A. try to run the kitchen without using any of these utensils
B. provide careful supervision of inmates using such utensils in the kitchen
C. assign only trusted inmates to kitchen duty and let them use the tools without regular supervision
D. take no special precautions since inmates are not likely to think of using these commonplace utensils as weapons

5. *Inmates may try to conceal objects that can be used as weapons or as escape devices. Therefore, routine searches of cells or dormitories are necessary for safety and security.* 5.___

Of the following, it would probably be MOST effective to schedule routine searches to take place

A. on regular days and always at the same time of day
B. on regular days but at different times of day
C. at frequent but irregular intervals, always at the same time of day
D. at frequent but irregular intervals and at different times of day

6. *One of the purposes of conducting routine searches for forbidden items is to discourage inmates from acquiring such items in the first place. Inmates should soon come to realize that only possessors of these items have reason to fear or resent such searches.* 6.___

Inmates are MOST likely to come to this realization if

A. the searching officer leaves every inmate's possessions in a mess to make it clear that a search has taken place
B. the searching officer confiscates something from every cell, though he may later return most of the items
C. other inmates are not told when a forbidden item is found in an inmate's possession
D. all inmates know that possession of a forbidden item will result in punishment

7. Suppose you are a correction officer supervising a work detail of 22 inmates. All 22 checked in at the start of the work period. Making an informal count an hour later, you count only 21 inmates. 7.___
What is the FIRST action to take?

A. Count again to make absolutely sure how many inmates are present.
B. Report immediately that an inmate has escaped.
C. Try to figure out where the missing inmate could be.
D. Wait until the end of the work period and then make a formal roll call.

8. *The officer who is making a count at night when inmates are in bed must make sure he sees each man. The rule "see living breathing flesh" must be followed in making accurate counts.* 8.____

Of the following, which is the MOST likely reason for this rule?

A. An inmate may be concealing a weapon in the bed.
B. A bed may be arranged to give the appearance of being occupied even when the inmate is not there.
C. Waking inmates for the count is a good disciplinary measure because it shows them that they are under constant guard.
D. It is important for officers on duty at night to have something to do to keep them busy.

9. *When counting a group of inmates on a work assignment, great care should be taken to insure accuracy. The count method should be adapted to the number of inmates and to the type of location.* 9.____

Suppose that you are supervising 15 inmates working in a kitchen. Most of them are moving about constantly, carrying dishes and equipment from one place to another. In order to make an accurate count, which of the following methods would be MOST suitable under these circumstances?

A. Have the inmates *freeze* where they are whenever you call for a count, even though some of them may be carrying hot pans or heavy stacks of dishes.
B. Have the inmates stop their work and gather in one place whenever it is necessary to make a count.
C. Circulate among the inmates and make an approximate count while they are working.
D. Divide the group into sections according to type of work and assign one inmate in each group to give you the number for this section.

10. *Officers on duty at entrances must exercise the greatest care to prevent movement of unauthorized persons. At vehicle entrances, all vehicles must be inspected and a record kept of their arrival and departure.* 10.____

Assume that, as a correction officer, you have been assigned to duty at a vehicle entrance. Which of the following is probably the BEST method of preventing the movement of unauthorized persons in vehicles?

A. If passenger identifications are checked when vehicle enters, no check is necessary when the vehicle leaves.
B. Passenger identifications should be checked for all vehicles when vehicle enters and when it leaves.

C. Passenger identifications need not be checked when vehicle enters, but should always be checked when vehicle leaves.
D. Except for official vehicles, passenger identifications should be checked when vehicle enters and when it leaves.

11. In making a routine search of an inmate's cell, an officer finds various items. Although there is no immediate danger, he is not sure whether the inmate is permitted to have one of the items.
Of the following, the BEST action for the officer to take is to 11._

A. confiscate the item immediately
B. give the inmate the benefit of the doubt, and let him keep the item
C. consult his rule book or his supervising officer to find out whether the inmate is permitted to have the item
D. leave the item in the inmate's cell, but plan to report him for an infraction of the rules

12. *It is almost certain that there will be occasional escape attempts or an occasional riot or disturbance that requires immediate emergency action. A well-developed emergency plan for dealing with these events includes not only planning for prevention and control and planning for action during the disturbance, but also planning steps that should be taken when the disturbance is over.* 12._

When a disturbance is ended, which of the following steps should be taken FIRST?

A. Punishing the ringleaders.
B. Giving first aid to inmates or other persons who were injured.
C. Making an institutional count of all inmates.
D. Adopting further security rules to make sure such an incident does not occur again.

13. *It is often important to make notes about an occurrence that will require a written report or personal testimony.* 13._

Assume that a correction officer has made the following notes for the warden of the institution about a certain occurrence: *10:45 A.M. March 16, 2007. Cellblock A. Robert Brown was attacked by another inmate and knocked to the floor. Brown's head hit the floor hard. He was knocked out. I reported a medical emergency. Dr. Thomas Nunez came and examined Brown. The doctor recommended that Brown be transferred to the infirmary for observation. Brown was taken to the infirmary at 11:15 A.M.*
Which of the following important items of information is MISSING or is INCOMPLETE in these notes? The

A. time that the incident occurred
B. place where the incident occurred
C. names of both inmates involved in the fight
D. name of the doctor who made the medical examination

14. A correction officer has made the following notes for the warden of his institution about an incident involving an infraction of the rules: *March 29, 2007. Cellblock B-4. Inmates involved were A. Whitman, T. Brach, M. Purlin, M. Verey. Whitman and Brach started the trouble around 7:30 P.M. I called for assistance. Officer Haley and Officer Blair responded. Officer Blair got cut, and blood started running down his face. The bleeding looked very bad. He was taken to the hospital and needed eight stitches.* Which of the following items of information is MISSING or is INCOMPLETE in these notes? 14.____

   A. The time and date of the incident
   B. The place of the incident
   C. Which inmates took part in the incident
   D. What the inmates did that broke the rules

15. Your supervising officer has instructed you to follow a new system for handling inmate requests. It seems to you that the new system is not going to work very well and that inmates may resent it. What should you do? 15.____

   A. Continue handling requests the old way but do not let your supervising officer know you are doing this.
   B. Continue using the old system until you have a chance to discuss the matter with your supervising officer.
   C. Begin using the new system but plan to discuss the matter with your supervising officer if the system really does not work well.
   D. Begin using the new system but make sure the inmates know that it is not your idea and you do not approve of it.

16. *Inmates who are prison-wise may know a good many tricks for putting something over. For instance, it is an officer's duty to stop fights among inmates. Therefore, inmates who want to distract the officer's attention from something that is going on in one place may arrange for a phony fight to take place some distance away.* 16.____

   To avoid being taken in by a trick like this, a correction officer should

   A. ignore any fights that break out among inmates
   B. always make an inspection tour to see what is going on elsewhere before breaking up a fight
   C. be alert for other suspicious activity when there is any disturbance
   D. refuse to report inmates involved in a fight if the fight seems to have been phony

17. *Copies of the regulations are posted at various locations in the cellblock so that inmates can refer to them.* 17.____

   Suppose that one of the regulations is changed and the correction officers receive revised copies to post in their cellblocks. Of the following, the MOST effective way of informing the inmates of the revision is to

   A. let the inmates know that you are taking down the old copies and putting up new ones in their place
   B. post the new copies next to the old ones so that inmates will be able to compare them and learn about the change for themselves

C. leave the old copies up until you have had a chance to explain the change to each inmate
D. post the new copies in place of the old ones and also explain the change orally to the inmates

18. *A fracture is a broken bone. In a simple fracture, the skin is not broken. In a compound fracture, a broken end of the bone pierces the skin. Whenever a fracture is feared, the first thing to do is to prevent motion of the broken part.* 18._

Suppose that an inmate has just tripped on a stairway and twisted his ankle. He says it hurts badly, but you cannot tell what is wrong merely by looking at it.
Of the following, the BEST action to take is to

A. tell the inmate to stand up and see whether he can walk
B. move the ankle gently to see whether you can feel any broken ends of bones
C. tell the inmate to rest a few minutes and promise to return later to see whether his condition has improved
D. tell the inmate not to move his foot and put in a call for medical assistance

19. *It is part of institutional procedure that at specified times during each 24-hour period all inmates in the institution are counted simultaneously. Each inmate must be counted at a specific place at a specified time. All movement of inmates ceases from the time the count starts until it is finished and cleared as correct.* 19._

Assume that, as a correction officer, you are making such a count when an inmate in your area suddenly remembers he has an important 9 A.M. clinic appointment. You check his clinic pass and find that this is true.
What should you do?

A. Let him go to the clinic even though he may be counted again there.
B. Take him off your count and tell him to be sure he is included in the count being made at the clinic.
C. Keep him in your count and tell him to inform the officer at the clinic that he has already been counted.
D. Ask him to wait a few minutes until the counting period is over and then let him go to the clinic.

20. *Except in the case of a serious illness or injury (when a doctor should see the inmate immediately), emergency sick calls should be kept to a minimum, and inmates should be encouraged to wait for regular sick-call hours.* 20._

In which of the following cases is an emergency sick call MOST likely to be justified?
A(n)

A. inmate has had very severe stomach pains for several hours
B. inmate has cut his hand, and the bleeding has now stopped
C. inmate's glasses have been broken, and he is nearly blind without them
D. normally healthy inmate has lost his appetite and does not want to eat

21. *People who have lost their freedom are likely to go through periods of depression or to become extremely resentful or unpleasant. A correction officer can help inmates who are undergoing such periods of depression by respecting their feelings and treating them in a reasonable and tactful manner.*

    Suppose that an inmate reacts violently to a single request made in a normal, routine manner by a correction officer. Of the following, which is likely to be the MOST effective way of handling the situation?

    A. Point out to the inmate that it is his own fault that he is in jail, and he has nobody to blame for his troubles but himself.
    B. Tell the inmate that he is acting childishly and that he had better straighten out.
    C. Tell the inmate in a friendly way that you can see he is feeling down, but that he should comply with your request.
    D. Let the inmate know that you are going to report his behavior unless he changes his attitude.

21.____

22. An inmate tells you, a correction officer, of his concern about the ability of his wife and children to pay for rent and food while he is in the institution.
    Of the following, which is the BEST action to take?

    A. Assure him that his wife and children are getting along fine, although you do not actually know this.
    B. Put him in touch with the social worker or the correction employee who handles such problems.
    C. Offer to lend him money yourself if his family is really in need.
    D. Advise him to forget about his family and start concentrating on his own problems.

22.____

23. *It is particularly important to notice changes in the general pattern of an inmate's behavior. When an inmate who has been generally unpleasant and who has not spoken to an officer unless absolutely necessary becomes very friendly and cooperative, something has happened, and the officer should take steps to make sure what.*

    Of the following possible explanations for this change in behavior, which one is the LEAST likely to be the real cause?

    A. The inmate may be planning some kind of disturbance or escape attempt and is trying to fool the officer.
    B. The inmate may be trying to get on the officer's good side for some reason of his own.
    C. His friendliness and cooperation may indicate a developing mental illness.
    D. He may be overcoming his initial hostile reactions to his imprisonment.

23.____

24. As a correction officer, you have an idea about a new way for handling a certain procedure. Your method would require a minor change in the regulations, but you are sure it would be a real improvement.
    The BEST thing for you to do is to

    A. discuss the idea with your supervising officer, explaining why it would work better than the present method
    B. try your idea on your own cellblock, telling inmates that it is just an experiment and not official

24.____

C. attempt to get officers on other cellblocks to use your methods on a strictly unofficial basis
D. forget the whole thing since it might be too difficult to change the regulations

25. *Correction officers assigned to visiting areas have a dual supervisory function since their responsibilities include receiving persons other than inmates, as well as handling inmates. Here, of all places, it is important for an officer to realize that he is acting as a representative of his institution and that what he is doing is very much like public relations work.* 25.___

Assume that you are a correction officer assigned to duty in a visiting area. Which of the following ways of carrying out this assignment is MOST likely to result in good public relations? You should

A. treat inmates and visitors sternly because this will let them know that the institution does not put up with any nonsense
B. be friendly to inmates but suspicious of visitors
C. be stern with inmates but polite and tactful with visitors
D. treat both inmates and visitors in a polite but tactful way

---

KEY (CORRECT ANSWERS)

1. A
2. C
3. A
4. B
5. D

6. D
7. A
8. B
9. B
10. B

11. C
12. B
13. C
14. D
15. C

16. C
17. D
18. D
19. D
20. A

21. C
22. B
23. C
24. A
25. D

TEST 2

DIRECTIONS: Each question or incomplete statement is followed by several suggested answers or completions. Select the one that BEST answers the question or completes the statement. *PRINT THE LETTER OF THE CORRECT ANSWER IN THE SPACE AT THE RIGHT.*

Questions 1-5.

DIRECTIONS: Answer Questions 1 through 5 on the basis of the following passage.

The handling of supplies is an important part of correctional administration. A good deal of planning and organization is involved in purchase, stock control, and issue of bulk supplies to the cell-block. This planning is meaningless, however, if the final link in the chain – the cell-block officer who is in charge of distributing supplies to the inmates – does not do his job in the proper way. First, when supplies are received, the officer himself should immediately check them or should personally supervise the checking, to make sure the count is correct. Nothing but trouble will result if an officer signs for 200 towels and discovers hours later that he is 20 towels short. Did the 20 towels "disappear," or did they never arrive in the first place? Second, all supplies should be locked up until they are actually distributed. Third, the officer must keep accurate records when supplies are issued. Complaints will be kept to a minimum if the officer makes sure that each inmate has received the supplies to which he is entitled, and if the officer can tell from his records when it is time to reorder to prevent a shortage. Fourth, the officer should either issue the supplies himself or else personally supervise the issuing. It is unfair and unwise to put an inmate in charge of supplies without giving him adequate supervision. A small thing like a bar of soap does not mean much to most people, but it means a great deal to the inmate who cannot even shave or wash up unless he receives the soap that is supposed to be issued to him.

1. Which one of the following jobs is NOT mentioned by the passage as the responsibility of a cellblock officer? 1.____

   A. Purchasing supplies
   B. Issuing supplies
   C. Counting supplies when they are delivered to the cellblock
   D. Keeping accurate records when supplies are issued

2. The passage says that supplies should be counted when they are delivered. Of the following, which is the BEST way of handling this job? 2.____

   A. The cellblock officer can wait until he has some free time and then count them himself.
   B. An inmate can start counting them right away, even if the cellblock officer cannot supervise his work.
   C. The cellblock officer can personally supervise an inmate who counts the supplies when they are delivered.
   D. Two inmates can count them when they are delivered, supervising each other's work.

3. The passage gives an example concerning a delivery of 200 towels that turned out to be 20 towels short. 3.___
The example is used to show that

   A. the missing towels were stolen
   B. the missing towels never arrived in the first place
   C. it is impossible to tell what happened to the missing towels because no count was made when they were delivered
   D. it does not matter that the missing towels were not accounted for because it is never possible to keep track of supplies accurately

4. The MAIN reason given by the passage for making a record when supplies are issued is that keeping records 4.___

   A. will discourage inmates from stealing supplies
   B. is a way of making sure that each inmate receives the supplies to which he is entitled
   C. will show the officer's superiors that he is doing his job in the proper way
   D. will enable the inmates to help themselves to any supplies they need

5. The passage says that it is unfair to put an inmate in charge of supplies without giving him adequate supervision. 5.___
Which of the following is the MOST likely explanation of why it would be *unfair* to do this?

   A. A privilege should not be given to one inmate unless it is given to all the other inmates too.
   B. It is wrong to make on inmate work when all the others can sit in their cells and do nothing.
   C. The cellblock officer should not be able to get out of doing a job by making an inmate do it for him.
   D. The inmate in charge of supplies could be put under pressure by other inmates to do them *special favors.*

Questions 6-10.

DIRECTIONS: Answer Questions 6 through 10 on the basis of the following passage.

The typical correction official must make predictions about the probable future behavior of his charges in order to make judgments affecting those individuals. In learning to predict behavior, the results of scientific studies of inmate behavior can be of some use. Most studies that have been made show that older men tend to obey rules and regulations better than younger men, and tend to be more reliable in carrying out assigned jobs. Men who had good employment records on the outside also tend to be more reliable than men whose records show haphazard employment or unemployment. Oddly enough, men convicted of crimes of violence are less likely to be troublemakers than men convicted of burglary or other crimes involving stealth. While it might be expected that first offenders would be much less likely to be troublemakers than men with previous convictions, the difference between the two groups is not very great. It must be emphasized, however, that predictions based on a man's background are only likelihoods – they are never certainties. A successful correction officer learns to give some weight to a man's background, but he should rely even more heavily on his own personal judgment of the individual in question. A good officer will develop in time a kind of sixth sense about human beings that is more reliable than any statistical predictions.

6. The passage suggests that knowledge of scientific studies of inmate behavior would PROBABLY help the correction officer to 6.____

   A. make judgments that affect the inmates in his charge
   B. write reports on all major infractions of the rules
   C. accurately analyze how an inmate's behavior is determined by his background
   D. change the personalities of the individuals in his charge

7. According to the information in the passage, which one of the following groups of inmates would tend to be MOST reliable in carrying out assigned jobs? 7.____

   A. Older men with haphazard employment records
   B. Older men with regular employment records
   C. Younger men with haphazard employment records
   D. Younger men with regular employment records

8. According to the information in the passage, which of the following are MOST likely to be troublemakers? 8.____

   A. Older men convicted of crimes of violence
   B. Younger men convicted of crimes of violence
   C. Younger men convicted of crimes involving stealth
   D. First offenders convicted of crimes of violence

9. The passage indicates that information about a man's background is 9.____

   A. a sure way of predicting his future behavior
   B. of no use at all in predicting his future behavior
   C. more useful in predicting behavior than a correction officer's expert judgment
   D. less reliable in predicting behavior than a correction officer's expert judgment

10. The passage names two groups of inmates whose behavior might be expected to be quite different, but who in fact behave only slightly differently.
    These two groups are 10.____

    A. older men and younger men
    B. first offenders and men with previous convictions
    C. men with good employment records and men with records of haphazard employment or unemployment
    D. men who obey the rules and men who do not

Questions 11-17.

DIRECTIONS: Questions 11 through 17 are based on the following pictures of objects found in Cells A, B, C, and D in a correctional institution.

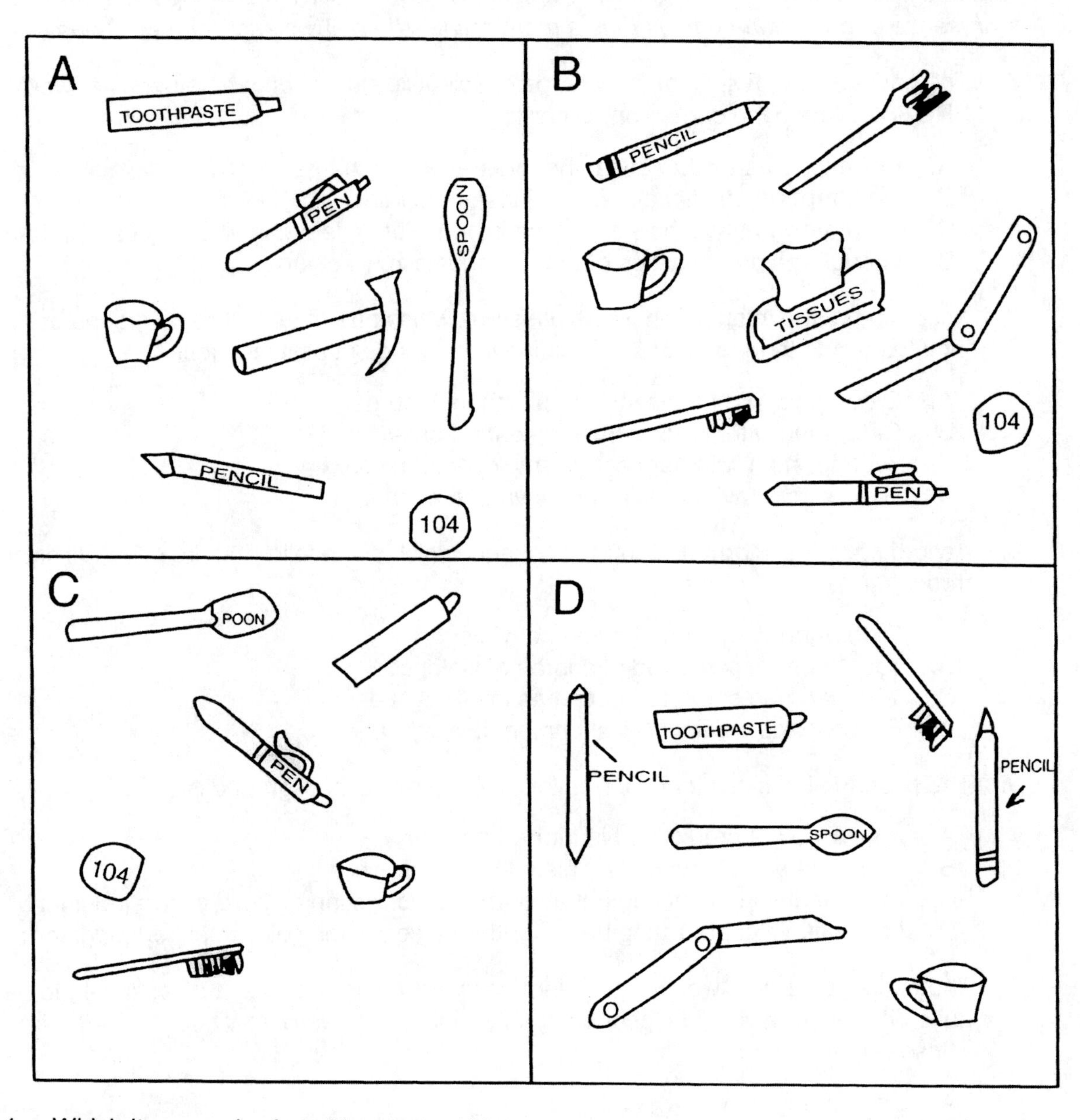

11. Which item can be found in every cell? 11.___

    A. Cup B. Money C. Pencil D. Toothpaste

12. Which cell has toothpaste but no toothbrush? 12.___

    A. A B. B C. C D. D

13. If knives and forks are prohibited in cells, how many cells are in violation of this rule? 13.___

    A. 1 B. 2 C. 3 D. 4

14. One inmate failed to return his tool in the woodworking shop before returning to his cell. That inmate is in Cell 14.___

    A. A B. B C. C D. D

15. The cell with the GREATEST number of objects is 15.____

A. A B. B C. C D. D

16. How many cells have AT LEAST one eating utensil? 16.____

A. 1 B. 2 C. 3 D. 4

17. Which cells contain money? 17.____

A. A, B, and C
B. A, B, and D
C. A, C, and D
D. B, C, and D

Questions 18-22.

DIRECTIONS: Answer Questions 18 through 22 on the basis of the following passage.

A large proportion of the people who are behind bars are not convicted criminals but people who have been arrested and are being held until their trial in court. Experts have often pointed out that this detention system does not operate fairly. For instance, a person who can afford to pay bail usually will not get looked up. The theory of the bail system is that the person will make sure to show up in court when he is supposed to since he knows that otherwise he will forfeit his bail -- he will lose the money he put up. Sometimes a person Who can show that he is a stable citizen with a job and a family will be released on "personal recognizance" (without bail). The result is that the well-to-do, the employed, and the family men can often avoid the detention system. The people who do wind up in detention tend to be the poor, the unemployed, the single, and the young.

18. According to the above passage, people who are put behind bars 18.____

A. are almost always dangerous criminals
B. include many innocent people who have been arrested by mistake
C. are often people who have been arrested but have not yet come to trial
D. are all poor people who tend to be young and single

19. The passage says that the detention system works *unfairly* against people who are 19.____

A. rich B. married C. old D. unemployed

20. The passage uses the expression *forfeit his bail.* Even if you have not seen the word *forfeit* before, you could figure out from the way it is used in the passage that *forfeiting* probably means ______ something. 20.____

A. losing track of
B. giving up
C. finding
D. avoiding

21. When someone is released on *personal recognizance,* this means that 21.____

A. the judge knows that he is innocent
B. he does not have to show up for a trial
C. he has a record of previous convictions
D. he does not have to pay bail

22. Suppose that two men were booked on the same charge at the same time, and that the same bail was set for both of them. One man was able to put up bail, and he was released. The second man was not able to put up bail, and he was held in detention. The reader of the passage would MOST likely feel that this result is 22.__

A. *unfair,* because it does not have any relation to guilt or innocence
B. *unfair,* because the first man deserves severe punishment
C. *fair,* because the first man is obviously innocent
D. *fair,* because the law should be tougher on poor people than on rich people

23. A certain cellblock has 240 inmates. From 8 A.M. to 9 A.M. on March 25, 120 inmates were assigned to cleanup work, and 25 inmates were sent for physical examinations. All the others remained in their cells. 23.__
How many inmates should have been in their cells during this hour?

A. 65
B. 85
C. 95
D. 105

24. There were 254 inmates in a certain cellblock at the beginning of the day. At 9:30 A.M., 12 inmates were checked out to the dispensary. At 10:00 A.M.,113 inmates were checked out to work details. At 10:30 A.M., 3 inmates were checked out to another cell-block. 24.__
How many inmates were present in this cellblock at 10:45 A.M. if none of the inmates who were checked out had returned?

A. 116
B. 126
C. 136
D. 226

25. There were 242 inmates in a certain cellblock at the beginning of the day. At 9:00 A.M., 116 inmates were checked out to a recreational program. At 9:15 A.M., 36 inmates were checked out to an educational program. At 9:30, 78 inmates were checked out on a work detail. By 10:15, the only inmates who had returned were 115 inmates who had been checked back in from the recreational program. A count made at 10:15 should show that the number of inmates present in the cellblock is 25.__

A. 127
B. 128
C. 135
D. 137

KEY (CORRECT ANSWERS)

1. A
2. C
3. C
4. B
5. D
6. A
7. B
8. C
9. D
10. B
11. A
12. A
13. B
14. A
15. B
16. D
17. A
18. C
19. D
20. B
21. D
22. A
23. C
24. B
25. A

EVALUATING INFORMATION AND EVIDENCE

EXAMINATION SECTION
TEST 1

DIRECTIONS: Each question or incomplete statement is followed by several suggested answers or completions. Select the one that BEST answers the question or completes the statement. *PRINT THE LETTER OF THE CORRECT ANSWER IN THE SPACE AT THE RIGHT.*

Questions 1 -9

Questions 1 through 9 measure your ability to (1) determine whether statements from witnesses say essentially the same thing and (2) determine the evidence needed to make it reasonably certain that a particular conclusion is true.

1. Which of the following pairs of statements say essentially the same thing in two different ways? 1.____

   I. Some employees at the water department have fully vested pensions.
   At least one employee at the water department has a pension that is not fully vested.

   II. All swans are white birds.
   A bird that is not white is not a swan.

   A. I only
   B. I and II
   C. II only
   D. Neither I nor II

2. Which of the following pairs of statements say essentially the same thing in two different ways? 2.____

   I. If you live in Humboldt County, your property taxes are high.
   If your property taxes are high, you live in Humboldt County.

   II. All the Hutchinsons live in Lindsborg.
   At least some Hutchinsons do not live in Lindsborg.

   A. I only
   B. I and II
   C. II only
   D. Neither I nor II

3. Which of the following pairs of statements say essentially the same thing in two different ways? 3.____

   I. Although Spike is a friendly dog, he is also one of the most unpopular dogs on the block.
   Although Spike is one of the most unpopular dogs on the block, he is a friendly dog.

   II. Everyone in Precinct 19 is taller than Officer Banks.
   Nobody in Precinct 19 is shorter than Officer Banks.

   A. I only
   B. I and II
   C. II only
   D. Neither I nor II

4. Which of the following pairs of statements say essentially the same thing in two different ways? 4._

   I. On Friday, every officer in Precinct 1 is assigned parking duty or crowd control, or both.
   If a Precinct 1 officer has been assigned neither parking duty nor crowd control, it is not Friday.

   II. Because the farmer mowed the hay fields today, his house will have mice tomorrow.
   Whenever the farmer mows his hay fields, his house has mice the next day.

   A. I only
   B. I and II
   C. II only
   D. Neither I nor II

5. Summary of Evidence Collected to Date: 5._

   I. Fishing in the Little Pony River is against the law.
   II. Captain Rick caught an 8-inch trout and ate it for dinner.

   Prematurely Drawn Conclusion: Captain Rick broke the law.
   Which of the following pieces of evidence, if any, would make it *reasonably certain* that the conclusion drawn is true?

   A. Captain Rick caught his trout in the Little Pony River
   B. There is no size limit on trout mentioned in the law
   C. A trout is a species of fish
   D. None of these

6. Summary of Evidence Collected to Date: 6._

   I. Some of the doctors in the ICU have been sued for malpractice
   II. Some of the doctors in the ICU are pediatricians

   Prematurely Drawn Conclusion: Some of the pediatricians in the ICU have never been sued for malpractice
   Which of the following pieces of evidence, if any, would make it *reasonably certain* that the conclusion drawn is true?

   A. The number of pediatricians in the ICU is the same as the number of doctors who have been sued for malpractice
   B. The number of pediatricians in the ICU is smaller than the number of doctors who have been sued for malpractice
   C. The number of ICU doctors who have been sued for malpractice is smaller than the number who are pediatricians
   D. None of these

7. Summary of Evidence Collected to Date: 7.____
   I. Along Paseo Boulevard, there are five convenience stores
   II. EZ-Go is east of Pop-a-Shop
   III. Kwik-E-Mart is west of Bob's Market
   IV. The Nightwatch is between EZ-Go and Kwik-E-Mart

   Prematurely Drawn Conclusion: Pop-a-Shop is the westernmost convenience store on Paseo Boulevard

   Which of the following pieces of evidence, if any, would make it *reasonably certain* that the conclusion drawn is true?

   A. Bob's Market is the easternmost convenience store on Paseo
   B. Kwik-E-Mart is the second store from the west
   C. The Nightwatch is west of the EZ-Go
   D. None of these

8. Summary of Evidence Collected to Date: 8.____
   Stark drove home from work at 70 miles an hour and wasn't breaking the law
   Prematurely Drawn Conclusion: Stark was either on an interstate highway or in the state of Montana
   Which of the following pieces of evidence, if any, would make it *reasonably certain* that the conclusion drawn is true?

   A. There are no interstate highways in Montana
   B. Montana is the only state that allows a speed of 70 miles an hour on roads other than interstate highways
   C. Most states don't allow speed of 70 miles an hour on state highways
   D. None of these

9. Summary of Evidence Collected to Date: 9.____
   I. Margaret, owner of *MetroWoman* magazine, signed a contract with each of her salespeople promising an automatic $200 bonus to any employee who sells more than 60 subscriptions in a calendar month
   II. Lynn sold 82 subscriptions to *MetroWoman* in the month of December

   Prematurely Drawn Conclusion: Lynn received a $200 bonus
   Which of the following pieces of evidence, if any, would make it *reasonably certain* that the conclusion drawn is true?

   A. Lynn is a salesperson
   B. Lynn works for Margaret
   C. Margaret offered only $200 regardless of the number of subscriptions sold
   D. None of these

Questions 10-14

Questions 10 through 14 refer to Map #3 and measure your ability to orient yourself within a given section of town, neighborhood or particular area. Each of the questions describes a starting point and a destination. Assume that you are driving a car in the area shown on the map accompanying the questions. Use the map as a basis for the shortest way to get from one point to another without breaking the law.

On the map, a street marked by arrows, or by arrows and the words "One Way," indicates one-way travel, and should be assumed to be one-way for the entire length, even when there are breaks or jogs in the street. EXCEPTION: A street that does not have the same name over the full length.

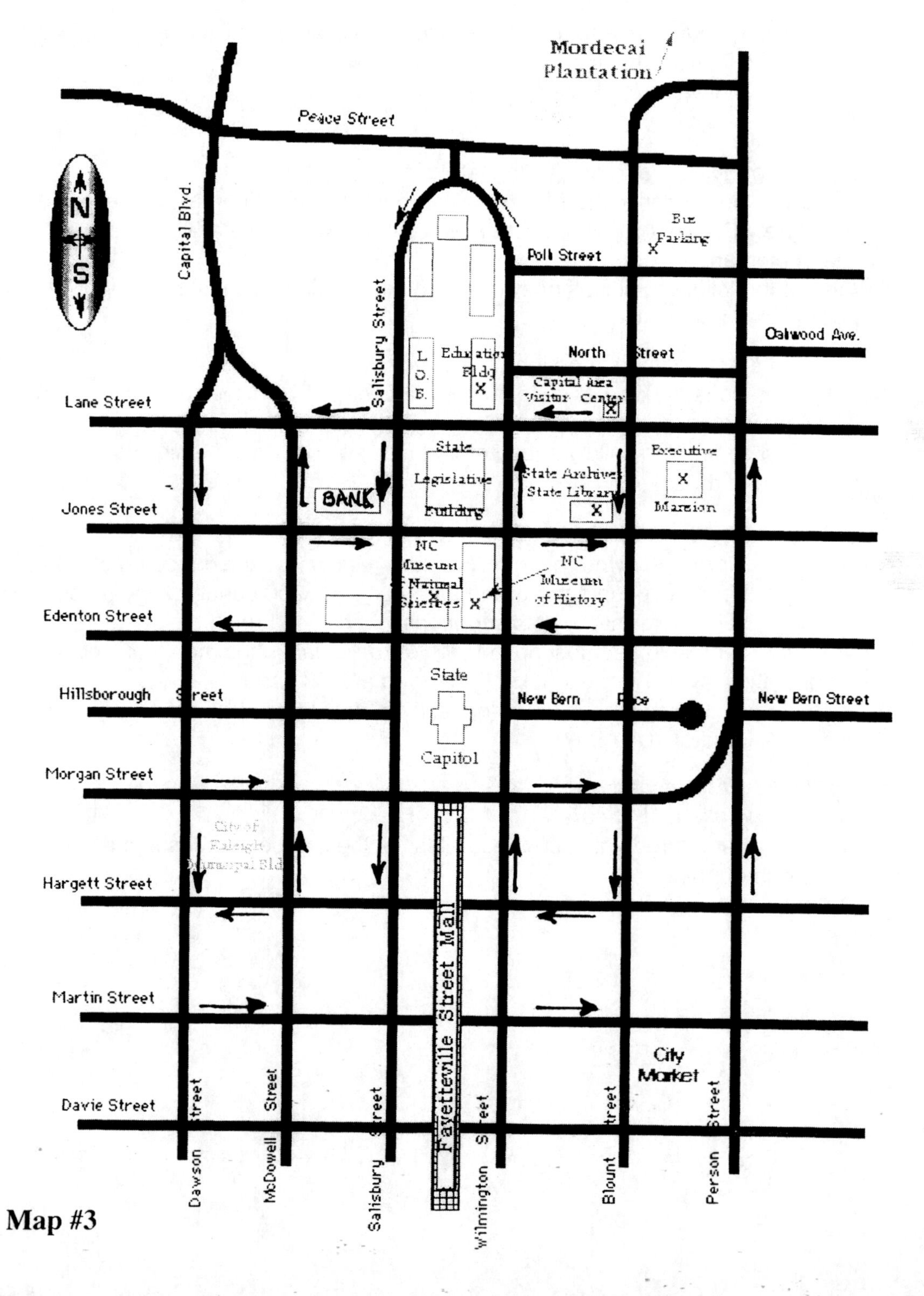

Map #3

10. The shortest legal way from the south end of the Fayetteville Street Mall, at Davie Street, to the city of Raleigh Municipal Building is 10.____

A. west on Davie, north on McDowell
B. west on Davie, north on Dawson
C. east on Davie, north on Wilmington, west on Morgan
D. east on Davie, north on Wilmington, west on Hargett

11. The shortest legal way from the City Market to the Education Building is 11.____

A. north on Blount, west on North
B. north on Person, west on Lane
C. north on Blount, west on Lane
D. west on Martin, north on Wilmington

12. The shortest legal way from the Education Building to the State Capitol is 12.____

A. south on Wilmington
B. north on Wilmington, west on Peace, south on Capitol, bear west to go south on Dawson, and east on Morgan
C. west on Lane, south on Salisbury
D. east on North, south on Blount, west on Edenton

13. The shortest legal way from the State Capitol to Peace College is 13.____

A. north on Wilmington, jog north, east on Peace
B. east on Morgan, north on Person, west on Peace
C. west on Edenton, north on McDowell, north on Capitol Blvd., east on Peace
D. east on Morgan, north on Blount, west on Peace

14. The shortest legal way from the State Legislative Building to the City Market is 14.____

A. south on Wilmington, east on Martin
B. east on Jones, south on Blount
C. south on Salisbury, east on Davie
D. east on Lane, south on Blount

Questions 15-19

Questions 15 through 19 refer to Figure #3, on the following page, and measure your ability to understand written descriptions of events. Each question presents a description of an accident or event and asks you which of the five drawings in Figure #3 BEST represents it. In the drawings, the following symbols are used:

Moving vehicle: Non-moving vehicle:

Pedestrian or bicyclist: ●

The path and direction of travel of a vehicle or pedestrian is indicated by a solid line.

The path and direction of travel of each vehicle or pedestrian directly involved in a collision from the point of impact is indicated by a dotted line.

In the space at the right, print the letter of the drawing that best fits the descriptions written below:

15. A driver headed north on Carson veers to the right and strikes a bicyclist who is also heading north. The bicyclist is thrown from the road. The driver flees north on Carson. 15._

16. A driver heading south on Carson runs the stop sign and barely misses colliding with an eastbound cyclist. The cyclist swerves to avoid the collision and continues traveling east. The driver swerves to avoid the collision and strikes a car parked in the northbound lane on Carson. 16._

17. A bicyclist heading west on Stone collides with a pedestrian in the crosswalk, then veers through the intersection and collides with the front of a car parked in the southbound lane on Carson. 17._

18. A driver traveling south on Carson runs over a bicyclist who has run the stop sign, and then flees south on Carson. 18._

19. A bicyclist heading west on Stone collides with the rear of a car parked in the westbound lane. 19._

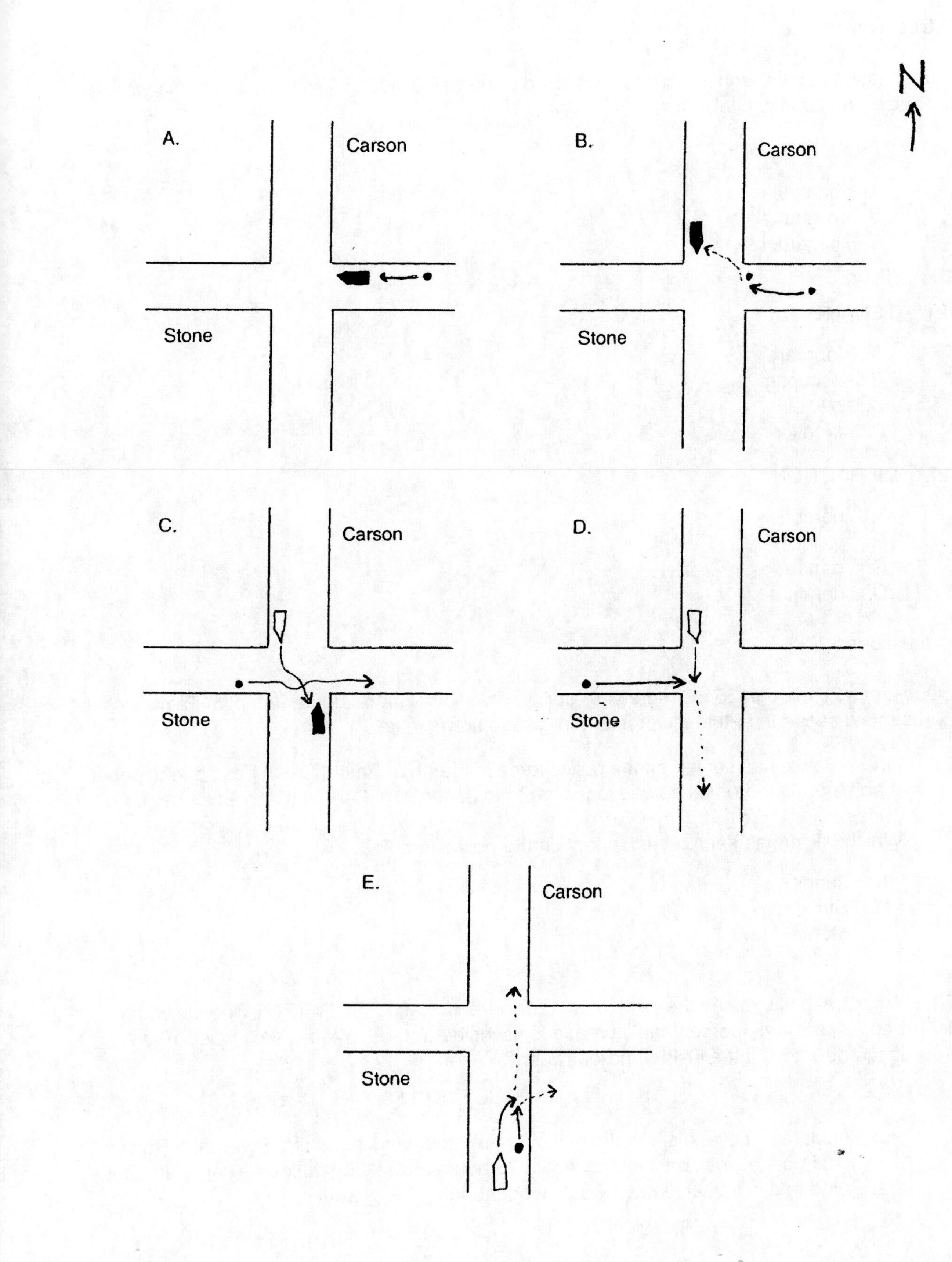
N
A.
Carson
Stone
B.
Carson
Stone
C.
Carson
Stone
D.
Carson
Stone
E.
Carson
Stone

Questions 20-22

In questions 20 through 22, choose the word or phrase CLOSEST in meaning to the word or phrase printed in capital letters.

20. INSOLVENT 20.___

A. bankrupt
B. vagrant
C. hazardous
D. illegal

21. TENANT 21.___

A. laborer
B. occupant
C. owner
D. creditor

22. INFRACTION 22.___

A. portion
B. violation
C. remark
D. detour

Questions 23-25

Questions 23 through 25 measure your ability to do fieldwork-related arithmetic. Each question presents a separate arithmetic problem for you to solve.

23. Officer Jones has served on the police force longer than Smith. Smith has served longer than Moore. Moore has served less time than Jones, and Park has served longer than Jones.
Which officer has served the longest on the police force? 23.___

A. Jones
B. Smith
C. Moore
D. Park

24. A car wash has raised the price of an outside-only wash from $4 to $5. The car wash applies the same percentage increase to its inside-and-out wash, which was $10. What is the new cost of the inside-and-out wash? 24.___

A. $8 B. $11 C. $12.50 D. $15

25. Ron and James, college students, make $10 an hour working at the restaurant. Ron works 13 hours a week and James works 20 hours a week. To make the same amount that Ron earns in a year, James would work about _______ weeks. 25.___

A. 18 B. 27 C. 34 D. 45

KEY (CORRECT ANSWERS)

1. C
2. D
3. B
4. B
5. A
6. D
7. B
8. B
9. B
10. A
11. B
12. C
13. A
14. B
15. E
16. C
17. B
18. D
19. A
20. A
21. B
22. B
23. D
24. C
25. C

TEST 2

DIRECTIONS: Each question or incomplete statement is followed by several suggested answers or completions. Select the one that BEST answers the question or completes the statement. *PRINT THE LETTER OF THE CORRECT ANSWER IN THE SPACE AT THE RIGHT.*

Questions 1 -9

Questions 1 through 9 measure your ability to (1) determine whether statements from witnesses say essentially the same thing and (2) determine the evidence needed to make it reasonably certain that a particular conclusion is true.

To do well on this part of the test, you do NOT have to have a working knowledge of police procedures and techniques. Nor do you have to have any more familiarity with criminals and criminal behavior than that acquired from reading newspapers, listening to radio or watching TV. To do well in this part, you must read and reason carefully.

1. Which of the following pairs of statements say essentially the same thing in two different ways? 1.___

   I. All of the teachers at Slater Middle School are intelligent, but some are irrational thinkers.
   Although some teachers at Slater Middle School are irrational thinkers, all of them are intelligent.

   II. Nobody has no friends.
   Everybody has at least one friend.

   A. I only
   B. I and II
   C. II only
   D. Neither I nor II

2. Which of the following pairs of statements say essentially the same thing in two different ways? 2.___

   I. Although bananas taste good to most people, they are also a healthy food.
   Bananas are a healthy food, but most people eat them because they taste good.

   II. If Dr. Jones is in, we should call at the office.
   Either Dr. Jones is in, or we should not call at the office.

   A. I only
   B. I and II
   C. II only
   D. Neither I nor II

3. Which of the following pairs of statements say essentially the same thing in two different ways? 3.___

   I. Some millworkers work two shifts.
   If someone works only one shift, he is probably not a millworker.

   II. If a letter carrier clocks in at nine, he can finish his route by the end of the day.
   If a letter carrier does not clock in at nine, he cannot finish his route by the end of the day.

   A. I only
   B. I and II
   C. II only
   D. Neither I nor II

4. Which of the following pairs of statements say essentially the same thing in two different ways? 4.____

   I. If a member of the swim team attends every practice, he will compete in the next meet.
   Either a swim team member will compete in the next meet, or he did not attend every practice.

   II. All the engineers in the drafting department who wear glasses know how to use AutoCAD.
   If an engineer wears glasses he will know how to use AutoCAD.

   A. I only
   B. I and II
   C. II only
   D. Neither I nor II

5. <u>Summary of Evidence Collected to Date:</u> 5.____
   All of the parents who attend the weekly parenting seminars are high school graduates.
   <u>Prematurely Drawn Conclusion:</u> Some parents who attend the weekly parenting seminars have been convicted of child abuse.
   Which of the following pieces of evidence, if any, would make it *reasonably certain* that the conclusion drawn is true?

   A. Those convicted of child abuse are often high school graduates
   B. Some high school graduates have been convicted of child abuse
   C. There is no correlation between education level and the incidence of child abuse
   D. None of these

6. <u>Summary of Evidence Collected to Date:</u> 6.____

   I. Mr. Cantwell promised to vote for new school buses if he was reelected to the board.
   II. If the new school buses are approved by the school board, then Mr. Cantwell was not reelected to the board.

   <u>Prematurely Drawn Conclusion:</u> Approval of the new school buses was defeated in spite of Mr. Cantwell's vote.
   Which of the following pieces of evidence, if any, would make it *reasonably certain* that the conclusion drawn is true?

   A. Mr. Cantwell decided not to run for reelection
   B. Mr. Cantwell was reelected to the board
   C. Mr. Cantwell changed his mind and voted against the new buses
   D. None of these

7. Summary of Evidence Collected to Date: 7.___

   I. The station employs three detectives: Francis, White and Stern. One of the detectives is a lieutenant, one is a sergeant and one is a major.
   II. Francis is not a lieutenant.

   Prematurely Drawn Conclusion: Jackson is a lieutenant.
   Which of the following pieces of evidence, if any, would make it *reasonably certain* that the conclusion drawn is true?

   A. Stern is not a sergeant
   B. Stern is a major
   C. Francis is a major
   D. None of these

8. Summary of Evidence Collected to Date: 8.___

   I. In the office building, every survival kit that contains a gas mask also contains anthrax vaccine.
   II. Some of the kits containing water purification tablets also contain anthrax vaccine.

   Prematurely Drawn Conclusion: If the survival kit near the typists' pool contains a gas mask, it does not contain water purification tablets.
   Which of the following pieces of evidence, if any, would make it *reasonably certain* that the conclusion drawn is true?

   A. Some survival kits contain all three items
   B. The survival kit near the typists' pool contains anthrax vaccine
   C. The survival kit near the typists' pool contains only two of these items
   D. None of these

9. Summary of Evidence Collected to Date: 9.___
   The shrink-wrap mechanism is designed to shut itself off if the heating coil temperature drops below 400 during the twin cycle.
   Prematurely Drawn Conclusion: If the machine was operating the twin cycle on Monday, it was not operating properly.
   Which of the following pieces of evidence, if any, would make it *reasonably certain* that the conclusion drawn is true?

   A. On Monday the heating coil temperature reached 450
   B. When the machine performs functions other than the twin cycle, the heating coil temperature sometimes drops below 400
   C. The shrink-wrap mechanism did not shut itself off on Monday
   D. None of these

Questions 10-14

Questions 10 through 14 refer to Map #4, located on the following page, and measure your ability to orient yourself within a given section of town, neighborhood or particular area. Each of the questions describes a starting point and a destination. Assume that you are driving a car in the area shown on the map accompanying the questions. Use the map as a basis for the shortest way to get from one point to another without breaking the law.

On the map, a street marked by arrows, or by arrows and the words "One Way," indicates one-way travel, and should be assumed to be one-way for the entire length, even when there are breaks or jogs in the street. EXCEPTION: A street that does not have the same name over the full length.

10. The shortest legal way from the State Capitol to Idaho Power is 10.____

A. south on Capitol Blvd., west on Main, north on 12th
B. south on 8th, west on Main
C. west on Jefferson, south on 12th
D. south on Capitol Blvd., west on Front, north on 12th

11. The shortest legal way from the Jefferson Place Building to the Statesman Building is 11.____

A. east on Jefferson, south on Capitol Blvd.
B. south on 8th, east on Main
C. east on Jefferson, south on 4th, west on Main
D. south on 9th, east on Main

12. The shortest legal way from Julia Davis Park to Owyhee Plaza Hotel is 12.____

A. north on 5th, west on Front, north on 11th
B. north on 6th, west on Main
C. west on Battery, north on 9th, west on Front, north on Main
D. north on 5th, west on Front, north on 13th, east on Main

13. The shortest legal way from the Big Easy to City Hall is 13.____

A. north on 9th, east on Main
B. east on Myrtle, north on Capitol Blvd.
C. north on 9th, east on Idaho
D. east on Myrtle, north on 6th

14. The shortest legal way from the Boise Contemporary Theater to the Pioneer Building is 14.____

A. north on 9th, east on Main
B. north on 9th, east on Myrtle, north on 6th
C. east on Fulton, north on Capitol Blvd., east on Main
D. east on Fulton, north on 6th

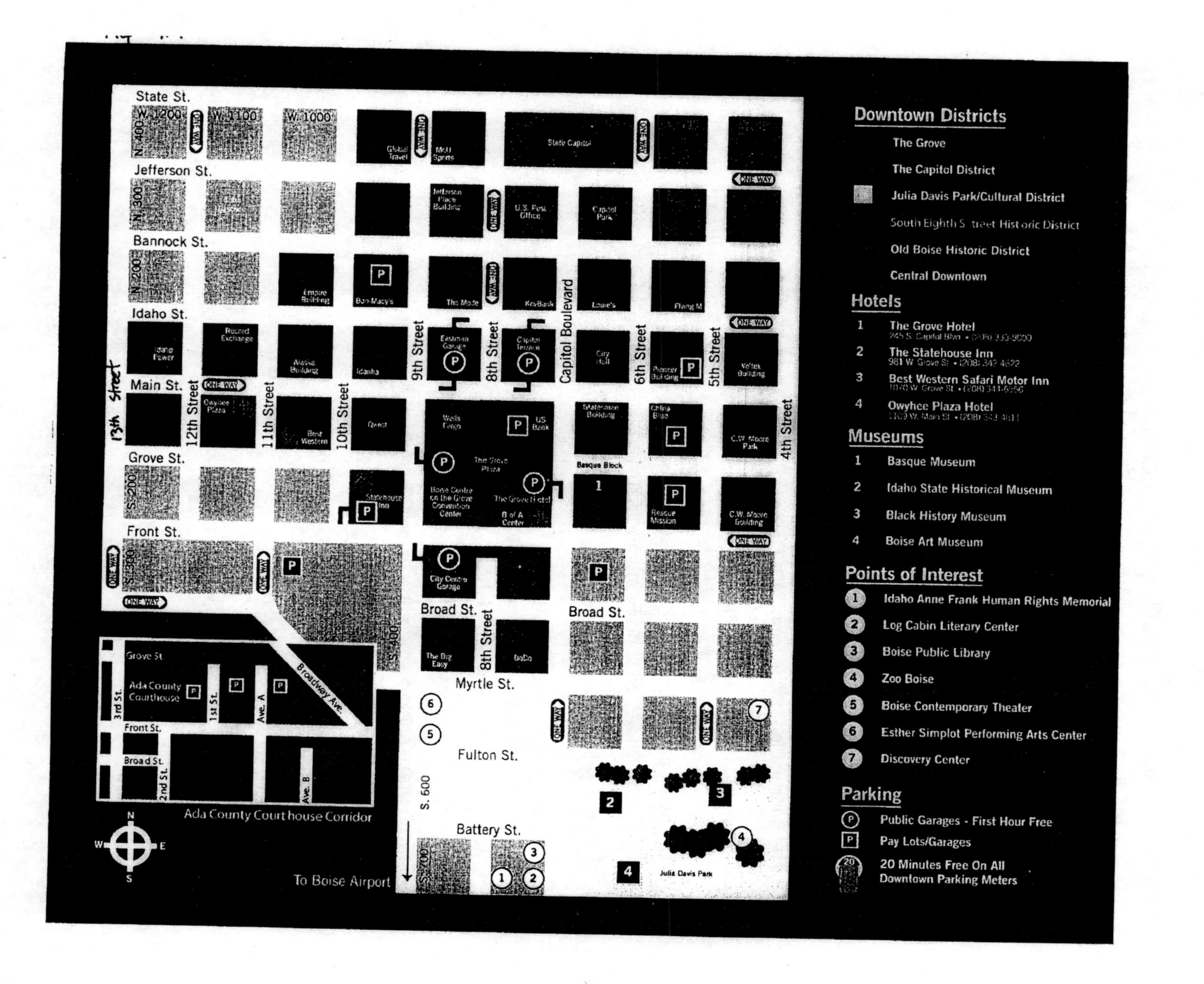

State St.
Jefferson St.
Bannock St.
Idaho St.
Main St.
Grove St.
Front St.
Broad St.
Myrtle St.
Fulton St.
Battery St.
W. 1200
W. 1100
W. 1000
N. 400
N. 300
N. 200
S. 200
S. 300
S. 400
S. 600
S. 700
13th Street
12th Street
11th Street
10th Street
9th Street
8th Street
Capitol Boulevard
6th Street
5th Street
4th Street
ONE WAY
Global Travel
McU Sports
State Capitol
Jefferson Place Building
U.S. Post Office
Capitol Park
Empire Building
Bon-Macy's
The Mode
KeyBank
Louie's
Flying M
Idaho Power
Record Exchange
Alaska Building
Idanha
Eastman Garage
Capitol Terrace
City Hall
Pioneer Building
Veltex Building
Owyhee Plaza
Best Western
Qwest
Wells Fargo
US Bank
Statesman Building
China Blue
C.W. Moore Park
The Grove Plaza
Boise Centre on the Grove Convention Center
The Grove Hotel
B of A Center
Statehouse Inn
Basque Block
Rescue Mission
C.W. Moore Building
City Centre Garage
The Big Easy
BoDo
Broadway Ave.
Grove St.
Ada County Courthouse
3rd St.
1st St.
Ave. A
Front St.
Broad St.
2nd St.
Ave. B
Ada County Courthouse Corridor
To Boise Airport
Julia Davis Park
N
W
E
S
Downtown Districts
The Grove
The Capitol District
Julia Davis Park/Cultural District
South Eighth Street Historic District
Old Boise Historic District
Central Downtown
Hotels
1 The Grove Hotel
2 The Statehouse Inn
3 Best Western Safari Motor Inn
4 Owyhee Plaza Hotel
Museums
1 Basque Museum
2 Idaho State Historical Museum
3 Black History Museum
4 Boise Art Museum
Points of Interest
1 Idaho Anne Frank Human Rights Memorial
2 Log Cabin Literary Center
3 Boise Public Library
4 Zoo Boise
5 Boise Contemporary Theater
6 Esther Simplot Performing Arts Center
7 Discovery Center
Parking
Public Garages - First Hour Free
Pay Lots/Garages
20 Minutes Free On All Downtown Parking Meters

Questions 15-19

Questions 15 through 19 refer to Figure #4, on the following page, and measure your ability to understand written descriptions of events. Each question presents a description of an accident or event and asks you which of the five drawings in Figure #4 BEST represents it.

In the drawings, the following symbols are used:

Moving vehicle: ⌂ Non-moving vehicle: ☗

Pedestrian or bicyclist: ●

The path and direction of travel of a vehicle or pedestrian is indicated by a solid line.

The path and direction of travel of each vehicle or pedestrian directly involved in a collision from the point of impact is indicated by a dotted line.

In the space at the right, print the letter of the drawing that best fits the descriptions written below:

15. A driver headed east on Union strikes a car that is pulling out from between two parked cars, and then continues east. 15.____

16. A driver headed north on Post strikes a car that is pulling out from in front of a parked car, then veers into the oncoming lane and collides head-on with a car that is parked in the southbound lane of Post. 16.____

17. A driver headed east on Union strikes a car that is pulling out from between two parked cars, travels through the intersection, and makes a sudden right turn onto Cherry, where he strikes a parked car in the rear. 17.____

18. A driver headed west on Union strikes a car that is pulling out from between two parked cars, and then swerves to the left. He cuts the corner and travels over the sidewalk at the intersection of Cherry and Post, and then strikes a car that is parked in the northbound lane on Post. 18.____

19. A driver headed east on Union strikes a car that is pulling out from between two parked cars, and then swerves to the left. He cuts the corner and travels over the sidewalk at the intersection of Oak and Post, and then flees north on Post. 19.____

FIGURE #4

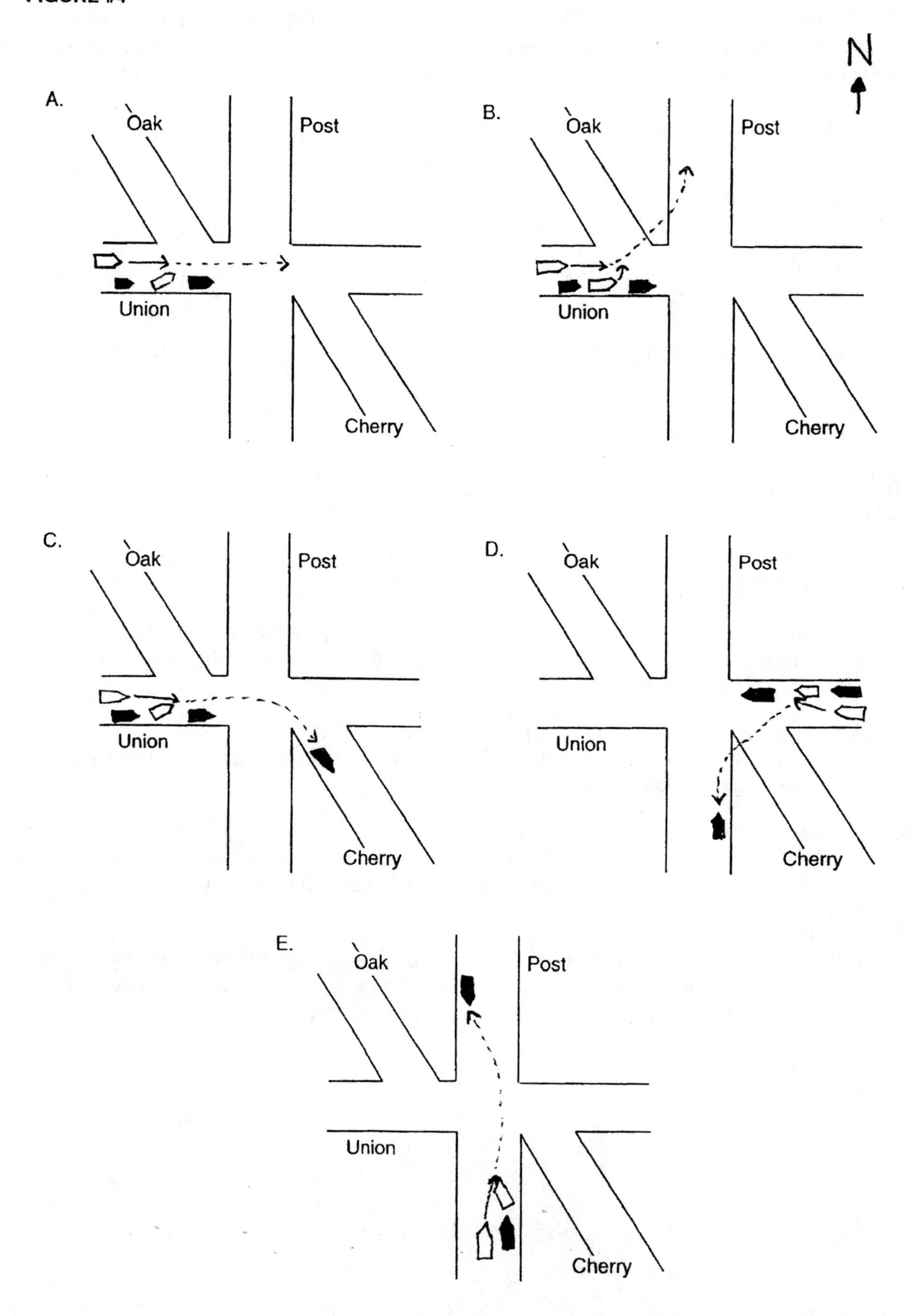
N
A.
Oak
Post
Union
Cherry
B.
Oak
Post
Union
Cherry
C.
Oak
Post
Union
Cherry
D.
Oak
Post
Union
Cherry
E.
Oak
Post
Union
Cherry

Questions 20-22

In questions 20 through 22, choose the word or phrase CLOSEST in meaning to the word or phrase printed in capital letters.

20. TITLE 20.____

A. danger
B. ownership
C. description
D. treatise

21. REVOKE 21.____

A. cancel
B. imagine
C. solicit
D. cause

22. BRIEF 22.____

A. summary
B. ruling
C. plea
D. motion

Questions 23-25

Questions 23 through 25 measure your ability to do fieldwork-related arithmetic. Each question presents a separate arithmetic problem for you to solve.

23. An investigator plans to drive from his home to Los Angeles, a trip of 2,800 miles. His car has a 24-gallon tank and gets 18 miles to the gallon. If he starts out with a full tank of gasoline, what is the FEWEST number of stops he will have to make for gasoline to complete his trip to Los Angeles? 23.____

A. 4 B. 5 C. 6 D. 7

24. A caseworker has 24 home visits to schedule for a week. She will visit three homes on Sunday, and on every day that follows she will visit one more home than she visited on the previous day. At the end of the day on ______, the caseworker will have completed all of her home visits. 24.____

A. Wednesday
B. Thursday
C. Friday
D. Saturday

25. Ms. Langhorn takes a cab from her house to the airport. The cab company charges $3.00 to start the meter and $.50 per mile after that. It's 15 miles from Ms. Langhorn's house to the airport. How much will she have to pay for a cab? 25.____

A. $10.50 B. $11.50 C. $14.00 D. $15.50

KEY (CORRECT ANSWERS)

1. A
2. C
3. D
4. A
5. D
6. B
7. B
8. C
9. D
10. C
11. D
12. A
13. B
14. C
15. A
16. E
17. C
18. D
19. B
20. B
21. A
22. A
23. C
24. B
25. A

READING COMPREHENSION
UNDERSTANDING AND INTERPRETING WRITTEN MATERIAL

EXAMINATION SECTION
TEST 1

DIRECTIONS: Each question or incomplete statement is followed by several suggested answers or completions. Select the one that BEST answers the question or completes the statement. *PRINT THE LETTER OF THE CORRECT ANSWER IN THE SPACE AT THE RIGHT.*

1. Custody in prison work used to be considered of such supreme importance that everything else was secondary. This statement implies MOST directly that 1.____

   A. formerly nothing was as important as custody in prison work
   B. formerly only custody was considered important in prison work
   C. today all aspects of prison work are considered equally important
   D. today reform of the prisoner is considered more important than custody

2. Since the total inmate treatment and training program is conditioned largely by custody requirements, its success is almost wholly dependent on flexibility of custody classification and handling of prisoners. 2.____
   Of the following, the MOST accurate statement based on the above statement is that the

   A. conditions of custody are completely dependent on the handling of inmates in accordance with their classification
   B. daily schedule at the institution should be flexible in order for the treatment and training program to succeed
   C. main factor influencing the inmate treatment and training program is the requirement for the proper safekeeping of inmates
   D. most important factor in the success of the treatment and training program is the cooperation of the inmates

3. An officer's revolver is a defensive and not offensive weapon. 3.____
   On the basis of this statement only, an officer should BEST draw his revolver to

   A. fire at an unarmed burglar
   B. force a suspect to confess
   C. frighten a juvenile delinquent
   D. protect his own life

4. Prevention of crime is of greater value to the community than the punishment of crime. 4.____
   If this statement is accepted as true, GREATEST emphasis should be placed on

   A. malingering
   B. medication
   C. imprisonment
   D. rehabilitation

5. The criminal is rarely or never reformed. Acceptance of this statement as true would mean that GREATEST emphasis should be placed on 5.____

   A. imprisonment
   B. parole
   C. probation
   D. malingering

6. Physical punishment of prison inmates has been shown by experience not only to be ineffective but to be dangerous and, in the long run, destructive of good discipline. According to the preceding statement, it is MOST reasonable to assume that, in the supervision of prison inmates, 6.__

   A. a good correction officer would not use physical punishment
   B. it is permissible for a good correction officer to use a limited amount of physical punishment to enforce discipline
   C. physical punishment improves discipline temporarily
   D. the danger of public scandal is basic in cases where physical punishment is used

7. There is no clear evidence that criminals, as a group, differ from non-criminals in their basic psychological needs.
   On the basis of this statement, it is MOST reasonable to assume that criminals and non-criminals 7.__

   A. are alike in some important respects
   B. are alike in their respective backgrounds
   C. differ but slightly in all respects
   D. differ in physical characteristics

8. Neither immediate protection for the community nor long-range reformation of the prisoner can be achieved by prison personnel who express toward the offender whatever feelings of frustration, fear, jealousy, or hunger for power they may have.
   Of the following, the CHIEF significance of this statement for correction officers is that, in their daily work, they should 8.__

   A. be on the constant lookout for opportunities to prove their courage to inmates
   B. not allow deeply personal problems to affect their relations with the inmates
   C. not try to advance themselves on the job because of personal motives
   D. spend a good part of their time examining their own feelings in order to understand better those of the inmates

9. Since ninety-five percent of prison inmates are released, and a great majority of these within two to three years, a prison which does nothing more than separate the criminal from society offers little promise of real protection to society.
   Of the following, the MOST valid reference which may be drawn from the preceding statement is that 9.__

   A. once it has been definitely established that a person has criminal tendencies, that person should be separated for the rest of his life from ordinary society
   B. prison sentences in general are much too short and should be lengthened to afford greater protection to society
   C. punishment, rather than separation of the criminal from society, should be the major objective of a correctional prison
   D. when a prison system produces no change in prisoners, and the period of imprisonment is short, the period during which society is protected is also short

10. A great handicap to successful correctional work lies in the negative response of the general community to the offender. Public attitudes of hostility toward, and rejection of, an ex-prisoner can undo the beneficial effects of even an ideal correctional system. Of the following, the CHIEF implication of this statement is that 10.____

    A. a friendly community attitude will insure the successful reformation of the ex-prisoner
    B. correctional efforts with most prisoners would generally prove successful if it were not for public hostility toward the former inmate
    C. in the long run, even an ideal correctional system cannot successfully reform criminals
    D. the attitude of the community toward an ex-prisoner is an important factor in determining whether or not an ex-prisoner reforms

11. While retribution and deterrence as a general philosophy in correction are widely condemned, no one raises any doubt as to the necessity for secure custody of some criminals. Of the following, the MOST valid conclusion based on the preceding statement is that the 11.____

    A. gradual change in the philosophy of correction has not affected custody practices
    B. need for safe custody of some criminals is not questioned by anyone
    C. philosophy of retribution, as shown in some correctional systems, has led to wide condemnation of custodial practices applied to all types of criminals

Questions 12-13.

DIRECTIONS: Questions 12 and 13 are to be answered SOLELY on the basis of the information contained in the following paragraph.

Those correction theorists who are in agreement with severe and rigid controls as a normal part of the correctional process are confronted with a contradiction; this is so because a responsibility which is consistent with freedom cannot be developed in a repressive atmosphere. They do not recognize this contradiction when they carry out their programs with dictatorial force and expect convicted criminals exposed to such programs to be reformed into free and responsible citizens.

12. According to the above paragraph, those correction theorists are faced with a contradiction who 12.____

    A. are in favor of the enforcement of strict controls in a prison
    B. believe that to develop a sense of responsibility, freedom must not be restricted
    C. take the position that the development of responsibility consistent with freedom is not possible in a repressive atmosphere
    D. think that freedom and responsibility can be developed only in a democratic atmosphere

13. According to the above paragraph, a repressive atmosphere in a prison 13.____

    A. does not conform to present day ideas of freedom of the individual
    B. is admitted by correction theorists to be in conflict with the basic principles of the normal correctional process

C. is advocated as the best method of maintaining discipline when rehabilitation is of secondary importance
D. is not suitable for the development of a sense of responsibility consistent with freedom

14. To state the matter in simplest terms, just as surely as some people are inclined to commit crimes, so some people are prevented from committing crimes by the fear of the consequences to themselves.
Of the following, the MOST logical conclusion based on this statement is that
14._

A. as many people are prevented from committing criminal acts as actually commit criminal acts
B. most men are not inclined to commit crimes
C. people who are inclined to violate the law are usually deterred from their purpose
D. there are people who have a tendency to commit crimes and people who are deterred from crime

15. Probation is a judicial instrument whereby a judge may withhold execution of a sentence upon a convicted person in order to give opportunity for rehabilitation in the community under the guidance of an officer of the court. According to the preceding statement, it is MOST reasonable to assume that
15._

A. a person on probation must report to the court at least once a month
B. a person who has been convicted of crime is sometimes placed on probation by the judge
C. criminals who have been rehabilitated in the community are placed on probation by the court after they are sentenced
D. the chief purpose of probation is to make the sentence easier to serve

Questions 16-19.

DIRECTIONS: Questions 16 through 19 are to be answered SOLELY on the basis of the following passage.

Traditional correctional institutions do not change or redirect the behavior of many of their inmates. Few of these establishments are equipped with adequate resources to treat the social and psychological handicaps of their wards. Too often, far removed ideologically from the world to which its charges must return, the institution often compounds the problems its corrective mechanisms are intended to cure. Training school academic programs, for example, range from poor to totally inadequate and usually reinforce negative feelings toward future learning experiences. Vocational programs are frequently designed to benefit the institution without regard to the inmate, and the usual low-key common denominator *treatment* program scarcely begins to meet the needs of many offenders.

Most correctional institutions must mobilize their limited resources in time and talent for purposes other than the ever-present concern about runaways or escapes. No one could quarrel rationally with the need to safeguard the community and control the behavior of people who may be of danger to themselves or others. It is ridiculous and tragic, however, that an overstated security approach is still the rule for the bulk of our correctional population.

16. The passage states that inmates of traditional correctional institutions are LIKELY to 16.____

    A. develop belief in radical political ideologies
    B. experience conditions that produce no betterment
    C. give major attention to devising plans of escape
    D. desire vocational training unrelated to their individual potential

17. The passage indicates that traditional training school academic programs lead inmates to 17.____

    A. adjust to the institutional setting
    B. avoid later formal learning
    C. develop respect for the values of education
    D. request more practical, vocational training

18. The passage indicates that most traditional correctional institutions, because of their ideological distance from the realities of the outside world, are MOST likely to 18.____

    A. ignore the safety of the outside community
    B. favor a minority of the inmate population
    C. lack properly motivated staff
    D. increase the problems of inmates

19. The passage states that the strong custodial function in most correctional institutions is MOST likely to be 19.____

    A. accorded excessive emphasis
    B. aimed at incorrigible inmates only
    C. necessary to redirect inmate behavior
    D. resented by the outside community

Questions 20-22.

DIRECTIONS: Questions 20 through 22 are to be answered SOLELY on the basis of the following passage.

The most widely accepted argument in favor of the death penalty is that the threat of its infliction deters people from committing capital offenses. Of course, since human behavior can be influenced through fear, and since man tends to fear death, it is possible to use capital punishment as a deterrent. But the real question is whether individuals think of the death penalty BEFORE they act, and whether they are thereby deterred from committing crimes. If for the moment we assume that the death penalty does this to some extent, we must also grant that certain human traits limit its effectiveness as a deterrent. Man tends to be a creature of habit and emotion, and when he is handicapped by poverty, ignorance, and malnutrition, as criminals often are, he becomes notoriously shortsighted. Many violators of the law give little thought to the possibility of detection and apprehension, and often they do not even consider the penalty. Moreover, it appears that most people do not regulate their lives in terms of the pleasure and pain that may result from their acts.

Human nature is very complex. A criminal may fear punishment, but he may fear the anger and contempt of his companions or his family even more, and the fear of economic insecurity or exclusion from the group whose respect he cherishes may drive him to commit the most daring crimes. Besides, fear is not the only emotion that motivates man. Love, loyalty, ambition, greed, lust, anger, and resentment may steel him to face even death in the perpetration of crime, and impel him to devise the most ingenious methods to get what he wants and to avoid detection.

If the death penalty were surely, quickly, uniformly, publicly, and painfully inflicted, it undoubtedly would prevent many capital offenses that are being committed by those who do consider the punishment that they may receive for their crimes. But this is precisely the point. Certainly, the way in which the death penalty has been administered in the United States is not fitted to produce this result.

20. Of the following, the MOST appropriate title for the above passage is 20.___

    A. CAPITAL OFFENSES IN THE UNITED STATES
    B. THE DEATH PENALTY AS A DETERRENT
    C. HUMAN NATURE AND FEAR
    D. EMOTION AS A CAUSE OF CRIME

21. The above passage implies that the death penalty, as it has been administered in the United States, 21.___

    A. was too prompt and uniform to be effective
    B. deterred many criminals who considered the possible consequences of their actions
    C. prevented crimes primarily among habitual criminals
    D. failed to prevent the commission of many capital offenses

22. According to the above passage, many violators of the law are 22.___

    A. intensely concerned with the pleasure or pain that may result from their acts
    B. influenced primarily by economic factors
    C. not influenced by the opinions of their family or friends
    D. not seriously concerned with the possibility of apprehension

Questions 23-25.

DIRECTIONS: Questions 23 through 25 are to be answered SOLELY on the basis of the information contained in the following paragraph.

As a secondary aspect of this revolutionary change in outlook resulting from the introduction of group counseling into the adult correctional institution, there must evolve a new type of prison employee, the true correctional or treatment worker. The top management will have to reorient their attitudes toward subordinate employees, respecting and accepting them as equal participants in the work of the institution. Rank may no longer be the measure of value in the inmate treatment program. Instead, the employee will be valuable whatever his location in the prison hierarchy or administrative plan in terms of his capacity constructively to relate himself to inmates as one human being to another. In group counseling, all employees must consider it their primary task to provide a wholesome environment for personality growth for the inmates in work crews, cell blocks, clerical pools, or classrooms. The above does not mean that custodial care and precautions regarding the prevention of disorders or escapes are cast aside or discarded by prison workers. On the contrary, the staff will be more acutely aware of the costs to the inmates of such infractions of institutional rules. Gradually, it is hoped, these instances of uncontrolled responses to over-powering feelings by inmates will become much less frequent in the treatment institution, In general, men in group counseling provide considerably fewer disciplinary infractions when compared with a control group of those still on a waiting list to enter group counseling, and especially fewer than those who do not choose to participate. It is optimistically anticipated that some day men in prison may have the same attitudes toward the staff, the same security in expecting treatment as do patients in a good general hospital.

23. According to the above paragraph, under a program of group counseling in an adult correctional institution, that employee will be MOST valuable in the inmate treatment program who 23.____

A. can establish a constructive relationship of one human being to another between himself and the inmate
B. gets top management to accept him as an equal participant in the work of the institution
C. is in contact with the inmate in work crews, cell blocks, clerical pools or classrooms
D. provides the inmate with a proper home environment for wholesome personality growth

24. According to the above paragraph, an effect that the group counseling program is expected to have on the problem of custody and discipline in a prison is that the staff will 24.____

A. be more acutely aware of the cost of maintaining strict prison discipline
B. discard old and outmoded notions of custodial care and the prevention of disorders and escapes
C. neglect this aspect of prison work unless proper safeguards are established
D. realize more deeply the harmful effect on the inmate of breaches of discipline

25. According to the above paragraph, a result that is expected from the group counseling method of inmate treatment in an adult correctional institution is 25.____

A. a greater desire on the part of potential delinquents to enter the correctional institution for the purpose of securing treatment
B. a large reduction in the number of infractions of institutional rules by inmates
C. a steady decrease in the crime rate
D. the introduction of hospital methods of organization and operation into the correctional institution

KEY (CORRECT ANSWERS)

1. A
2. C
3. D
4. D
5. A
6. A
7. A
8. B
9. D
10. D
11. B
12. A
13. D
14. D
15. B
16. B
17. B
18. D
19. A
20. B
21. D
22. D
23. A
24. D
25. B

TEST 2

DIRECTIONS: Each question or incomplete statement is followed by several suggested answers or completions. Select the one that BEST answers the question or completes the statement. *PRINT THE LETTER OF THE CORRECT ANSWER IN THE SPACE AT THE RIGHT.*

Questions 1-7.

DIRECTIONS: Questions 1 through 7 are to be answered on the basis of the following paragraph.

FLAGGING RULES

When a track gang is going to work under flagging protection at a given location, the Desk Trainmaster of the division must be notified. Work on trainways must not be performed on operating tracks between 6:00 A.M. and 9:00 A.M., or between 4:00 P.M. and 7:00 P.M. A flagman must be selected from the list of flagmen qualified as such by the Assistant General Superintendent. No person acting as a flagman may be assigned any duties other than those of a flagman. For underground flagging signals, lighted lanterns must be used. Out of doors, flags at least 23" x 29" in dimensions must be used between sunrise and sunset. Moving a red light across the track is the prescribed stop signal under normal flagging conditions. Moving a white light up and down means proceed slowly. A red light must never be used to give a proceed signal. Moving a yellow light up and down is a signal to a motorman to proceed very slowly. On the track to be worked on, two yellow lights must be displayed at a point not less than 500 feet, nor more than 700 feet, in approach to the flagman's station. On any track where caution lights are displayed, one green light must be displayed a safe distance beyond the farthest point of work. Caution lights must be displayed on the right hand side of the track.

1. Before starting work on a track, the transit official who should be notified is the 1.____

   A. General Superintendent
   B. Assistant General Superintendent
   C. Desk Trainmaster
   D. Yardmaster

2. It is permissible to start work on an operating track at 2.____

   A. 8 A.M. B. 11 A.M. C. 8 P.M. D. 6 P.M.

3. A flagman for a track gang MUST be selected from 3.____

   A. men on light duty
   B. disabled men
   C. a list of qualified men
   D. senior trackmen

4. The flagman who is protecting a working gang of trackmen 4.____

   A. should lend a hand when needed in heavy lifting
   B. should clean up the track area while awaiting trains
   C. must not be assigned to other duties
   D. can collect scrap iron while awaiting trains

5. The prescribed *stop* signal is given by moving a 5.____

   A. red light up and down
   B. green light up and down
   C. red light across the tracks
   D. green light across the tracks

6. The normal *proceed slowly* signal is given by moving a

   A. red light up and down
   B. white light up and down
   C. yellow light across the tracks
   D. green light across the tracks

6.___

7. Of the following, an ACCEPTABLE distance between a work area and the yellow lights is _______ feet.

   A. 300   B. 600   C. 800   D. 1,000

7.___

Questions 8-12.

DIRECTIONS: Questions 8 through 12 are to be answered on the basis of the following passage.

The handling of supplies is an important part of correctional administration. A good deal of planning and organization is involved in purchase, stock control, and issue of bulk supplies to the cell-block. This planning is meaningless, however, if the final link in the chain -- the cell-block officer who is in charge of distributing supplies to the inmates -- does not do his job in the proper way. First, when supplies are received, the officer himself should immediately check them or should personally supervise the checking, to make sure the count is correct. Nothing but trouble will result if an officer signs for 200 towels and discovers hours later that he is 20 towels short. Did the 20 towels *disappear,* or did they never arrive in the first place? Second, all supplies should be locked up until they are actually distributed. Third, the officer must keep accurate records when supplies are issued. Complaints will be kept to a minimum if the officer makes sure that each inmate has received the supplies to which he is entitled, and if the officer can tell from his records when it is time to reorder to prevent a shortage. Fourth, the officer should either issue the supplies himself or else personally supervise the issuing. It is unfair and unwise to put an inmate in charge of supplies without giving him adequate supervision. A small thing like a bar of soap does not mean much to most people, but it means a great deal to the inmate who cannot even shave or wash up unless he receives the soap that is supposed to be issued to him.

8. Which one of the following jobs is NOT mentioned by the above passage as the responsibility of a cellblock officer?

   A. Purchasing supplies
   B. Issuing supplies
   C. Counting supplies when they are delivered to the cell-block
   D. Keeping accurate records when supplies are issued

8.___

9. The above passage says that supplies should be counted when they are delivered. Of the following, which is the BEST way of handling this job?

   A. The cellblock officer can wait until he has some free time, and then count them himself.
   B. An inmate can start counting them right away, even if the cellblock officer cannot supervise his work.
   C. The cellblock officer can personally supervise an inmate who counts the supplies when they are delivered.
   D. Two inmates can count them when they are delivered, supervising each other's work.

9.___

10. The above passage gives an example concerning a delivery of 200 towels that turned out to be 20 towels short. The example is used to show that 10.____

    A. the missing towels were stolen
    B. the missing towels never arrived in the first place
    C. it is impossible to tell what happened to the missing towels because no count was made when they were delivered
    D. it does not matter that the missing towels were not accounted for because it is never possible to keep track of supplies accurately

11. The MAIN reason given by the above passage for making a record when supplies are issued is that keeping records 11.____

    A. will discourage inmates from stealing supplies
    B. is a way of making sure that each inmate receives the supplies to which he is entitled
    C. will show the officer's superiors that he is doing his job in the proper way
    D. will enable the inmates to help themselves to any supplies they need

12. The above passage says that it is unfair to put an inmate in charge of supplies without giving him adequate supervision. 12.____
    Which of the following is the MOST likely explanation of why it would be *unfair* to do this?

    A. A privilege should not be given to one inmate unless it is given to all the other inmates too.
    B. It is wrong to make one inmate work when all the others can sit in their cells and do nothing.
    C. The cellblock officer should not be able to get out of doing a job by making an inmate do it for him.
    D. The inmate in charge of supplies could be put under pressure by other inmates to do them *special favors.*

Questions 13-17.

DIRECTIONS: Questions 13 through 17 are to be answered on the basis of the following passage.

The typical correction official must make predictions about the probable future behavior of his charges in order to make judgments affecting those individuals. In learning to predict behavior, the results of scientific studies of inmate behavior can be of some use. Most studies that have been made show that older men tend to obey rules and regulations better than younger men, and tend to be more reliable in carrying out assigned jobs. Men who had good employment records on the outside also tend to be more reliable than men whose records show haphazard employment or unemployment. Oddly enough, men convicted of crimes of violence are less likely to be troublemakers than men convicted of burglary or other crimes involving stealth. While it might be expected that first offenders would be much less likely to be troublemakers than men with previous convictions, the difference between the two groups is not very great. It must be emphasized, however, that predictions based on a man's background are only likelihoods -- they are never certainties. A successful correction officer learns to give some weight to a man's background, but he should rely even more heavily on his own personal judgment of the individual in question. A good officer will develop in time a kind of sixth sense about human beings that is more reliable than any statistical predictions.

13. The above passage suggests that knowledge of scientific studies of inmate behavior would PROBABLY help the correction officer to 13._

   A. make judgments that affect the inmates in his charge
   B. write reports on all major infractions of the rules
   C. accurately analyze how an inmate's behavior is determined by his background
   D. change the personalities of the individuals in his charge

14. According to the information in the above passage, which one of the following groups of inmates would tend to be MOST reliable in carrying out assigned jobs? 14._

   A. Older men with haphazard employment records
   B. Older men with regular employment records
   C. Younger men with haphazard employment records
   D. Younger men with regular employment records

15. According to the information in the above passage, which of the following are MOST likely to be troublemakers? 15._

   A. Older men convicted of crimes of violence
   B. Younger men convicted of crimes of violence
   C. Younger men convicted of crimes involving stealth
   D. First offenders convicted of crimes of violence

16. The above passage indicates that information about a man's background is 16._

   A. a sure way of predicting his future behavior
   B. of no use at all in predicting his future behavior
   C. more useful in predicting behavior than a correction officer's expert judgment
   D. less reliable in predicting behavior than a correction officer's expert judgment

17. The above passage names two groups of inmates whose behavior might be expected to be quite different, but who in fact behave only slightly differently. 17._
These two groups are

   A. older men and younger men
   B. first offenders and men with previous convictions
   C. men with good employment records and men with records of haphazard employment or unemployment
   D. men who obey the rules and men who do not

Questions 18-22.

DIRECTIONS: Questions 18 through 22 are to be answered on the basis of the following passage.

A large proportion of the people who are behind bars are not convicted criminals, but people who have been arrested and are being held until their trial in court. Experts have often pointed out that this detention system does not operate fairly. For instance, a person who can afford to pay bail usually will not get locked up. The theory of the bail system is that the person will make sure to show up in court when he is supposed to since he knows that otherwise he will forfeit his bail -- he will lose the money he put up. Sometimes a person who can show that he is a stable citizen with a job and a family will be released on *personal recognizance* (without bail). The result is that the well-to-do, the employed, and the family men can often avoid the detention system. The people who do wind up in detention tend to be the poor, the unemployed, the single, and the young.

18. According to the above passage, people who are put behind bars 18.____

A. are almost always dangerous criminals
B. include many innocent people who have been arrested by mistake
C. are often people who have been arrested but have not yet come to trial
D. are all poor people who tend to be young and single

19. The above passage says that the detention system works UNFAIRLY against people 19.____

A. rich B. married C. old D. unemployed

20. The above passage uses the expression *forfeit his bail.* Even if you have not seen the word *forfeit* before, you could figure out from the way it is used in the passage that *forfeiting* PROBABLY means _________ something. 20.____

A. losing track of
B. giving up
C. finding
D. avoiding

21. When someone is released on *personal recognizance,* this means that 21.____

A. the judge knows that he is innocent
B. he does not have to show up for a trial
C. he has a record of previous convictions
D. he does not have to pay bail

22. Suppose that two men were booked on the same charge at the same time, and that the same bail was set for both of them. One man was able to put up bail, and he was released. The second man was not able to put up bail, and he was held in detention. The reader of the above passage would MOST likely feel that this result is 22.____

A. *unfair,* because it does not have any relation to guilt or innocence
B. *unfair,* because the first man deserves severe punishment
C. *fair,* because the first man is obviously innocent
D. *fair,* because the law should be tougher on poor people than on rich people

Questions 23-25.

DIRECTIONS: Questions 23 through 25 are to be answered on the basis of the information contained in the following paragraph,

Group counseling may contain potentialities of an extraordinary character for the philosophy and especially the management and operation of the adult correctional institution. Primarily, the change may be based upon the valued and respected participation of the rank-and-file of employees in the treatment program. Group counseling provides new treatment functions for correctional workers. The older, more conventional duties and activities of correctional officers, teachers, maintenance foremen, and other employees, which they currently perform, may be fortified and improved by their participation in group counseling. Psychologists, psychiatrists, and classification officers may also need to revise their attitudes toward others on the staff and toward their own procedure in treating inmates to accord with the new type of treatment program which may evolve if group counseling were to become accepted practice in the prison. The primary locale of the psychological treatment program may move from the clinical center to all places in the institution where inmates are in contact with employees. The thoughtful guidance and steering of the program, figuratively its pilot-house, may still be the clinical center. The actual points of contact of the treatment program will, however, be wherever inmates are in personal relationship, no matter how superficial, with employees of the prison.

23. According to the above paragraph, a basic change that may be brought about by the introduction of a group counseling program into an adult correctional institution would be that the 23.____

    A. educational standards for correctional employees would be raised
    B. management of the institution would have to be selected primarily on the basis of ability to understand and apply the counseling program
    C. older and conventional duties of correctional employees would assume less importance
    D. rank-and-file employees would play an important part in the treatment program for inmates

24. According to the above paragraph, the one of the following that is NOT mentioned specifically as a change that may be required by or result from the introduction of group counseling in an adult correctional institution is a change in the 24.____

    A. attitude of the institution's classification officers toward their own procedures in treating inmates
    B. attitudes of the institution's psychologists toward correction officers
    C. place where the treatment program is planned and from which it is directed
    D. principal place where the psychological treatment program makes actual contact with the inmate

25. According to the above paragraph, under a program of group counseling in an adult correctional institution, treatment of inmates takes place 25.____

    A. as soon as they are admitted to the prison
    B. chiefly in the clinical center
    C. mainly where inmates are in continuing close and personal relationship with the technical staff
    D. wherever inmates come in contact with prison employees

KEY (CORRECT ANSWERS)

1. C
2. B
3. C
4. C
5. C

6. B
7. B
8. A
9. C
10. C

11. B
12. D
13. A
14. B
15. C

16. D
17. B
18. C
19. D
20. B

21. D
22. A
23. D
24. C
25. D

RECORD KEEPING
EXAMINATION SECTION
TEST 1

DIRECTIONS: Each question or incomplete statement is followed by several suggested answers or completions. Select the one that BEST answers the question or completes the statement. *PRINT THE LETTER OF THE CORRECT ANSWER IN THE SPACE AT THE RIGHT.*

Questions 1-15.

DIRECTIONS: Questions 1 through 15 are to be answered on the basis of the following list of company names below. Arrange a file alphabetically, word-by-word, disregarding punctuation, conjunctions, and apostrophes. Then answer the questions.

A Bee C Reading Materials
ABCO Parts
A Better Course for Test Preparation
AAA Auto Parts Co.
A-Z Auto Parts, Inc.
Aabar Books
Abbey, Joanne
Boman-Sylvan Law Firm
BMW Autowerks
C Q Service Company
Chappell-Murray, Inc.
E&E Life Insurance
Emcrisco
Gigi Arts
Gordon, Jon & Associates
SOS Plumbing
Schmidt, J.B. Co.

1. Which of these files should appear FIRST? 1.____

   A. ABCO Parts
   B. A Bee C Reading Materials
   C. A Better Course for Test Preparation
   D. AAA Auto Parts Co.

2. Which of these files should appear SECOND? 2.____

   A. A-Z Auto Parts, Inc.
   B. A Bee C Reading Materials
   C. A Better Course for Test Preparation
   D. AAA Auto Parts Co.

3. Which of these files should appear THIRD? 3.____

   A. ABCO Parts
   B. A Bee C Reading Materials
   C. Aabar Books
   D. AAA Auto Parts Co.

4. Which of these files should appear FOURTH? 4._

   A. Aabar Books
   B. ABCO Parts
   C. Abbey, Joanne
   D. AAA Auto Parts Co.

5. Which of these files should appear LAST? 5._

   A. Gordon, Jon & Associates
   B. Gigi Arts
   C. Schmidt, J.B. Co.
   D. SOS Plumbing

6. Which of these files should appear between A-Z Auto Parts, Inc. and Abbey, Joanne? 6._

   A. A Bee C Reading Materials
   B. AAA Auto Parts Co.
   C. ABCO Parts
   D. A Better Course for Test Preparation

7. Which of these files should appear between ABCO Parts and Aabar Books? 7._

   A. A Bee C Reading Materials
   B. Abbey, Joanne
   C. Aabar Books
   D. A-Z Auto Parts

8. Which of these files should appear between Abbey, Joanne and Boman-Sylvan Law Firm? 8._

   A. A Better Course for Test Preparation
   B. BMW Autowerks
   C. Chappell-Murray, Inc.
   D. Aabar Books

9. Which of these files should appear between Abbey, Joanne and C Q Service? 9._

   A. A-Z Auto Parts,Inc.
   B. BMW Autowerks
   C. Choices A and B
   D. Chappell-Murray, Inc.

10. Which of these files should appear between C Q Service Company and Emcrisco? 10._

    A. Chappell-Murray, Inc.
    B. E&E Life Insurance
    C. Gigi Arts
    D. Choices A and B

11. Which of these files should NOT appear between C Q Service Company and E&E Life Insurance? 11._

    A. Gordon, Jon & Associates
    B. Emcrisco
    C. Gigi Arts
    D. All of the above

12. Which of these files should appear between Chappell-Murray Inc., and Gigi Arts? 12.____

    A. CQ Service Inc. E&E Life Insurance, and Emcrisco
    B. Emcrisco, E&E Life Insurance, and Gordon, Jon & Associates
    C. E&E Life Insurance and Emcrisco
    D. Emcrisco and Gordon, Jon & Associates

13. Which of these files should appear between Gordon, Jon & Associates and SOS Plumbing? 13.____

    A. Gigi Arts
    B. Schmidt, J.B. Co.
    C. Choices A and B
    D. None of the above

14. Each of the choices lists the four files in their proper alphabetical order except 14.____

    A. E&E Life Insurance; Gigi Arts; Gordon, Jon & Associates; SOS Plumbing
    B. E&E Life Insurance; Emcrisco; Gigi Arts; SOS Plumbing
    C. Emcrisco; Gordon, Jon & Associates; SOS Plumbing; Schmidt, J.B. Co.
    D. Emcrisco; Gigi Arts; Gordon, Jon & Associates; SOS Plumbing

15. Which of the choices lists the four files in their proper alphabetical order? 15.____

    A. Gigi Arts; Gordon, Jon & Associates; SOS Plumbing; Schmidt, J.B. Co.
    B. Gordon, Jon & Associates; Gigi Arts; Schmidt, J.B. Co.; SOS Plumbing
    C. Gordon, Jon & Associates; Gigi Arts; SOS Plumbing; Schmidt, J.B. Co.
    D. Gigi Arts; Gordon, Jon & Associates; Schmidt, J.B. Co.; SOS Plumbing

16. The alphabetical filing order of two businesses with identical names is determined by the 16.____

    A. length of time each business has been operating
    B. addresses of the businesses
    C. last name of the company president
    D. none of the above

17. In an alphabetical filing system, if a business name includes a number, it should be 17.____

    A. disregarded
    B. considered a number and placed at the end of an alphabetical section
    C. treated as though it were written in words and alphabetized accordingly
    D. considered a number and placed at the beginning of an alphabetical section

18. If a business name includes a contraction (such as *don't* or *it's*), how should that word be treated in an alphabetical filing system? 18.____

    A. Divide the word into its separate parts and treat it as two words.
    B. Ignore the letters that come after the apostrophe.
    C. Ignore the word that contains the contraction.
    D. Ignore the apostrophe and consider all letters in the contraction.

19. In what order should the parts of an address be considered when using an alphabetical filing system? 19.____

    A. City or town; state; street name; house or building number
    B. State; city or town; street name; house or building number
    C. House or building number; street name; city or town; state
    D. Street name; city or town; state

20. A business record should be cross-referenced when a(n) 20

A. organization is known by an abbreviated name
B. business has a name change because of a sale, incorporation, or other reason
C. business is known by a *coined* or common name which differs from a dictionary spelling
D. all of the above

21. A geographical filing system is MOST effective when 21.

A. location is more important than name
B. many names or titles sound alike
C. dealing with companies who have offices all over the world
D. filing personal and business files

Questions 22-25.

DIRECTIONS: Questions 22 through 25 are to be answered on the basis of the list of items below, which are to be filed geographically. Organize the items geographically and then answer the questions.

1. University Press at Berkeley, U.S.
2. Maria Sanchez, Mexico City, Mexico
3. Great Expectations Ltd. in London, England
4. Justice League, Cape Town, South Africa, Africa
5. Crown Pearls Ltd. in London, England
6. Joseph Prasad in London, England

22. Which of the following arrangements of the items is composed according to the policy of: *Continent, Country, City, Firm or Individual Name?* 22._

A. 5, 3, 4, 6, 2, 1
B. 4, 5, 3, 6, 2, 1
C. 1, 4, 5, 3, 6, 2
D. 4, 5, 3, 6, 1, 2

23. Which of the following files is arranged according to the policy of: *Continent, Country, City, Firm or Individual Name?* 23._

A. South Africa. Africa. Cape Town. Justice League
B. Mexico. Mexico City, Maria Sanchez
C. North America. United States. Berkeley. University Press
D. England. Europe. London. Prasad, Joseph

24. Which of the following arrangements of the items is composed according to the policy of: *Country, City, Firm or Individual Name*? 24._

A. 5, 6, 3, 2, 4, 1
B. 1, 5, 6, 3, 2, 4
C. 6, 5, 3, 2, 4, 1
D. 5, 3, 6, 2, 4, 1

25. Which of the following files is arranged according to a policy of: *Country, City, Firm or Individual Name*? 25._

A. England. London. Crown Pearls Ltd.
B. North America. United States. Berkeley. University Press
C. Africa. Cape Town. Justice League
D. Mexico City. Mexico. Maria Sanchez

26. Under which of the following circumstances would a phonetic filing system be MOST effective? 26.____

   A. When the person in charge of filing can't spell very well
   B. With large files with names that sound alike
   C. With large files with names that are spelled alike
   D. All of the above

Questions 27-29.

DIRECTIONS: Questions 27 through 29 are to be answered on the basis of the following list of numerical files.

1. 391-023-100
2. 361-132-170
3. 385-732-200
4. 381-432-150
5. 391-632-387
6. 361-423-303
7. 391-123-271

27. Which of the following arrangements of the files follows a consecutive-digit system? 27.____

   A. 2, 3, 4, 1
   B. 1, 5, 7, 3
   C. 2, 4, 3, 1
   D. 3, 1, 5, 7

28. Which of the following arrangements follows a terminal-digit system? 28.____

   A. 1, 7, 2, 4, 3
   B. 2, 1, 4, 5, 7
   C. 7, 6, 5, 4, 3
   D. 1, 4, 2, 3, 7

29. Which of the following lists follows a middle-digit system? 29.____

   A. 1, 7, 2, 6, 4, 5, 3
   B. 1, 2, 7, 4, 6, 5, 3
   C. 7, 2, 1, 3, 5, 6, 4
   D. 7, 1, 2, 4, 6, 5, 3

Questions 30-31.

DIRECTIONS: Questions 30 and 31 are to be answered on the basis of the following information.

1. Reconfirm Laura Bates appointment with James Caldecort on December 12 at 9:30 A.M.
2. Laurence Kinder contact Julia Lucas on August 3 and set up a meeting for week of September 23 at 4 P.M.
3. John Lutz contact Larry Waverly on August 3 and set up appointment for September 23 at 9:30 A.M.
4. Call for tickets for Gerry Stanton August 21 for New Jersey on September 23, flight 143 at 4:43 P.M.

30. A chronological file for the above information would be 30.___

A. 4, 3, 2, 1
B. 3, 2, 4, 1
C. 4, 2, 3, 1
D. 3, 1, 2, 4

31. Using the above information, a chronological file for the date of September 23 would be 31.___

A. 2, 3, 4 B. 3, 1, 4 C. 3, 2, 4 D. 4, 3, 2

Questions 32-34.

DIRECTIONS: Questions 32 through 34 are to be answered on the basis of the following information.

1. Call Roger Epstein, Ashoke Naipaul, Jon Anderson, and Sarah Washington on April 19 at 1:00 P.M. to set up meeting with Alika D'Ornay for June 6 in New York.
2. Call Martin Ames before noon on April 19 to confirm afternoon meeting with Bob Greenwood on April 20th
3. Set up meeting room at noon for 2:30 P.M. meeting on April 19th;
4. Ashley Stanton contact Bob Greenwood at 9:00 A.M. on April 20 and set up meeting for June 6 at 8:30 A.M.
5. Carol Guiland contact Shelby Van Ness during afternoon of April 20 and set up meeting for June 6 at 10:00 A.M.
6. Call airline and reserve tickets on June 6 for Roger Epstein trip *to* Denver on July 8
7. Meeting at 2:30 P.M. on April 19th

32. A chronological file for all of the above information would be 32.___

A. 2, 1, 3, 7, 5, 4, 6
B. 3, 7, 2, 1, 4, 5, 6
C. 3, 7, 1, 2, 5, 4, 6
D. 2, 3, 1, 7, 4, 5, 6

33. A chronological file for the date of April 19th would be 33.___

A. 2, 3, 7, 1
B. 2, 3, 1, 7
C. 7, 1, 3, 2
D. 3, 7, 1, 2

34. Add the following information to the file, and then create a chronological file for April 20th: 34.___
8. April 20: 3:00 P.M. meeting between Bob Greenwood and Martin Ames.

A. 4, 5, 8 B. 4, 8, 5 C. 8, 5, 4 D. 5, 4, 8

35. The PRIMARY advantage of computer records filing over a manual system is 35.___

A. speed of retrieval
B. accuracy
C. cost
D. potential file loss

KEY (CORRECT ANSWERS)

1. B
2. C
3. D
4. A
5. D

6. C
7. B
8. B
9. C
10. D

11. D
12. C
13. B
14. C
15. D

16. B
17. C
18. D
19. A
20. D

21. A
22. B
23. C
24. D
25. A

26. B
27. C
28. D
29. A
30. B

31. C
32. D
33. B
34. A
35. A

PREPARING WRITTEN MATERIAL

EXAMINATION SECTION
TEST 1

Questions 1-15.

DIRECTIONS: For each of Questions 1 through 15, select from the options given below the MOST applicable choice, and mark your answer accordingly.

A. The sentence is correct.
B. The sentence contains a spelling error *only.*
C. The sentence contains an English grammar error *only.*
D. The sentence contains both a spelling error and an English grammar error.

1. He is a very dependible person whom we expect will be an asset to this division. 1.____

2. An investigator often finds it necessary to be very diplomatic when conducting an interview. 2.____

3. Accurate detail is especially important if court action results from an investigation. 3.____

4. The report was signed by him and I since we conducted the investigation jointly. 4.____

5. Upon receipt of the complaint, an inquiry was begun. 5.____

6. An employee has to organize his time so that he can handle his workload efficiantly. 6.____

7. It was not apparant that anyone was living at the address given by the client. 7.____

8. According to regulations, there is to be at least three attempts made to locate the client. 8.____

9. Neither the inmate nor the correction officer was willing to sign a formal statement. 9.____

10. It is our opinion that one of the persons interviewed were lying. 10.____

11. We interviewed both clients and departmental personel in the course of this investigation. 11.____

12. It is concievable that further research might produce additional evidence. 12.____

13. There are too many occurences of this nature to ignore. 13.____

14. We cannot accede to the candidate's request. 14.____

15. The submission of overdue reports is the reason that there was a delay in completion of this investigation. 15.____

Questions 16-25.

DIRECTIONS: Each of Questions 16 through 25 may be classified under one of the following four categories:

A. Faulty because of incorrect grammar or sentence structure
B. Faulty because of incorrect punctuation
C. Faulty because of incorrect spelling
D. Correct

Examine each sentence carefully to determine under which of the above four options it is best classified. Then, in the space at the right, write the letter preceding the option which is the BEST of the four suggested above. Each incorrect sentence contains but one type of error. Consider a sentence to be correct if it contains none of the types of errors mentioned, even though there may be other correct ways of expressing the same thought.

16. Although the department's supply of scratch pads and stationary have diminished considerably, the allotment for our division has not been reduced. 16.___

17. You have not told us whom you wish to designate as your secretary. 17.___

18. Upon reading the minutes of the last meeting, the new proposal was taken up for consideration. 18.___

19. Before beginning the discussion, we locked the door as a precautionery measure. 19.___

20. The supervisor remarked, “Only those clerks, who perform routine work, are permitted to take a rest period.” 20.___

21. Not only will this duplicating machine make accurate copies, but it will also produce a quantity of work equal to fifteen transcribing typists. 21.___

22. “Mr. Jones,” said the supervisor, “we regret our inability to grant you an extention of your leave of absence.” 22.___

23. Although the employees find the work monotonous and fatigueing, they rarely complain. 23.___

24. We completed the tabulation of the receipts on time despite the fact that Miss Smith our fastest operator was absent for over a week. 24.___

25. The reaction of the employees who attended the meeting, as well as the reaction of those who did not attend, indicates clearly that the schedule is satisfactory to everyone concerned. 25.___

KEY (CORRECT ANSWERS)

1. D
2. A
3. A
4. C
5. A
6. B
7. B
8. C
9. A
10. C
11. B
12. B
13. B
14. A
15. C
16. A
17. D
18. A
19. C
20. B
21. A
22. C
23. C
24. B
25. D

TEST 2

Questions 1-15.

DIRECTIONS: Questions 1 through 15 consist of two sentences. Some are correct according to ordinary formal English usage. Others are incorrect because they contain errors in English usage, spelling, or punctuation. Consider a sentence correct if it contains no errors in English usage, spelling, or punctuation, even if there may be other ways of writing the sentence correctly. Mark your answer:

A. If only sentence I is correct
B. If only sentence II is correct
C. If sentences I and II are correct
D. If neither sentence I nor II is correct

1. I. The influence of recruitment efficiency upon administrative standards is readily apparant. 1.___
   II. Rapid and accurate thinking are an essential quality of the police officer.

2. I. The administrator of a police department is constantly confronted by the demands of subordinates for increased personnel in their respective units. 2.___
   II. Since a chief executive must work within well-defined fiscal limits, he must weigh the relative importance of various requests.

3. I. The two men whom the police arrested for a parking violation were wanted for robbery in three states. 3.___
   II. Strong executive control from the top to the bottom of the enterprise is one of the basic principals of police administration.

4. I. When he gave testimony unfavorable to the defendant loyalty seemed to mean very little. 4.___
   II. Having run off the road while passing a car, the patrolman gave the driver a traffic ticket.

5. I. The judge ruled that the defendant's conversation with his doctor was a priviliged communication. 5.___
   II. The importance of our training program is widely recognized; however, fiscal difficulties limit the program's effectiveness.

6. I. Despite an increase in patrol coverage, there were less arrests for crimes against property this year. 6.___
   II. The investigators could hardly have expected greater cooperation from the public.

7. I. Neither the patrolman nor the witness could identify the defendant as the driver of the car. 7.___
   II. Each of the officers in the class received their certificates at the completion of the course.

8. I. The new commander made it clear that those kind of procedures would no longer be permitted. 8.____
   II. Giving some weight to performance records is more advisable then making promotions solely on the basis of test scores.

9. I. A deputy sheriff must ascertain whether the debtor, has any property. 9.____
   II. A good deputy sheriff does not cause histerical excitement when he executes a process.

10. I. Having learned that he has been assigned a judgment debtor, the deputy sheriff should call upon him. 10.____
    II. The deputy sheriff may seize and remove property without requiring a bond.

11. I. If legal procedures are not observed, the resulting contract is not enforseable. 11.____
    II. If the directions from the creditor's attorney are not in writing, the deputy sheriff should request a letter of instructions from the attorney.

12. I. The deputy sheriff may confer with the defendant and may enter this defendants' place of business. 12.____
    II. A deputy sheriff must ascertain from the creditor's attorney whether the debtor has any property against which he may proceede.

13. I. The sheriff has a right to do whatever is reasonably necessary for the purpose of executing the order of the court. 13.____
    II. The written order of the court gives the sheriff general authority and he is governed in his acts by a very simple principal.

14. I. Either the patrolman or his sergeant are always ready to help the public. 14.____
    II. The sergeant asked the patrolman when he would finish the report.

15. I. The injured man could not hardly talk. 15.____
    II. Every officer had ought to hand in their reports on time.

Questions 16-25.

DIRECTIONS: For each of the sentences given below, numbered 16 through 25, select from the following choices the MOST correct choice and print your choice in the space at the right. Select as your answer:

A. If the statement contains an unnecessary word or expression
B. If the statement contains a slang term or expression ordinarily not acceptable in government report writing
C. If the statement contains an old-fashioned word or expression, where a concrete, plain term would be more useful
D. If the statement contains no major faults

16. Every one of us should try harder 16.____

17. Yours of the first instant has been received. 17.____

18. We will have to do a real snow job on him. 18.____

19. I shall contact him next Thursday. 19.____

20. None of us were invited to the meeting with the community. 20.__
21. We got this here job to do. 21.__
22. She could not help but see the mistake in the checkbook. 22.__
23. Don't bug the Director about the report. 23.__
24. I beg to inform you that your letter has been received. 24.__
25. This project is all screwed up. 25.__

KEY (CORRECT ANSWERS)

1. D
2. C
3. A
4. D
5. B
6. B
7. A
8. D
9. D
10. C
11. B
12. D
13. A
14. D
15. D
16. D
17. C
18. B
19. D
20. D
21. B
22. D
23. B
24. C
25. B

TEST 3

DIRECTIONS: Questions 1 through 25 are sentences taken from reports. Some are correct according to ordinary formal English usage. Others are incorrect because they contain errors in English usage, spelling, or punctuation. Consider a sentence correct if it contains no errors in English usage, spelling, or punctuation, even if there may be other ways of writing the sentence correctly. Mark your answer:

A. If only sentence I is correct
B. If only sentence II is correct
C. If sentences I and II are correct
D. If neither sentence I nor II is correct.

1. I. The Neighborhood Police Team Commander and Team Patrol- men are encouraged to give to the public the widest possible verbal and written disemination of information regarding the existence and purposes of the program. 1.____
   II. The police must be vitally interelated with every segment of the public they serve.

2. I. If social gambling, prostitution, and other vices are to be prohibited, the law makers should provide the manpower and method for enforcement. 2.____
   II. In addition to checking on possible crime locations such as hallways, roofs yards and other similar locations, Team Patrolmen are encouraged to make known their presence to members of the community.

3. I. The Neighborhood Police Team Commander is authorized to secure, the cooperation of local publications, as well as public and private agencies, to further the goals of the program. 3.____
   II. Recruitment from social minorities is essential to effective police work among minorities and meaningful relations with them.

4. I. The Neighborhood Police Team Commander and his men have the responsibility for providing patrol service within the sector territory on a twenty-four hour basis. 4.____
   II. While the patrolman was walking his beat at midnight he noticed that the clothing stores' door was partly open.

5. I. Authority is granted to the Neighborhood Police Team to device tactics for coping with the crime in the sector. 5.____
   II. Before leaving the scene of the accident, the patrolman drew a map showing the positions of the automobiles and indicated the time of the accident as 10 M. in the morning.

6. I. The Neighborhood Police Team Commander and his men must be kept apprised of conditions effecting their sector. 6.____
   II. Clear, continuous communication with every segment of the public served based on the realization of mutual need and founded on trust and confidence is the basis for effective law enforcement.

7. I. The irony is that the police are blamed for the laws they enforce when they are doing their duty.
   II. The Neighborhood Police Team Commander is authorized to prepare and distribute literature with pertinent information telling the public whom to contact for assistance.

7.___

8. I. The day is not far distant when major parts of the entire police compliment will need extensive college training or degrees.
   II. Although driving under the influence of alcohol is a specific charge in making arrests, drunkeness is basically a health and social problem.

8.___

9. I. If a deputy sheriff finds that property he has to attach is located on a ship, he should notify his supervisor.
   II. Any contract that tends to interfere with the administration of justice is illegal.

9.___

10. I. A mandate or official order of the court to the sheriff or other officer directs it to take into possession property of the judgment debtor.
    II. Tenancies from month-to-month, week-to-week, and sometimes year-to-year are termenable.

10.___

11. I. A civil arrest is an arrest pursuant to an order issued by a court in civil litigation.
    II. In a criminal arrest, a defendant is arrested for a crime he is alleged to have committed.

11.___

12. I. Having taken a defendant into custody, there is a complete restraint of personal liberty.
    II. Actual force is unnecessary when a deputy sheriff makes an arrest.

12.___

13. I. When a husband breaches a separation agreement by failing to supply to the wife the amount of money to be paid to her periodically under the agreement, the same legal steps may be taken to enforce his compliance as in any other breach of contract.
    II. Having obtained the writ of attachment, the plaintiff is then in the advantageous position of selling the very property that has been held for him by the sheriff while he was obtaining a judgment.

13.___

14. I. Being locked in his desk, the investigator felt sure that the records would be safe.
    II. The reason why the witness changed his statement was because he had been threatened.

14.___

15. I. The investigation had just began then an important witness disappeared.
    II. The check that had been missing was located and returned to its owner, Harry Morgan, a resident of Suffolk County, New York.

15.___

16. I. A supervisor will find that the establishment of standard procedures enables his staff to work more efficiently.
    II. An investigator hadn't ought to give any recommendations in his report if he is in doubt.

16.___

17. I. Neither the investigator nor his supervisor is ready to interview the witnesses.
    II. Interviewing has been and always will be an important asset in investigation.

17.___

18. I. One of the investigator's reports has been forwarded to the wrong person. 18.____
    II. The investigator stated that he was not familiar with those kind of cases.

19. I. Approaching the victim of the assault, two large bruises were noticed by me. 19.____
    II. The prisoner was arrested for assault, resisting arrest, and use of a deadly weapon.

20. I. A copy of the orders, which had been prepared by the captain, was given to each patrolman. 20.____
    II. It's always necessary to inform an arrested person of his constitutional rights before asking him any questions.

21. I. To prevent further bleeding, I applied a tourniquet to the wound. 21.____
    II. John Rano a senior officer was on duty at the time of the accident.

22. I. Limiting the term "property" to tangible property, in the criminal mischief setting, accords with prior case law holding that only tangible property came within the purview of the offense of malicious mischief. 22.____
    II. Thus, a person who intentionally destroys the property of another, but under an honest belief that he has title to such property, cannot be convicted of criminal mischief under the Revised Penal Law.

23. I. Very early in it's history, New York enacted statutes from time to time punishing, either as a felony or as a misdemeanor, malicious injuries to various kinds of property: piers, booms, dams, bridges, etc. 23.____
    II. The application of the statute is necessarily restricted to trespassory takings with larcenous intent: namely with intent permanently or virtually permanently to "appropriate" property or "deprive" the owner of its use.

24. I. Since the former Penal Law did not define the instruments of forgery in a general fashion, its crime of forgery was held to be narrower than the common law offense in this respect and to embrace only those instruments explicitly specified in the substantive provisions. 24.____
    II. After entering the barn through an open door for the purpose of stealing, it was closed by the defendants.

25. I. The use of fire or explosives to destroy tangible property is proscribed by the criminal mischief provisions of the Revised Penal Law. 25.____
    II. The defendant's taking of a taxicab for the immediate purpose of affecting his escape did not constitute grand larceny.

KEY (CORRECT ANSWERS)

1. D
2. D
3. B
4. A
5. D
6. D
7. C
8. D
9. C
10. D
11. C
12. B
13. C
14. D
15. B
16. A
17. C
18. A
19. B
20. C
21. A
22. C
23. B
24. A
25. A

TEST 4

Questions 1-4.

DIRECTIONS: Each of the two sentences in Questions 1 through 4 may be correct or may contain errors in punctuation, capitalization, or grammar. Mark your answer:

A. If there is an error only in sentence I
B. If there is an error only in sentence II
C. If there is an error in both sentences I and II
D. If both sentences are correct.

1. I. It is very annoying to have a pencil sharpener, which is not in working order.
II. Patrolman Blake checked the door of Joe's Restaurant and found that the lock has been jammed.
1.____

2. I. When you are studying a good textbook is important.
II. He said he would divide the money equally between you and me.
2.____

3. I. Since he went on the city council a year ago, one of his primary concerns has been safety in the streets.
II. After waiting in the doorway for about 15 minutes, a black sedan appeared.
3.____

Questions 5-9.

DIRECTIONS: Each of the sentences in Questions 5 through 9 may be classified under one of the following four categories:

A. Faulty because of incorrect grammar
B. Faulty because of incorrect punctuation
C. Faulty because of incorrect capitalization or incorrect spelling
D. Correct

Examine each sentence carefully to determine under which of the above four options it is BEST classified. Then, in the space at the right, print the capitalized letter preceding the option which is the BEST of the four suggested above. Each faulty sentence contains but one type of error. Consider a sentence to be correct if it contains none of the types of errors mentioned, even though there may be other correct ways of expressing the same thought.

5. They told both he and I that the prisoner had escaped. 5.____

6. Any superior officer, who, disregards the just complaints of his subordinates, is remiss in the performance of his duty. 6.____

7. Only those members of the national organization who resided in the Middle west attended the conference in Chicago. 7.____

8. We told him to give the investigation assignment to whoever was available. 8.____

9. Please do not disappoint and embarass us by not appearing in court. 9.____

Questions 10-14.

DIRECTIONS: Each of Questions 10 through 14 consists of three sentences lettered A, B, and C. In each of these questions, one of the sentences may contain an error in grammar, sentence structure, or punctuation, or all three sentences may be correct. If one of the sentences in a question contains an error in grammar, sentence structure, or punctuation, print in the space at the right the capital letter preceding the sentence which contains the error. If all three sentences are correct, print the letter D.

10. A. Mr. Smith appears to be less competent than I in performing these duties. 10.___
    B. The supervisor spoke to the employee, who had made the error, but did not reprimand him.
    C. When he found the book lying on the table, he immediately notified the owner.

11. A. Being locked in the desk, we were certain that the papers would not be taken. 11.___
    B. It wasn't I who dictated the telegram; I believe it was Eleanor.
    C. You should interview whoever comes to the office today.

12. A. The clerk was instructed to set the machine on the table before summoning the manager. 12.___
    B. He said that he was not familiar with those kind of activities.
    C. A box of pencils, in addition to erasers and blotters, was included in the shipment of supplies.

13. A. The supervisor remarked, "Assigning an employee to the proper type of work is not always easy." 13.___
    B. The employer found that each of the applicants were qualified to perform the duties of the position.
    C. Any competent student is permitted to take this course if he obtains the consent of the instructor.

14. A. The prize was awarded to the employee whom the judges believed to be most deserving. 14.___
    B. Since the instructor believes this book is the better of the two, he is recommending it for use in the school.
    C. It was obvious to the employees that the completion of the task by the scheduled date would require their working overtime.

Questions 15-21.

DIRECTIONS: In answering Questions 15 through 21, choose the sentence which is BEST from the point of view of English usage suitable for a business report.

15. A. The client's receiving of public assistance checks at two different addresses were disclosed by the investigation.
B. The investigation disclosed that the client was receiving public assistance checks at two different addresses.
C. The client was found out by the investigation to be receiving public assistance checks at two different addresses.
D. The client has been receiving public assistance checks at two different addresses, disclosed the investigation.

15.____

16. A. The investigation of complaints are usually handled by this unit, which deals with internal security problems in the department.
B. This unit deals with internal security problems in the department usually investigating complaints.
C. Investigating complaints is this unit's job, being that it handles internal security problems in the department.
D. This unit deals with internal security problems in the department and usually investigates complaints.

16.____

17. A. The delay in completing this investigation was caused by difficulty in obtaining the required documents from the candidate.
B. Because of difficulty in obtaining the required documents from the candidate is the reason that there was a delay in completing this investigation.
C. Having had difficulty in obtaining the required documents from the candidate, there was a delay in completing this investigation.
D. Difficulty in obtaining the required documents from the candidate had the affect of delaying the completion of this investigation.

17.____

18. A. This report, together with documents supporting our recommendation, are being submitted for your approval.
B. Documents supporting our recommendation is being submitted with the report for your approval.
C. This report, together with documents supporting our recommendation, is being submitted for your approval.
D. The report and documents supporting our recommendation is being submitted for your approval.

18.____

19. A. The chairman himself, rather than his aides, has reviewed the report.
B. The chairman himself, rather than his aides, have reviewed the report.
C. The chairmen, not the aide, has reviewed the report.
D. The aide, not the chairmen, have reviewed the report.

19.____

20. A. Various proposals were submitted but the decision is not been made.
B. Various proposals has been submitted but the decision has not been made.
C. Various proposals were submitted but the decision is not been made.
D. Various proposals have been submitted but the decision has not been made.

20.____

21. A. Everyone were rewarded for his successful attempt.
B. They were successful in their attempts and each of them was rewarded.
C. Each of them are rewarded for their successful attempts.
D. The reward for their successful attempts were made to each of them.

21.____

22. The following is a paragraph from a request for departmental recognition consisting of five numbered sentences submitted to a Captain for review. These sentences may or may not have errors in spelling, grammar, and punctuation: 22.___

1. The officers observed the subject Mills surreptitiously remove a wallet from the woman's handbag and entered his automobile. 2. As they approached Mills, he looked in their direction and drove away. 3. The officers pursued in their car. 4. Mills executed a series of complicated manuvers to evade the pursuing officers. 5. At the corner of Broome and Elizabeth Streets, Mills stopped the car, got out, raised his hands and surrendered to the officers.

Which one of the following BEST classifies the above with regard to spelling, grammar and punctuation?

A. 1, 2, and 3 are correct, but 4 and 5 have errors.
B. 2, 3, and 5 are correct, but 1 and 4 have errors.
C. 3, 4, and 5 are correct, but 1 and 2 have errors.
D. 1, 2, 3, and 5 are correct, but 4 has errors.

23. The one of the following sentences which is grammatically PREFERABLE to the others is: 23.___

A. Our engineers will go over your blueprints so that you may have no problems in construction.
B. For a long time he had been arguing that we, not he, are to blame for the confusion.
C. I worked on this automobile for two hours and still cannot find out what is wrong with it.
D. Accustomed to all kinds of hardships, fatigue seldom bothers veteran policemen.

24. The MOST accurate of the following sentences is: 24.___

A. The commissioner, as well as his deputy and various bureau heads, were present.
B. A new organization of employers and employees have been formed.
C. One or the other of these men have been selected.
D. The number of pages in the book is enough to discourage a reader.

25. The MOST accurate of the following sentences is: 25.___

A. Between you and me, I think he is the better man.
B. He was believed to be me.
C. Is it us that you wish to see?
D. The winners are him and her.

KEY (CORRECT ANSWERS)

1. C
2. A
3. C
4. B
5. A
6. B
7. C
8. D
9. C
10. B
11. A
12. B
13. B
14. D
15. B
16. D
17. A
18. C
19. A
20. D
21. B
22. B
23. A
24. D
25. A

PREPARING WRITTEN MATERIAL

PARAGRAPH REARRANGEMENT COMMENTARY

The sentences which follow are in scrambled order. You are to rearrange them in proper order and indicate the letter choice containing the correct answer at the space at the right.

Each group of sentences in this section is actually a paragraph presented in scrambled order. Each sentence in the group has a place in that paragraph; no sentence is to be left out. You are to read each group of sentences and decide upon the best order in which to put the sentences so as to form as well-organized paragraph.

The questions in this section measure the ability to solve a problem when all the facts relevant to its solution are not given.

More specifically, certain positions of responsibility and authority require the employee to discover connections between events sometimes, apparently, unrelated. In order to do this, the employee will find it necessary to correctly infer that unspecified events have probably occurred or are likely to occur. This ability becomes especially important when action must be taken on incomplete information.

Accordingly, these questions require competitors to choose among several suggested alternatives, each of which presents a different sequential arrangement of the events. Competitors must choose the MOST logical of the suggested sequences.

In order to do so, they may be required to draw on general knowledge to infer missing concepts or events that are essential to sequencing the given events. Competitors should be careful to infer only what is essential to the sequence. The plausibility of the wrong alternatives will always require the inclusion of unlikely events or of additional chains of events which are NOT essential to sequencing the given events.

It's very important to remember that you are looking for the best of the four possible choices, and that the best choice of all may not even be one of the answers you're given to choose from.

There is no one right way to these problems. Many people have found it helpful to first write out the order of the sentences, as they would have arranged them, on their scrap paper before looking at the possible answers. If their optimum answer is there, this can save them some time. If it isn't, this method can still give insight into solving the problem. Others find it most helpful to just go through each of the possible choices, contrasting each as they go along. You should use whatever method feels comfortable, and works, for you.

While most of these types of questions are not that difficult, we've added a higher percentage of the difficult type, just to give you more practice. Usually there are only one or two questions on this section that contain such subtle distinctions that you're unable to answer confidently, and you then may find yourself stuck deciding between two possible choices, neither of which you're sure about.

EXAMINATION SECTION
TEST 1

DIRECTIONS: Each question consists of several sentences which can be arranged in a logical sequence. For each question, select the choice which places the numbered sentences in the MOST logical sequence. *PRINT THE LETTER OF THE CORRECT ANSWER IN THE SPACE AT THE RIGHT.*

1. I. A body was found in the woods.
   II. A man proclaimed innocence.
   III. The owner of a gun was located.
   IV. A gun was traced.
   V. The owner of a gun was questioned.

   The CORRECT answer is:

   A. IV, III, V, II, I
   B. II, I, IV, III, V
   C. I, IV, III, V, II
   D. I, III, V, II, IV
   E. I, II, IV, III, V

   1.____

2. I. A man was in a hunting accident.
   II. A man fell down a flight of steps.
   III. A man lost his vision in one eye.
   IV. A man broke his leg.
   V. A man had to walk with a cane.

   The CORRECT answer is:

   A. II, IV, V, I, III
   B. IV, V, I, III, II
   C. III, I, IV, V, II
   D. I, III, V, II, IV
   E. I, III, II, IV, V

   2.____

3. I. A man is offered a new job.
   II. A woman is offered a new job.
   III. A man works as a waiter.
   IV. A woman works as a waitress.
   V. A woman gives notice.

   The CORRECT answer is:

   A. IV, II, V, III, I
   B. IV, II, V, I, III
   C. II, IV, V, III, I
   D. III, I, IV, II, V
   E. IV, III, II, V, I

   3.____

4. I. A train left the station late.
   II. A man was late for work.
   III. A man lost his job.
   IV. Many people complained because the train was late.
   V. There was a traffic jam.

   The CORRECT answer is:

   A. V, II, I, IV, III
   B. V, I, IV, II, III
   C. V, I, II, IV, III
   D. I, V, IV, II, III
   E. II, I, IV, V, III

   4.____

5. I. The burden of proof as to each issue is determined before trial and remains upon the same party throughout the trial.
   II. The jury is at liberty to believe one witness' testimony as against a number of contradictory witnesses.
   III. In a civil case, the party bearing the burden of proof is required to prove his contention by a fair preponderance of the evidence.
   IV. However, it must be noted that a fair preponderance of evidence does not necessarily mean a greater number of witnesses.
   V. The burden of proof is the burden which rests upon one of the parties to an action to persuade the trier of the facts, generally the jury, that a proposition he asserts is true.
   VI. If the evidence is equally balanced, or if it leaves the jury in such doubt as to be unable to decide the controversy either way, judgment must be given against the party upon whom the burden of proof rests.

   The CORRECT answer is:

   A. III, II, V, IV, I, VI
   B. I, II,VI,V,III,IV
   C. III, IV, V, I, II, VI
   D. V, I, III,VI, IV, II
   E. I,V, III, VI, IV, II

5.___

6. I. If a parent is without assets and is unemployed, he cannot be convicted of the crime of non-support of a child.
   II. The term *sufficient ability* has been held to mean sufficient financial ability.
   III. It does not matter if his unemployment is by choice or unavoidable circumstances.
   IV. If he fails to take any steps at all, he may be liable to prosecution for endangering the welfare of a child.
   V. Under the penal law, a parent is responsible for the support of his minor child only if the parent is *of* sufficient ability.
   VI. An indigent parent may meet his obligation by borrowing money or by seeking aid under the provisions of the Social Welfare Law.

   The CORRECT answer is:

   A. VI, I, V, III, II, IV
   B. I, III, V, II, IV, VI
   C. V, II, I, III, VI, IV
   D. I, VI, IV, V, II, III
   E. II, V, I, III, VI, IV

6.___

7. I. Consider, for example, the case of a rabble rouser who urges a group of twenty people to go out and break the windows of a nearby factory.
   II. Therefore, the law fills the indicated gap with the crime of *inciting to riot*.
   III. A person is considered guilty of inciting to riot when he urges ten or more persons to engage in tumultuous and violent conduct of a kind likely to create public alarm.
   IV. However, if he has not obtained the cooperation of at least four people, he cannot be charged with unlawful assembly.
   V. The charge of inciting to riot was added to the law to cover types of conduct which cannot be classified as either the crime of *riot* or the crime of *unlawful assembly*.
   VI. If he acquires the acquiescence of at least four of them, he is guilty of unlawful assembly even if the project does not materialize.

   The CORRECT answer is:

7.___

A. III, V, I, VI, IV, II
B. V, I, IV, VI, II, III
C. III, IV, I, V, II, VI
D. V, I, IV, VI, III, II
E. V, III, I, VI, IV, II

8. I. If, however, the rebuttal evidence presents an issue of credibility, it is for the jury to determine whether the presumption has, in fact, been destroyed. 8.____
II. Once sufficient evidence to the contrary is introduced, the presumption disappears from the trial.
III. The effect of a presumption is to place the burden upon the adversary to come forward with evidence to rebut the presumption.
IV. When a presumption is overcome and ceases to exist in the case, the fact or facts which gave rise to the presumption still remain.
V. Whether a presumption has been overcome is ordinarily a question for the court.
VI. Such information may furnish a basis for a logical inference.
The CORRECT answer is:

A. IV, VI, II, V, I, III
B. III, II, V, I, IV, VI
C. V, III, VI, IV, II, I
D. V, IV, I, II, VI, III
E. II, III, V, I, IV, VI

9. I. An executive may answer a letter by writing his reply on the face of the letter itself instead of having a return letter typed. 9.____
II. This procedure is efficient because it saves the executive's time, the typist's time, and saves office file space.
III. Copying machines are used in small offices as well as large offices to save time and money in making brief replies to business letters.
IV. A copy is made on a copying machine to go into the company files, while the original is mailed back to the sender.
The CORRECT answer is:

A. I, II, IV, III
B. I, IV, II, III
C. III, I, IV, II
D. III, IV, II, I

10. I. Most organizations favor one of the types but always include the others to a lesser degree. 10.____
II. However, we can detect a definite trend toward greater use of symbolic control.
III. We suggest that our local police agencies are today primarily utilizing material control.
IV. Control can be classified into three types: physical, material, and symbolic.
The CORRECT answer is:

A. IV, II, III, I
B. II, I, IV, III
C. III, IV, II, I
D. IV, I, III, II

11. I. Project residents had first claim to this use, followed by surrounding neighborhood children. 11.____
II. By contrast, recreation space within the project's interior was found to be used more often by both groups.
III. Studies of the use of project grounds in many cities showed grounds left open for public use were neglected and unused, both by residents and by members of the surrounding community.

IV. Project residents had clearly laid claim to the play spaces, setting up and enforcing unwritten rules for use.
V. Each group, by experience, found their activities easily disrupted by other groups, and their claim to the use of space for recreation difficult to enforce.

The CORRECT answer is:

A. IV, V, I, II, III
B. V, II, IV, III, I
C. I, IV, III, II, V
D. III, V, II, IV, I

12. I. They do not consider the problems correctable within the existing subsidy formula and social policy of accepting all eligible applicants regardless of social behavior and lifestyle.
II. A recent survey, however, indicated that tenants believe these problems correctable by local housing authorities and management within the existing financial formula.
III. Many of the problems and complaints concerning public housing management and design have created resentment between the tenant and the landlord.
IV. This same survey indicated that administrators and managers do not agree with the tenants.

The CORRECT answer is:

A. II, I, III, IV
B. I, III, IV, II
C. III, II, IV, I
D. IV, II, I, III

12.___

13. I. In single-family residences, there is usually enough distance between tenants to prevent occupants from annoying one another.
II. For example, a certain small percentage of tenant families has one or more members addicted to alcohol.
III. While managers believe in the right of individuals to live as they choose, the manager becomes concerned when the pattern of living jeopardizes others' rights.
IV. Still others turn night into day, staging lusty entertainments which carry on into the hours when most tenants are trying to sleep.
V. In apartment buildings, however, tenants live so closely together that any misbehavior can result in unpleasant living conditions.
VI. Other families engage in violent argument.

The CORRECT answer is:

A. III, II, V, IV, VI, I
B. I, V, II, VI, IV, III
C. II, V, IV, I, III, VI
D. IV, II, V, VI, III, I

13.___

14. I. Congress made the commitment explicit in the Housing Act of 1949, establishing as a national goal the realization of *a decent home and suitable environment for every American family.*
II. The result has been that the goal of decent home and suitable environment is still as far distant as ever for the disadvantaged urban family.
III. In spite of this action by Congress, federal housing programs have continued to be fragmented and grossly underfunded.
IV. The passage of the National Housing Act signalled a new federal commitment to provide housing for the nation's citizens.

The CORRECT answer is:

A. I, IV, III, II
B. IV, I, III, II
C. IV, I, II, III
D. II, IV, I, III

14.___

15. I. The greater expense does not necessarily involve *exploitation,* but it is often perceived as exploitative and unfair by those who are aware of the price differences involved, but unaware of operating costs.

II. Ghetto residents believe they are *exploited* by local merchants, and evidence substantiates some of these beliefs.

III. However, stores in low-income areas were more likely to be small independents, which could not achieve the economies available to supermarket chains and were, therefore, more likely to charge higher prices, and the customers were more likely to buy smaller-sized packages which are more expensive per unit of measure.

IV. A study conducted in one city showed that distinctly higher prices were charged for goods sold in ghetto stores than in other areas.

The CORRECT answer is:

A. IV, II, I, III
B. IV, I, III, II
C. II, IV, III, I
D. II, III, IV, I

15.____

KEY (CORRECT ANSWERS)

1. C
2. E
3. B
4. D
5. D
6. C
7. A
8. B
9. C
10. D
11. D
12. C
13. B
14. B
15. C

EXAMINATION SECTION
TEST 1

DIRECTIONS: Each question or incomplete statement is followed by several suggested answers or completions. Select the one that BEST answers the question or completes the statement. *PRINT THE LETTER OF THE CORRECT ANSWER IN THE SPACE AT THE RIGHT.*

Questions 1-50.

DIRECTIONS: Each of Questions 1 through 50 consists of a word in capital letters followed by four suggested meanings of the word. For each question, choose the word or phrase which means MOST NEARLY the same as the word in capital letters.

1. ABUT 1.___
   A. abandon B. assist C. border on D. renounce

2. ABSCOND 2.___
   A. draw in B. give up
   C. refrain from D. deal off

3. BEQUEATH 3.___
   A. deaden B. hand down C. make sad D. scold

4. BOGUS 4.___
   A. sad B. false C. shocking D. stolen

5. CALAMITY 5.___
   A. disaster B. female C. insanity D. patriot

6. COMPULSORY 6.___
   A. binding B. ordinary C. protected D. ruling

7. CONSIGN 7.___
   A. agree with B. benefit
   C. commit D. drive down

8. DEBILITY 8.___
   A. failure B. legality
   C. quality D. weakness

9. DEFRAUD 9.___
   A. cheat B. deny
   C. reveal D. tie

10. DEPOSITION 10.___
    A. absence B. publication
    C. removal D. testimony

11. DOMICILE 11.___
    A. anger B. dwelling
    C. tame D. willing

12. HEARSAY
    A. selfish B. serious C. rumor D. unlikely
    12.____

13. HOMOGENEOUS
    A. human B. racial C. similar D. unwise
    13.____

14. ILLICIT
    A. understood B. uneven C. unkind D. unlawful
    14.____

15. LEDGER
    A. book of accounts B. editor
    C. periodical D. shelf
    15.____

16. NARRATIVE
    A. gossip B. natural C. negative D. story
    16.____

17. PLAUSIBLE
    A. reasonable B. respectful C. responsible D. rightful
    17.____

18. RECIPIENT
    A. absentee B. receiver C. speaker D. substitute
    18.____

19. SUBSTANTIATE
    A. appear for B. arrange
    C. confirm D. combine
    19.____

20. SURMISE
    A. aim B. break C. guess D. order
    20.____

21. ALTER EGO
    A. business partner B. confidential friend
    C. guide D. subconscious conflict
    21.____

22. FOURTH ESTATE
    A. the aristocracy B. the clergy
    C. the judiciary D. the newspapers
    22.____

23. IMPEACH
    A. accuse B. find guilty
    C. remove D. try
    23.____

24. PROPENSITY
    A. dislike B. helpfulness
    C. inclination D. supervision
    24.____

25. SPLENETIC
    A. charming B. peevish C. shining D. sluggish
    25.____

26. SUBORN
    A. bribe someone to commit perjury
    B. demote someone several levels in rank
    C. deride
    D. substitute
    26.____

27. TALISMAN 27.___
    A. charm B. juror
    C. prayer shawl D. native

28. VITREOUS 28.___
    A. corroding B. glassy
    C. nourishing D. sticky

29. WRY 29.___
    A. comic B. grained C. resilient D. twisted

30. SIGNATORY 30.___
    A. lawyer who draws up a legal document
    B. document that must be signed by a judge
    C. person who signs a document
    D. true copy of a signature

31. RETAINER 31.___
    A. fee paid to a lawyer for his services
    B. document held by a third party
    C. court decision to send a prisoner back to custody pending trial
    D. legal requirement to keep certain types of files

32. BEQUEATH 32.___
    A. to receive assistance from a charitable organization
    B. to give personal property by will to another
    C. to transfer real property from one person to another
    D. to receive an inheritance upon the death of a relative

33. RATIFY 33.___
    A. approve and sanction B. forego
    C. produce evidence D. summarize

34. CODICIL 34.___
    A. document introduced in evidence in a civil action
    B. subsection of a law
    C. type of legal action that can be brought by a plaintiff
    D. supplement or an addition to a will

35. ALIAS 35.___
    A. assumed name B. in favor of C. against D. a writ

36. PROXY 36.___
    A. a phony document in a real estate transaction
    B. an opinion by a judge of a civil court
    C. a document containing appointment of an agent
    D. a summons in a lawsuit

37. ALLEGED 37.___
    A. innocent B. asserted C. guilty D. called upon

38. EXECUTE 38.
   A. to complete a legal document by signing it
   B. to set requirements
   C. to render services to a duly elected executive of a municipality
   D. to initiate legal action such as a lawsuit

39. NOTARY PUBLIC 39.___
   A. lawyer who is running for public office
   B. judge who hears minor cases
   C. public officer, one of whose functions is to administer oaths
   D. lawyer who gives free legal services to persons unable to pay

40. WAIVE 40.___
   A. to disturb a calm state of affairs
   B. to knowingly renounce a right or claim
   C. to pardon someone for a minor fault
   D. to purposely mislead a person during an investigation

41. ARRAIGN 41.___
   A. to prevent an escape
   B. to defend a prisoner
   C. to verify a document
   D. to accuse in a court of law

42. VOLUNTARY 42.___
   A. by free choice
   B. necessary
   C. important
   D. by design

43. INJUNCTION 43.___
   A. act of prohibiting
   B. process of inserting
   C. means of arbitrating
   D. freedom of action

44. AMICABLE 44.___
   A. compelled
   B. friendly
   C. unimportant
   D. insignificant

45. CLOSED SHOP 45.___
   A. one that employs only members of a union
   B. one that employs union members and unaffiliated employees
   C. one that employs only employees with previous experience
   D. one that employs skilled and unskilled workers

46. ABDUCT 46.___
   A. lead B. kidnap C. sudden D. worthless

47. BIAS 47.___
   A. ability B. envy C. prejudice D. privilege

48. COERCE 48.___
   A. cancel B. force C. rescind D. rugged

49. CONDONE 49.___

A. combine B. pardon C. revive D. spice

50. CONSISTENCY 50.___

A. bravery
B. readiness
C. strain
D. uniformity

KEY (CORRECT ANSWERS)

1. C	11. B	21. B	31. A	41. D
2. D	12. C	22. D	32. B	42. A
3. B	13. C	23. A	33. A	43. A
4. B	14. D	24. C	34. D	44. B
5. A	15. A	25. B	35. A	45. A
6. A	16. D	26. A	36. C	46. B
7. C	17. A	27. A	37. B	47. C
8. D	18. B	28. B	38. A	48. B
9. A	19. C	29. D	39. C	49. B
10. D	20. C	30. C	40. B	50. D

TEST 2

DIRECTIONS: Each question or incomplete statement is followed by several suggested answers or completions. Select the one that BEST answers the question or completes the statement. *PRINT THE LETTER OF THE CORRECT ANSWER IN THE SPACE AT THE RIGHT.*

1. In the sentence, *The prisoner was fractious when brought to the station house*, the word *fractious* means MOST NEARLY 1.___
   A. penitent B. talkative
   C. irascible D. broken-hearted

2. In the sentence, *The judge was implacable when the attorney pleaded for leniency*, the word *implacable* means MOST NEARLY 2.___
   A. inexorable B. disinterested
   C. inattentive D. indifferent

3. In the sentence, *The court ordered the mendacious statements stricken from the record*, the word *mendacious* means MOST NEARLY 3.___
   A. begging B. lying
   C. threatening D. lengthy

4. In the sentence, *The district attorney spoke in a strident voice*, the word *strident* means MOST NEARLY 4.___
   A. loud B. harsh-sounding
   C. sing-song D. low

5. In the sentence, *The speaker had a predilection for long sentences*, the word *predilection* means MOST NEARLY 5.___
   A. aversion B. talent
   C. propensity D. diffidence

6. A person who has an uncontrollable desire to steal without need is called a 6.___
   A. dipsomaniac B. kleptomaniac
   C. monomaniac D. pyromaniac

7. In the sentence, *Malice was immanent in all his remarks*, the word *immanent* means MOST NEARLY 7.___
   A. elevated B. inherent
   C. threatening D. foreign

8. In the sentence, *The extant copies of the document were found in the safe*, the word *extant* means MOST NEARLY 8.___
   A. existing B. original
   C. forged D. duplicate

9. In the sentence, *The recruit was more complaisant after the captain spoke to him*, the word *complaisant* means MOST NEARLY 9.___
   A. calm B. affable
   C. irritable D. confident

10. In the sentence, *The man was captured under highly creditable circumstances*, the word *creditable* means MOST NEARLY 10.___

A. doubtful B. believable
C. praiseworthy D. unexpected

11. In the sentence, *His superior officers were more sagacious than he*, the word *sagacious* means MOST NEARLY 11.___

A. shrewd B. obtuse
C. absurd D. verbose

12. In the sentence, *He spoke with impunity*, the word *impunity* means MOST NEARLY 12.___

A. rashness B. caution
C. without fear D. immunity

13. In the sentence, *The new officer displayed unusual temerity during the emergency*, the word *temerity* means MOST NEARLY 13.___

A. fear B. rashness
C. calmness D. anxiety

14. In the sentence, *The portions of food were parsimoniously served*, the word *parsimoniously* means MOST NEARLY 14.___

A. stingily B. piously
C. elaborately D. generously

15. In the sentence, *Generally the speaker's remarks were sententious*, the word *sententious* means MOST NEARLY 15.___

A. verbose B. witty
C. argumentative D. pithy

Questions 16-20.

DIRECTIONS: Next to the number which corresponds with the number of each item in Column I, place the letter preceding the adjective in Column II which BEST describes the persons in Column I.

COLUMN I	COLUMN II	
16. Talkative woman	A. abstemious	16.___
17. Person on a reducing diet	B. pompous	17.___
18. Scholarly professor	C. erudite	18.___
19. Man who seldom speaks	D. benevolent	19.___
20. Charitable person	E. docile	20.___
	F. loquacious	
	G. indefatigable	
	H. taciturn	

Questions 21-25.

DIRECTIONS: Next to the number which corresponds with the number preceding each profession in Column I, place the letter preceding the word in Column II which BEST explains the subject matter of that profession.

COLUMN I	COLUMN II	
21. Geologist	A. animals	21
22. Oculist	B. eyes	22
23. Podiatrist	C. feet	23
24. Palmist	D. fortune-telling	24
25. Zoologist	E. language	25
	F. rocks	
	G. stamps	
	H. woman	

Questions 26-30.

DIRECTIONS: Next to the number corresponding to the number of each of the words in Column I, place the letter preceding the word in Column II that is MOST NEARLY OPPOSITE to it in meaning.

COLUMN I	COLUMN II	
26. comely	A. beautiful	26.
27. eminent	B. cowardly	27.
28. frugal	C. kind	28.
29. gullible	D. sedate	29.
30. valiant	E. shrewd	30.
	F. ugly	
	G. unknown	
	H. wasteful	

KEY (CORRECT ANSWERS).

1.	C	11.	A	21.	F
2.	A	12.	D	22.	B
3.	B	13.	B	23.	C
4.	B	14.	A	24.	D
5.	C	15.	D	25.	A
6.	B	16.	F	26.	F
7.	B	17.	A	27.	G
8.	A	18.	C	28.	H
9.	B	19.	H	29.	E
10.	C	20.	D	30.	B

GLOSSARY OF LEGAL TERMS

TABLE OF CONTENTS

	Page
Action ... Affiant	1
Affidavit ... At Bar	2
At Issue ... Burden of Proof	3
Business ... Commute	4
Complainant ... Conviction	5
Cooperative ... Demur (v.)	6
Demurrage ... Endorsement	7
Enjoin ... Facsimile	8
Factor ... Guilty	9
Habeas Corpus ... Incumbrance	10
Indemnify ... Laches	11
Landlord and Tenant ... Malice	12
Mandamus ... Obiter Dictum	13
Object (v.) ... Perjury	14
Perpetuity ... Proclamation	15
Proffered Evidence ... Referee	16
Referendum ... Stare Decisis	17
State ... Term	18
Testamentary ... Warrant (Warranty) (v.)	19
Warrant (n.) ... Zoning	20

GLOSSARY OF LEGAL TERMS

A

ACTION - "Action" includes a civil action and a criminal action.
A FORTIORI - A terra meaning you can reason one thing from the existence of certain facts.
A POSTERIORI - From what goes after; from effect to cause.
A PRIORI - From what goes before; from cause to effect.
AB INITIO - From the beginning.
ABATE - To diminish or put an end to.
ABET - To encourage the commission of a crime.
ABEYANCE - Suspension, temporary suppression.
ABIDE - To accept the consequences of.
ABJURE - To renounce; give up.
ABRIDGE - To reduce; contract; diminish.
ABROGATE - To annul, repeal, or destroy.
ABSCOND - To hide or absent oneself to avoid legal action.
ABSTRACT - A summary.
ABUT - To border on, to touch.
ACCESS - Approach; in real property law it means the right of the owner of property to the use of the highway or road next to his land, without obstruction by intervening property owners.
ACCESSORY - In criminal law, it means the person who contributes or aids in the commission of a crime.
ACCOMMODATED PARTY - One to whom credit is extended on the strength of another person signing a commercial paper.
ACCOMMODATION PAPER - A commercial paper to which the accommodating party has put his name.
ACCOMPLICE - In criminal law, it means a person who together with the principal offender commits a crime.
ACCORD - An agreement to accept something different or less than that to which one is entitled, which extinguishes the entire obligation.
ACCOUNT - A statement of mutual demands in the nature of debt and credit between parties.
ACCRETION - The act of adding to a thing; in real property law, it means gradual accumulation of land by natural causes.
ACCRUE - To grow to; to be added to.
ACKNOWLEDGMENT - The act of going before an official authorized to take acknowledgments, and acknowledging an act as one's own.
ACQUIESCENCE - A silent appearance of consent.
ACQUIT - To legally determine the innocence of one charged with a crime.
AD INFINITUM - Indefinitely.
AD LITEM - For the suit.
AD VALOREM - According to value.
ADJECTIVE LAW - Rules of procedure.
ADJUDICATION - The judgment given in a case.
ADMIRALTY - Court having jurisdiction over maritime cases.
ADULT - Sixteen years old or over (in criminal law).
ADVANCE - In commercial law, it means to pay money or render other value before it is due.
ADVERSE - Opposed; contrary.
ADVOCATE - (v.) To speak in favor of;
(n.) One who assists, defends, or pleads for another.
AFFIANT - A person who makes and signs an affidavit.

AFFIDAVIT - A written and sworn to declaration of facts, voluntarily made.
AFFINITY- The relationship between persons through marriage with the kindred of each other; distinguished from consanguinity, which is the relationship by blood.
AFFIRM - To ratify; also when an appellate court affirms a judgment, decree, or order, it means that it is valid and right and must stand as rendered in the lower court.
AFOREMENTIONED; AFORESAID - Before or already said.
AGENT - One who represents and acts for another.
AID AND COMFORT - To help; encourage.
ALIAS - A name not one's true name.
ALIBI - A claim of not being present at a certain place at a certain time.
ALLEGE - To assert.
ALLOTMENT - A share or portion.
AMBIGUITY - Uncertainty; capable of being understood in more than one way.
AMENDMENT - Any language made or proposed as a change in some principal writing.
AMICUS CURIAE - A friend of the court; one who has an interest in a case, although not a party in the case, who volunteers advice upon matters of law to the judge. For example, a brief amicus curiae.
AMORTIZATION - To provide for a gradual extinction of (a future obligation) in advance of maturity, especially, by periodical contributions to a sinking fund which will be adequate to discharge a debt or make a replacement when it becomes necessary.
ANCILLARY - Aiding, auxiliary.
ANNOTATION - A note added by way of comment or explanation.
ANSWER - A written statement made by a defendant setting forth the grounds of his defense.
ANTE - Before.
ANTE MORTEM - Before death.
APPEAL - The removal of a case from a lower court to one of superior jurisdiction for the purpose of obtaining a review.
APPEARANCE - Coming into court as a party to a suit.
APPELLANT - The party who takes an appeal from one court or jurisdiction to another (appellate) court for review.
APPELLEE - The party against whom an appeal is taken.
APPROPRIATE - To make a thing one's own.
APPROPRIATION - Prescribing the destination of a thing; the act of the legislature designating a particular fund, to be applied to some object of government expenditure.
APPURTENANT - Belonging to; accessory or incident to.
ARBITER - One who decides a dispute; a referee.
ARBITRARY - Unreasoned; not governed by any fixed rules or standard.
ARGUENDO - By way of argument.
ARRAIGN - To call the prisoner before the court to answer to a charge.
ASSENT - A declaration of willingness to do something in compliance with a request.
ASSERT - Declare.
ASSESS - To fix the rate or amount.
ASSIGN - To transfer; to appoint; to select for a particular purpose.
ASSIGNEE - One who receives an assignment.
ASSIGNOR - One who makes an assignment.
AT BAR - Before the court.

AT ISSUE - When parties in an action come to a point where one asserts something and the other denies it.
ATTACH - Seize property by court order and sometimes arrest a person.
ATTEST - To witness a will, etc.; act of attestation.
AVERMENT - A positive statement of facts.

B

BAIL - To obtain the release of a person from legal custody by giving security and promising that he shall appear in court; to deliver (goods, etc.) in trust to a person for a special purpose.
BAILEE - One to whom personal property is delivered under a contract of bailment.
BAILMENT - Delivery of personal property to another to be held for a certain purpose and to be returned when the purpose is accomplished.
BAILOR - The party who delivers goods to another, under a contract of bailment.
BANC (OR BANK) - Bench; the place where a court sits permanently or regularly; also the assembly of all the judges of a court.
BANKRUPT - An insolvent person, technically, one declared to be bankrupt after a bankruptcy proceeding.
BAR - The legal profession.
BARRATRY - Exciting groundless judicial proceedings.
BARTER - A contract by which parties exchange goods for other goods.
BATTERY - Illegal interfering with another's person.
BEARER - In commercial law, it means the person in possession of a commercial paper which is payable to the bearer.
BENCH - The court itself or the judge.
BENEFICIARY - A person benefiting under a will, trust, or agreement.
BEST EVIDENCE RULE,THE - Except as otherwise provided by statute, no evidence other than the writing itself is admissible to prove the content of a writing. This section shall be known and may be cited as the best evidence rule.
BEQUEST - A gift of personal property under a will.
BILL - A formal written statement of complaint to a court of justice; also, a draft of an act of the legislature before it becomes a law; also, accounts for goods sold, services rendered, or work done.
BONA FIDE - In or with good faith; honestly.
BOND - An instrument by which the maker promises to pay a sum of money to another, usually providing that upon performances of a certain condition the obligation shall be void.
BOYCOTT - A plan to prevent the carrying on of a business by wrongful means.
BREACH - The breaking or violating of a law, or the failure to carry out a duty.
BRIEF - A written document, prepared by a lawyer to serve as the basis of an argument upon a case in court, usually an appellate court.
BURDEN OF PRODUCING EVIDENCE - The obligation of a party to introduce evidence sufficient to avoid a ruling against him on the issue.
BURDEN OF PROOF - The obligation of a party to establish by evidence a requisite degree of belief concerning a fact in the mind of the trier of fact or the court. The burden of proof may require a party to raise a reasonable doubt concerning the existence of nonexistence of a fact or that he establish the existence or nonexistence of a fact by a preponderance of the evidence, by clear and convincing proof, or by proof beyond a reasonable doubt.

Except as otherwise provided by law, the burden of proof requires proof by a preponderance of the evidence.

BUSINESS, A - Shall include every kind of business, profession, occupation, calling or operation of institutions, whether carried on for profit or not.
BY-LAWS - Regulations, ordinances, or rules enacted by a corporation, association, etc., for its own government.

C

CANON - A doctrine; also, a law or rule, of a church or association in particular.
CAPIAS - An order to arrest.
CAPTION - In a pleading, deposition or other paper connected with a case in court, it is the heading or introductory clause which shows the names of the parties, name of the court, number of the case on the docket or calendar, etc.
CARRIER - A person or corporation undertaking to transport persons or property.
CASE - A general term for an action, cause, suit, or controversy before a judicial body.
CAUSE - A suit, litigation or action before a court.
CAVEAT EMPTOR - Let the buyer beware. This term expresses the rule that the purchaser of an article must examine, judge, and test it for himself, being bound to discover any obvious defects or imperfections.
CERTIFICATE - A written representation that some legal formality has been complied with.
CERTIORARI - To be informed of; the name of a writ issued by a superior court directing the lower court to send up to the former the record and proceedings of a case.
CHANGE OF VENUE - To remove place of trial from one place to another.
CHARGE - An obligation or duty; a formal complaint; an instruction of the court to the jury upon a case.
CHARTER - (n.) The authority by virtue of which an organized body acts;
(v.) in mercantile law, it means to hire or lease a vehicle or vessel for transportation.
CHATTEL - An article of personal property.
CHATTEL MORTGAGE - A mortgage on personal property.
CIRCUIT - A division of the country, for the administration of justice; a geographical area served by a court.
CITATION - The act of the court by which a person is summoned or cited; also, a reference to legal authority.
CIVIL (ACTIONS)- It indicates the private rights and remedies of individuals in contrast to the word "criminal" (actions) which relates to prosecution for violation of laws.
CLAIM (n.) - Any demand held or asserted as of right.
CODICIL - An addition to a will.
CODIFY - To arrange the laws of a country into a code.
COGNIZANCE - Notice or knowledge.
COLLATERAL - By the side; accompanying; an article or thing given to secure performance of a promise.
COMITY - Courtesy; the practice by which one court follows the decision of another court on the same question.
COMMIT - To perform, as an act; to perpetrate, as a crime; to send a person to prison.
COMMON LAW - As distinguished from law created by the enactment of the legislature (called statutory law), it relates to those principles and rules of action which derive their authority solely from usages and customs of immemorial antiquity, particularly with reference to the ancient unwritten law of England. The written pronouncements of the common law are found in court decisions.
COMMUTE - Change punishment to one less severe.

COMPLAINANT - One who applies to the court for legal redress.
COMPLAINT - The pleading of a plaintiff in a civil action; or a charge that a person has committed a specified offense.
COMPROMISE - An arrangement for settling a dispute by agreement.
CONCUR - To agree, consent.
CONCURRENT - Running together, at the same time.
CONDEMNATION - Taking private property for public use on payment therefor.
CONDITION - Mode or state of being; a qualification or restriction.
CONDUCT - Active and passive behavior; both verbal and nonverbal.
CONFESSION - Voluntary statement of guilt of crime.
CONFIDENTIAL COMMUNICATION BETWEEN CLIENT AND LAWYER - Information transmitted between a client and his lawyer in the course of that relationship and in confidence by a means which, so far as the client is aware, discloses the information to no third persons other than those who are present to further the interest of the client in the consultation or those to whom disclosure is reasonably necessary for the transmission of the information or the accomplishment of the purpose for which the lawyer is consulted, and includes a legal opinion formed and the advice given by the lawyer in the course of that relationship.
CONFRONTATION - Witness testifying in presence of defendant.
CONSANGUINITY - Blood relationship.
CONSIGN - To give in charge; commit; entrust; to send or transmit goods to a merchant, factor, or agent for sale.
CONSIGNEE - One to whom a consignment is made.
CONSIGNOR - One who sends or makes a consignment.
CONSPIRACY - In criminal law, it means an agreement between two or more persons to commit an unlawful act.
CONSPIRATORS - Persons involved in a conspiracy.
CONSTITUTION - The fundamental law of a nation or state.
CONSTRUCTION OF GENDERS - The masculine gender includes the feminine and neuter.
CONSTRUCTION OF SINGULAR AND PLURAL - The singular number includes the plural; and the plural, the singular.
CONSTRUCTION OF TENSES - The present tense includes the past and future tenses; and the future, the present.
CONSTRUCTIVE - An act or condition assumed from other parts or conditions.
CONSTRUE - To ascertain the meaning of language.
CONSUMMATE - To complete.
CONTIGUOUS - Adjoining; touching; bounded by.
CONTINGENT - Possible, but not assured; dependent upon some condition.
CONTINUANCE - The adjournment or postponement of an action pending in a court.
CONTRA - Against, opposed to; contrary.
CONTRACT - An agreement between two or more persons to do or not to do a particular thing.
CONTROVERT - To dispute, deny.
CONVERSION - Dealing with the personal property of another as if it were one's own, without right.
CONVEYANCE - An instrument transferring title to land.
CONVICTION - Generally, the result of a criminal trial which ends in a judgment or sentence that the defendant is guilty as charged.

COOPERATIVE - A cooperative is a voluntary organization of persons with a common interest, formed and operated along democratic lines for the purpose of supplying services at cost to its members and other patrons, who contribute both capital and business.
CORPUS DELICTI - The body of a crime; the crime itself.
CORROBORATE - To strengthen; to add weight by additional evidence.
COUNTERCLAIM - A claim presented by a defendant in opposition to or deduction from the claim of the plaintiff.
COUNTY - Political subdivision of a state.
COVENANT - Agreement.
CREDIBLE - Worthy of belief.
CREDITOR - A person to whom a debt is owing by another person, called the "debtor."
CRIMINAL ACTION - Includes criminal proceedings.
CRIMINAL INFORMATION - Same as complaint.
CRITERION (sing.)
CRITERIA (plural) - A means or tests for judging; a standard or standards.
CROSS-EXAMINATION - Examination of a witness by a party other than the direct examiner upon a matter that is within the scope of the direct examination of the witness.
CULPABLE - Blamable.
CY-PRES - As near as (possible). The rule of *cy-pres* is a rule for the construction of instruments in equity by which the intention of the party is carried out *as near as may be*, *when it* would be impossible or illegal to give it literal effect.

D

DAMAGES - A monetary compensation, which may be recovered in the courts by any person who has suffered loss, or injury, whether to his person, property or rights through the unlawful act or omission or negligence of another.
DECLARANT - A person who makes a statement.
DE FACTO - In fact; actually but without legal authority.
DE JURE - Of right; legitimate; lawful.
DE MINIMIS - Very small or trifling.
DE NOVO - Anew; afresh; a second time.
DEBT - A specified sum of money owing to one person from another, including not only the obligation of the debtor to pay, but the right of the creditor to receive and enforce payment.
DECEDENT - A dead person.
DECISION - A judgment or decree pronounced by a court in determination of a case.
DECREE - An order of the court, determining the rights of all parties to a suit.
DEED - A writing containing a contract sealed and delivered; particularly to convey real property.
DEFALCATION - Misappropriation of funds.
DEFAMATION - Injuring one's reputation by false statements.
DEFAULT - The failure to fulfill a duty, observe a promise, discharge an obligation, or perform an agreement.
DEFENDANT - The person defending or denying; the party against whom relief or recovery is sought in an action or suit.
DEFRAUD - To practice fraud; to cheat or trick.
DELEGATE (v.)- To entrust to the care or management of another.
DELICTUS - A crime.
DEMUR (v.) - To dispute the sufficiency in law of the pleading of the other side.

DEMURRAGE - In maritime law, it means, the sum fixed or allowed as remuneration to the owners of a ship for the detention of their vessel beyond the number of days allowed for loading and unloading or for sailing; also used in railroad terminology.
DENIAL - A form of pleading; refusing to admit the truth of a statement, charge, etc.
DEPONENT - One who gives testimony under oath reduced to writing.
DEPOSITION - Testimony given under oath outside of court for use in court or for the purpose of obtaining information in preparation for trial of a case.
DETERIORATION - A degeneration such as from decay, corrosion or disintegration.
DETRIMENT - Any loss or harm to person or property.
DEVIATION - A turning aside.
DEVISE - A gift of real property by the last will and testament of the donor.
DICTUM (sing.)
DICTA (plural) - Any statements made by the court in an opinion concerning some rule of law not necessarily involved nor essential to the determination of the case.
DIRECT EVIDENCE - Evidence that directly proves a fact, without an inference or presumption, and which in itself if true, conclusively establishes that fact.
DIRECT EXAMINATION - The first examination of a witness upon a matter that is not within the scope of a previous examination of the witness.
DISAFFIRM - To repudicate.
DISMISS - In an action or suit, it means to dispose of the case without any further consideration or hearing.
DISSENT - To denote disagreement of one or more judges of a court with the decision passed by the majority upon a case before them.
DOCKET (n.) - A formal record, entered in brief, of the proceedings in a court.
DOCTRINE - A rule, principle, theory of law.
DOMICILE - That place where a man has his true, fixed and permanent home to which whenever he is absent he has the intention of returning.
DRAFT (n.) - A commercial paper ordering payment of money drawn by one person on another.
DRAWEE - The person who is requested to pay the money.
DRAWER - The person who draws the commercial paper and addresses it to the drawee.
DUPLICATE - A counterpart produced by the same impression as the original enlargements and miniatures, or by mechanical or electronic re-recording, or by chemical reproduction, or by other equivalent technique which accurately reproduces the original.
DURESS - Use of force to compel performance or non-performance of an act.

E

EASEMENT - A liberty, privilege, or advantage without profit, in the lands of another.
EGRESS - Act or right of going out or leaving; emergence.
EIUSDEM GENERIS - Of the same kind, class or nature. A rule used in the construction of language in a legal document.
EMBEZZLEMENT - To steal; to appropriate fraudulently to one's own use property entrusted to one's care.
EMBRACERY - Unlawful attempt to influence jurors, etc., but not by offering value.
EMINENT DOMAIN - The right of a state to take private property for public use.
ENACT - To make into a law.
ENDORSEMENT - Act of writing one's name on the back of a note, bill or similar written instrument.

ENJOIN - To require a person, by writ of injunction from a court of equity, to perform or to abstain or desist from some act.
ENTIRETY - The whole; that which the law considers as one whole, and not capable of being divided into parts.
ENTRAPMENT - Inducing one to commit a crime so as to arrest him.
ENUMERATED - Mentioned specifically; designated.
ENURE - To operate or take effect.
EQUITY - In its broadest sense, this term denotes the spirit and the habit of fairness, justness, and right dealing which regulate the conduct of men.
ERROR - A mistake of law, or the false or irregular application of law as will nullify the judicial proceedings.
ESCROW - A deed, bond or other written engagement, delivered to a third person, to be delivered by him only upon the performance or fulfillment of some condition.
ESTATE - The interest which any one has in lands, or in any other subject of property.
ESTOP - To stop, bar, or impede.
ESTOPPEL - A rule of law which prevents a man from alleging or denying a fact, because of his own previous act.
ET AL. (alii) - And others.
ET SEQ. (sequential) - And the following.
ET UX. (uxor) - And wife.
EVIDENCE - Testimony, writings, material objects, or other things presented to the senses that are offered to prove the existence or non-existence of a fact.
Means from which inferences may be drawn as a basis of proof in duly constituted judicial or fact finding tribunals, and includes testimony in the form of opinion and hearsay.
EX CONTRACTU
EX DELICTO - In law, rights and causes of action are divided into two classes, those arising *ex contractu* (from a contract) and those arising *ex delicto* (from a delict or tort).
EX OFFICIO - From office; by virtue of the office.
EX PARTE - On one side only; by or for one.
EX POST FACTO - After the fact.
EX POST FACTO LAW - A law passed after an act was done which retroactively makes such act a crime.
EX REL. (relations) - Upon relation or information.
EXCEPTION - An objection upon a matter of law to a decision made, either before or after judgment by a court.
EXECUTOR (male)
EXECUTRIX (female) - A person who has been appointed by will to execute the will.
EXECUTORY - That which is yet to be executed or performed.
EXEMPT - To release from some liability to which others are subject.
EXONERATION - The removal of a burden, charge or duty.
EXTRADITION - Surrender of a fugitive from one nation to another.

F

F.A.S.- "Free alongside ship"; delivery at dock for ship named.
F.O.B.- "Free on board"; seller will deliver to car, truck, vessel, or other conveyance by which goods are to be transported, without expense or risk of loss to the buyer or consignee.
FABRICATE - To construct; to invent a false story.
FACSIMILE - An exact or accurate copy of an original instrument.

FACTOR - A commercial agent.
FEASANCE - The doing of an act.
FELONIOUS - Criminal, malicious.
FELONY - Generally, a criminal offense that may be punished by death or imprisonment for more than one year as differentiated from a misdemeanor.
FEME SOLE - A single woman.
FIDUCIARY - A person who is invested with rights and powers to be exercised for the benefit of another person.
FIERI FACIAS - A writ of execution commanding the sheriff to levy and collect the amount of a judgment from the goods and chattels of the judgment debtor.
FINDING OF FACT - Determination from proof or judicial notice of the existence of a fact. A ruling implies a supporting finding of fact; no separate or formal finding is required unless required by a statute of this state.
FISCAL - Relating to accounts or the management of revenue.
FORECLOSURE (sale) - A sale of mortgaged property to obtain satisfaction of the mortgage out of the sale proceeds.
FORFEITURE - A penalty, a fine.
FORGERY - Fabricating or producing falsely, counterfeited.
FORTUITOUS - Accidental.
FORUM - A court of justice; a place of jurisdiction.
FRAUD - Deception; trickery.
FREEHOLDER - One who owns real property.
FUNGIBLE - Of such kind or nature that one specimen or part may be used in the place of another.

G

GARNISHEE - Person garnished.
GARNISHMENT - A legal process to reach the money or effects of a defendant, in the possession or control of a third person.
GRAND JURY - Not less than 16, not more than 23 citizens of a county sworn to inquire into crimes committed or triable in the county.
GRANT - To agree to; convey, especially real property.
GRANTEE - The person to whom a grant is made.
GRANTOR - The person by whom a grant is made.
GRATUITOUS - Given without a return, compensation or consideration.
GRAVAMEN - The grievance complained of or the substantial cause of a criminal action.
GUARANTY (n.) - A promise to answer for the payment of some debt, or the performance of some duty, in case of the failure of another person, who, in the first instance, is liable for such payment or performance.
GUARDIAN - The person, committee, or other representative authorized by law to protect the person or estate or both of an incompetent (or of a *sui juris* person having a guardian) and to act for him in matters affecting his person or property or both. An incompetent is a person under disability imposed by law.
GUILTY - Establishment of the fact that one has committed a breach of conduct; especially, a violation of law.

H

HABEAS CORPUS - You have the body; the name given to a variety of writs, having for their object to bring a party before a court or judge for decision as to whether such person is being lawfully held prisoner.
HABENDUM - In conveyancing; it is the clause in a deed conveying land which defines the extent of ownership to be held by the grantee.
HEARING - A proceeding whereby the arguments of the interested parties are heared.
HEARSAY - A type of testimony given by a witness who relates, not what he knows personally, but what others have told hi, or what he has heard said by others.
HEARSAY RULE, THE - (a) "Hearsay evidence" is evidence of a statement that was made other than by a witness while testifying at the hearing and that is offered to prove the truth of the matter stated; (b) Except as provided by law, hearsay evidence is inadmissible; (c) This section shall be known and may be cited as the hearsay rule.
HEIR - Generally, one who inherits property, real or personal.
HOLDER OF THE PRIVILEGE - (a) The client when he has no guardian or conservator; (b) A guardian or conservator of the client when the client has a guardian or conservator; (c) The personal representative of the client if the client is dead; (d) A successor, assign, trustee in dissolution, or any similar representative of a firm, association, organization, partnership, business trust, corporation, or public entity that is no longer in existence.
HUNG JURY - One so divided that they can't agree on a verdict.
HUSBAND-WIFE PRIVILEGE - An accused in a criminal proceeding has a privilege to prevent his spouse from testifying against him.
HYPOTHECATE - To pledge a thing without delivering it to the pledgee.
HYPOTHESIS - A supposition, assumption, or toehry.

I

I.E. (id est) - That is.
IB., OR IBID.(ibidem) - In the same place; used to refer to a legal reference previously cited to avoid repeating the entire citation.
ILLICIT - Prohibited; unlawful.
ILLUSORY - Deceiving by false appearance.
IMMUNITY - Exemption.
IMPEACH - To accuse, to dispute.
IMPEDIMENTS - Disabilities, or hindrances.
IMPLEAD - To sue or prosecute by due course of law.
IMPUTED - Attributed or charged to.
IN LOCO PARENTIS - In place of parent, a guardian.
IN TOTO - In the whole; completely.
INCHOATE - Imperfect; unfinished.
INCOMMUNICADO - Denial of the right of a prisoner to communicate with friends or relatives.
INCOMPETENT - One who is incapable of caring for his own affairs because he is mentally deficient or undeveloped.
INCRIMINATION - A matter will incriminate a person if it constitutes, or forms an essential part of, or, taken in connection with other matters disclosed, is a basis for a reasonable inference of such a violation of the laws of this State as to subject him to liability to punishment therefor, unless he has become for any reason permanently immune from punishment for such violation.
INCUMBRANCE - Generally a claim, lien, charge or liability attached to and binding real property.

INDEMNIFY - To secure against loss or damage; also, to make reimbursement to one for a loss already incurred by him.
INDEMNITY - An agreement to reimburse another person in case of an anticipated loss falling upon him.
INDICIA - Signs; indications.
INDICTMENT - An accusation in writing found and presented by a grand jury charging that a person has committed a crime.
INDORSE - To write a name on the back of a legal paper or document, generally, a negotiable instrument
INDUCEMENT - Cause or reason why a thing is done or that which incites the person to do the act or commit a crime; the motive for the criminal act.
INFANT - In civil cases one under 21 years of age.
INFORMATION - A formal accusation of crime made by a prosecuting attorney.
INFRA - Below, under; this word occurring by itself in a publication refers the reader to a future part of the publication.
INGRESS - The act of going into.
INJUNCTION - A writ or order by the court requiring a person, generally, to do or to refrain from doing an act.
INSOLVENT - The condition of a person who is unable to pay his debts.
INSTRUCTION - A direction given by the judge to the jury concerning the law of the case.
INTERIM - In the meantime; time intervening.
INTERLOCUTORY - Temporary, not final; something intervening between the commencement and the end of a suit which decides some point or matter, but is not a final decision of the whole controversy.
INTERROGATORIES - A series of formal written questions used in the examination of a party or a witness usually prior to a trial.
INTESTATE - A person who dies without a will.
INURE - To result, to take effect.
IPSO FACTO - By the fact iself; by the mere fact.
ISSUE (n.) The disputed point or question in a case,

J

JEOPARDY - Danger, hazard, peril.
JOINDER - Joining; uniting with another person in some legal steps or proceeding.
JOINT - United; combined.
JUDGE - Member or members or representative or representatives of a court conducting a trial or hearing at which evidence is introduced.
JUDGMENT - The official decision of a court of justice.
JUDICIAL OR JUDICIARY - Relating to or connected with the administration of justice.
JURAT - The clause written at the foot of an affidavit, stating when, where and before whom such affidavit was sworn.
JURISDICTION - The authority to hear and determine controversies between parties.
JURISPRUDENCE - The philosophy of law.
JURY - A body of persons legally selected to inquire into any matter of fact, and to render their verdict according to the evidence.

L

LACHES - The failure to diligently assert a right, which results in a refusal to allow relief.

LANDLORD AND TENANT - A phrase used to denote the legal relation existing between the owner and occupant of real estate.
LARCENY - Stealing personal property belonging to another.
LATENT - Hidden; that which does not appear on the face of a thing.
LAW - Includes constitutional, statutory, and decisional law.
LAWYER-CLIENT PRIVILEGE - (1) A "client" is a person, public officer, or corporation, association, or other organization or entity, either public or private, who is rendered professional legal services by a lawyer, or who consults a lawyer with a view to obtaining professional legal services from him; (2) A "lawyer" is a person authorized, or reasonably believed by the client to be authorized, to practice law in any state or nation; (3) A "representative of the lawyer" is one employed to assist the lawyer in the rendition of professional legal services; (4) A communication is "confidential" if not intended to be disclosed to third persons other than those to whom disclosure is in furtherance of the rendition of professional legal services to the client or those reasonably necessary for the transmission of the communication.

General rule of privilege - A client has a privilege to refuse to disclose and to prevent any other person from disclosing confidential communications made for the purpose of facilitating the rendition of professional legal services to the client, (1) between himself or his representative and his lawyer or his lawyer's representative, or (2) between his lawyer and the lawyer's representative, or (3) by him or his lawyer to a lawyer representing another in a matter of common interest, or (4) between representatives of the client or between the client and a representative of the client, or (5) between lawyers representing the client.

LEADING QUESTION - Question that suggests to the witness the answer that the examining party desires.
LEASE - A contract by which one conveys real estate for a limited time usually for a specified rent; personal property also may be leased.
LEGISLATION - The act of enacting laws.
LEGITIMATE - Lawful.
LESSEE - One to whom a lease is given.
LESSOR - One who grants a lease
LEVY - A collecting or exacting by authority.
LIABLE - Responsible; bound or obligated in law or equity.
LIBEL (v.) - To defame or injure a person's reputation by a published writing.
(n.) - The initial pleading on the part of the plaintiff in an admiralty proceeding.
LIEN - A hold or claim which one person has upon the property of another as a security for some debt or charge.
LIQUIDATED - Fixed; settled.
LIS PENDENS - A pending civil or criminal action.
LITERAL - According to the language.
LITIGANT - A party to a lawsuit.
LITATION - A judicial controversy.
LOCUS - A place.
LOCUS DELICTI - Place of the crime.
LOCUS POENITENTIAE - The abandoning or giving up of one's intention to commit some crime before it is fully completed or abandoning a conspiracy before its purpose is accomplished.

M

MALFEASANCE - To do a wrongful act.
MALICE - The doing of a wrongful act Intentionally without just cause or excuse.

MANDAMUS - The name of a writ issued by a court to enforce the performance of some public duty.
MANDATORY (adj.) Containing a command.
MARITIME - Pertaining to the sea or to commerce thereon.
MARSHALING - Arranging or disposing of in order.
MAXIM - An established principle or proposition.
MINISTERIAL - That which involves obedience to instruction, but demands no special discretion, judgment or skill.
MISAPPROPRIATE - Dealing fraudulently with property entrusted to one.
MISDEMEANOR - A crime less than a felony and punishable by a fine or imprisonment for less than one year.
MISFEASANCE - Improper performance of a lawful act.
MISREPRESENTATION - An untrue representation of facts.
MITIGATE - To make or become less severe, harsh.
MITTIMUS - A warrant of commitment to prison.
MOOT (adj.) Unsettled, undecided, not necessary to be decided.
MORTGAGE - A conveyance of property upon condition, as security for the payment of a debt or the performance of a duty, and to become void upon payment or performance according to the stipulated terms.
MORTGAGEE - A person to whom property is mortgaged.
MORTGAGOR - One who gives a mortgage.
MOTION - In legal proceedings, a "motion" is an application, either written or oral, addressed to the court by a party to an action or a suit requesting the ruling of the court on a matter of law.
MUTUALITY - Reciprocation.

N

NEGLIGENCE - The failure to exercise that degree of care which an ordinarily prudent person would exercise under like circumstances.
NEGOTIABLE (instrument) - Any instrument obligating the payment of money which is transferable from one person to another by endorsement and delivery or by delivery only.
NEGOTIATE - To transact business; to transfer a negotiable instrument; to seek agreement for the amicable disposition of a controversy or case.
NOLLE PROSEQUI - A formal entry upon the record, by the plaintiff in a civil suit or the prosecuting officer in a criminal action, by which he declares that he "will no further prosecute" the case.
NOLO CONTENDERE - The name of a plea in a criminal action, having the same effect as a plea of guilty; but not constituting a direct admission of guilt.
NOMINAL - Not real or substantial.
NOMINAL DAMAGES - Award of a trifling sum where no substantial injury is proved to have been sustained.
NONFEASANCE - Neglect of duty.
NOVATION - The substitution of a new debt or obligation for an existing one.
NUNC PRO TUNC - A phrase applied to acts allowed to be done after the time when they should be done, with a retroactive effect.("Now for then.")

O

OATH - Oath includes affirmation or declaration under penalty of perjury.
OBITER DICTUM - Opinion expressed by a court on a matter not essentially -involved in a case and hence not a decision; also called dicta, if plural.

OBJECT (v.) - To oppose as improper or illegal and referring the question of its propriety or legality to the court.
OBLIGATION - A legal duty, by which a person is bound to do or not to do a certain thing.
OBLIGEE - The person to whom an obligation is owed.
OBLIGOR - The person who is to perform the obligation.
OFFER (v.) - To present for acceptance or rejection.
(n.) - A proposal to do a thing, usually a proposal to make a contract.
OFFICIAL INFORMATION - Information within the custody or control of a department or agency of the government the disclosure of which is shown to be contrary to the public interest.
OFFSET - A deduction.
ONUS PROBANDI - Burden of proof.
OPINION - The statement by a judge of the decision reached in a case, giving the law as applied to the case and giving reasons for the judgment; also a belief or view.
OPTION - The exercise of the power of choice; also a privilege existing in one person, for which he has paid money, which gives him the right to buy or sell real or personal property at a given price within a specified time.
ORDER - A rule or regulation; every direction of a court or judge made or entered in writing but not including a judgment.
ORDINANCE - Generally, a rule established by authority; also commonly used to designate the legislative acts of a municipal corporation.
ORIGINAL - Writing or recording itself or any counterpart intended to have the same effect by a person executing or issuing it. An "original" of a photograph includes the negative or any print therefrom. If data are stored in a computer or similar device, any printout or other output readable by sight, shown to reflect the data accurately, is an "original."
OVERT - Open, manifest.

P

PANEL - A group of jurors selected to serve during a term of the court.
PARENS PATRIAE - Sovereign power of a state to protect or be a guardian over children and incompetents.
PAROL - Oral or verbal.
PAROLE - To release one in prison before the expiration of his sentence, conditionally.
PARITY - Equality in purchasing power between the farmer and other segments of the economy.
PARTITION - A legal division of real or personal property between one or more owners.
PARTNERSHIP - An association of two or more persons to carry on as co-owners a business for profit.
PATENT (adj.) - Evident.
(n.) - A grant of some privilege, property, or authority, made by the government or sovereign of a country to one or more individuals.
PECULATION - Stealing.
PECUNIARY - Monetary.
PENULTIMATE - Next to the last.
PER CURIAM - A phrase used in the report of a decision to distinguish an opinion of the whole court from an opinion written by any one judge.
PER SE - In itself; taken alone.
PERCEIVE - To acquire knowledge through one's senses.
PEREMPTORY - Imperative; absolute.
PERJURY - To lie or state falsely under oath.

PERPETUITY - Perpetual existence; also the quality or condition of an estate limited so that it will not take effect or vest within the period fixed by law.
PERSON - Includes a natural person, firm, association, organization, partnership, business trust, corporation, or public entity.
PERSONAL PROPERTY - Includes money, goods, chattels, things in action, and evidences of debt.
PERSONALTY - Short term for personal property.
PETITION - An application in writing for an order of the court, stating the circumstances upon which it is founded and requesting any order or other relief from a court.
PLAINTIFF - A person who brings a court action.
PLEA - A pleading in a suit or action.
PLEADINGS - Formal allegations made by the parties of their respective claims and defenses, for the judgment of the court.
PLEDGE - A deposit of personal property as a security for the performance of an act.
PLEDGEE - The party to whom goods are delivered in pledge.
PLEDGOR - The party delivering goods in pledge.
PLENARY - Full; complete.
POLICE POWER - Inherent power of the state or its political subdivisions to enact laws within constitutional limits to promote the general welfare of society or the community.
POLLING THE JURY - Call the names of persons on a jury and requiring each juror to declare what his verdict is before it is legally recorded.
POST MORTEM - After death.
POWER OF ATTORNEY - A writing authorizing one to act for another.
PRECEPT - An order, warrant, or writ issued to an officer or body of officers, commanding him or them to do some act within the scope of his or their powers.
PRELIMINARY FACT - Fact upon the existence or nonexistence of which depends the admissibility or inadmissibility of evidence. The phrase "the admissibility or inadmissibility of evidence" includes the qualification or disqualification of a person to be a witness and the existence or nonexistence of a privilege.
PREPONDERANCE - Outweighing.
PRESENTMENT - A report by a grand jury on something they have investigated on their own knowledge.
PRESUMPTION - An assumption of fact resulting from a rule of law which requires such fact to be assumed from another fact or group of facts found or otherwise established in the action.
PRIMA FACUE - At first sight.
PRIMA FACIE CASE - A case where the evidence is very patent against the defendant.
PRINCIPAL - The source of authority or rights; a person primarily liable as differentiated from "principle" as a primary or basic doctrine.
PRO AND CON - For and against.
PRO RATA - Proportionally.
PROBATE - Relating to proof, especially to the proof of wills.
PROBATIVE - Tending to prove.
PROCEDURE - In law, this term generally denotes rules which are established by the Federal, State, or local Governments regarding the types of pleading and courtroom practice which must be followed by the parties involved in a criminal or civil case.
PROCLAMATION - A public notice by an official of some order, intended action, or state of facts.

PROFFERED EVIDENCE - The admissibility or inadmissibility of which is dependent upon the existence or nonexistence of a preliminary fact.
PROMISSORY (NOTE) - A promise in writing to pay a specified sum at an expressed time, or on demand, or at sight, to a named person, or to his order, or bearer.
PROOF - The establishment by evidence of a requisite degree of belief concerning a fact in the mind of the trier of fact or the court.
PROPERTY - Includes both real and personal property.
PROPRIETARY (adj.) - Relating or pertaining to ownership; usually a single owner.
PROSECUTE - To carry on an action or other judicial proceeding; to proceed against a person criminally.
PROVISO - A limitation or condition in a legal instrument.
PROXIMATE - Immediate; nearest
PUBLIC EMPLOYEE - An officer, agent, or employee of a public entity.
PUBLIC ENTITY - Includes a national, state, county, city and county, city, district, public authority, public agency, or any other political subdivision or public corporation, whether foreign or domestic.
PUBLIC OFFICIAL - Includes an official of a political dubdivision of such state or territory and of a municipality.
PUNITIVE - Relating to punishment.

Q

QUASH - To make void.
QUASI - As if; as it were.
QUID PRO QUO - Something for something; the giving of one valuable thing for another.
QUITCLAIM (v.) - To release or relinquish claim or title to, especially in deeds to realty.
QUO WARRANTO - A legal procedure to test an official's right to a public office or the right to hold a franchise, or to hold an office in a domestic corporation.

R

RATIFY - To approve and sanction.
REAL PROPERTY - Includes lands, tenements, and hereditaments.
REALTY - A brief term for real property.
REBUT - To contradict; to refute, especially by evidence and arguments.
RECEIVER - A person who is appointed by the court to receive, and hold in trust property in litigation.
RECIDIVIST - Habitual criminal.
RECIPROCAL - Mutual.
RECOUPMENT - To keep back or get something which is due; also, it is the right of a defendant to have a deduction from the amount of the plaintiff's damages because the plaintiff has not fulfilled his part of the same contract.
RECROSS EXAMINATION - Examination of a witness by a cross-examiner subsequent to a redirect examination of the witness.
REDEEM - To release an estate or article from mortgage or pledge by paying the debt for which it stood as security.
REDIRECT EXAMINATION - Examination of a witness by the direct examiner subsequent to the cross-examination of the witness.
REFEREE - A person to whom a cause pending in a court is referred by the court, to take testimony, hear the parties, and report thereon to the court.

REFERENDUM - A method of submitting an important legislative or administrative matter to a direct vote of the people.
RELEVANT EVIDENCE - Evidence including evidence relevant to the credulity of a witness or hearsay declarant, having any tendency in reason to prove or disprove any disputed fact that is of consequence to the determination of the action.
REMAND - To send a case back to the lower court from which it came, for further proceedings.
REPLEVIN - An action to recover goods or chattels wrongfully taken or detained.
REPLY (REPLICATION) - Generally, a reply is what the plaintiff or other person who has instituted proceedings says in answer to the defendant's case.
RE JUDICATA - A thing judicially acted upon or decided.
RES ADJUDICATA - Doctrine that an issue or dispute litigated and determined in a case between the opposing parties is deemed permanently decided between these parties.
RESCIND (RECISSION) - To avoid or cancel a contract.
RESPONDENT - A defendant in a proceeding in chancery or admiralty; also, the person who contends against the appeal in a case.
RESTITUTION - In equity, it is the restoration of both parties to their original condition (when practicable), upon the rescission of a contract for fraud or similar cause.
RETROACTIVE (RETROSPECTIVE) - Looking back; effective as of a prior time.
REVERSED - A term used by appellate courts to indicate that the decision of the lower court in the case before it has been set aside.
REVOKE - To recall or cancel.
RIPARIAN (RIGHTS) - The rights of a person owning land containing or bordering on a water course or other body of water, such as lakes and rivers.

S

SALE - A contract whereby the ownership of property is transferred from one person to another for a sum of money or for any consideration.
SANCTION - A penalty or punishment provided as a means of enforcing obedience to a law; also, an authorization.
SATISFACTION - The discharge of an obligation by paying a party what is due to him; or what is awarded to him by the judgment of a court or otherwise.
SCIENTER - Knowingly; also, it is used in pleading to denote the defendant 's guilty knowledge.
SCINTILLA - A spark; also the least particle.
SECRET OF STATE - Governmental secret relating to the national defense or the international relations of the United States.
SECURITY - Indemnification; the term is applied to an obligation, such as a mortgage or deed of trust, given by a debtor to insure the payment or performance of his debt, by furnishing the creditor with a resource to be used in case of the debtor's failure to fulfill the principal obligation.
SENTENCE - The judgment formally pronounced by the court or judge upon the defendant after his conviction in a criminal prosecution.
SET-OFF - A claim or demand which one party in an action credits against the claim of the opposing party.
SHALL and MAY - "Shall" is mandatory and "may" is permissive.
SITUS - Location.
SOVEREIGN - A person, body or state in which independent and supreme authority is vested.
STARE DECISIS - To follow decided cases.

STATE - "State" means this State, unless applied to the different parts of the United States. In the latter case, it includes any state, district, commonwealth, territory or insular possession of the United States, including the District of Columbia.

STATEMENT - (a) Oral or written verbal expression or (b) nonverbal conduct of a person intended by him as a substitute for oral or written verbal expression.

STATUTE - An act of the legislature. Includes a treaty.

STATUTE OF LIMITATION - A statute limiting the time to bring an action after the right of action has arisen.

STAY - To hold in abeyance an order of a court.

STIPULATION - Any agreement made by opposing attorneys regulating any matter incidental to the proceedings or trial.

SUBORDINATION (AGREEMENT) - An agreement making one's rights inferior to or of a lower rank than another's.

SUBORNATION - The crime of procuring a person to lie or to make false statements to a court.

SUBPOENA - A writ or order directed to a person, and requiring his attendance at a particular time and place to testify as a witness.

SUBPOENA DUCES TECUM - A subpoena used, not only for the purpose of compelling witnesses to attend in court, but also requiring them to bring with them books or documents which may be in their possession, and which may tend to elucidate the subject matter of the trial.

SUBROGATION - The substituting of one for another as a creditor, the new creditor succeeding to the former's rights.

SUBSIDY - A government grant to assist a private enterprise deemed advantageous to the public.

SUI GENERIS - Of the same kind.

SUIT - Any civil proceeding by a person or persons against another or others in a court of justice by which the plaintiff pursues the remedies afforded him by law.

SUMMONS - A notice to a defendant that an action against him has been commenced and requiring him to appear in court and answer the complaint.

SUPRA - Above; this word occurring by itself in a book refers the reader to a previous part of the book.

SURETY - A person who binds himself for the payment of a sum of money, or for the performance of something else, for another.

SURPLUSAGE - Extraneous or unnecessary matter.

SURVIVORSHIP - A term used when a person becomes entitled to property by reason of his having survived another person who had an interest in the property.

SUSPEND SENTENCE - Hold back a sentence pending good behavior of prisoner.

SYLLABUS - A note prefixed to a report, especially a case, giving a brief statement of the court's ruling on different issues of the case.

T

TALESMAN - Person summoned to fill a panel of jurors.

TENANT - One who holds or possesses lands by any kind of right or title; also, one who has the temporary use and occupation of real property owned by another person (landlord), the duration and terms of his tenancy being usually fixed by an instrument called "a lease."

TENDER - An offer of money; an expression of willingness to perform a contract according to its terms.

TERM - When used with reference to a court, it signifies the period of time during which the court holds a session, usually of several weeks or months duration.

TESTAMENTARY - Pertaining to a will or the administration of a will.
TESTATOR (male)
TESTATRIX (female) - One who makes or has made a testament or will.
TESTIFY (TESTIMONY) - To give evidence under oath as a witness.
TO WIT - That is to say; namely.
TORT - Wrong; injury to the person.
TRANSITORY - Passing from place to place.
TRESPASS - Entry into another's ground, illegally.
TRIAL - The examination of a cause, civil or criminal, before a judge who has jurisdiction over it, according to the laws of the land.
TRIER OF FACT - Includes (a) the jury and (b) the court when the court is trying an issue of fact other than one relating to the admissibility of evidence.
TRUST - A right of property, real or personal, held by one party for the benefit of another.
TRUSTEE - One who lawfully holds property in custody for the benefit of another.

U

UNAVAILABLE AS A WITNESS - The declarant is (1) Exempted or precluded on the ground of privilege from testifying concerning the matter to which his statement is relevant; (2) Disqualified from testifying to the matter; (3) Dead or unable to attend or to testify at the hearing because of then existing physical or mental illness or infirmity; (4) Absent from the hearing and the court is unable to compel his attendance by its process; or (5) Absent from the hearing and the proponent of his statement has exercised reasonable diligence but has been unable to procure his attendance by the court's process.
ULTRA VIRES - Acts beyond the scope and power of a corporation, association, etc.
UNILATERAL - One-sided; obligation upon, or act of one party.
USURY - Unlawful interest on a loan.

V

VACATE - To set aside; to move out.
VARIANCE - A discrepancy or disagreement between two instruments or two aspects of the same case, which by law should be consistent.
VENDEE - A purchaser or buyer.
VENDOR - The person who transfers property by sale, particularly real estate; the term "seller" is used more commonly for one who sells personal property.
VENIREMEN - Persons ordered to appear to serve on a jury or composing a panel of jurors.
VENUE - The place at which an action is tried, generally based on locality or judicial district in which an injury occurred or a material fact happened.
VERDICT - The formal decision or finding of a jury.
VERIFY - To confirm or substantiate by oath.
VEST - To accrue to.
VOID - Having no legal force or binding effect.
VOIR DIRE - Preliminary examination of a witness or a juror to test competence, interest, prejudice, etc.

W

WAIVE - To give up a right.
WAIVER - The intentional or voluntary relinquishment of a known right.
WARRANT (WARRANTY) (v.) - To promise that a certain fact or state of facts, in relation to the subject matter, is, or shall be, as it is represented to be.

WARRANT (n.) - A writ issued by a judge, or other competent authority, addressed to a sheriff, or other officer, requiring him to arrest the person therein named, and bring him before the judge or court to answer or be examined regarding the offense with which he is charged.
WRIT - An order or process issued in the name of the sovereign or in the name of a court or judicial officer, commanding the performance or nonperformance of some act.
WRITING - Handwriting, typewriting, printing, photostating, photographing and every other means of recording upon any tangible thing any form of communication or representation, including letters, words, pictures, sounds, or symbols, or combinations thereof.
WRITINGS AND RECORDINGS - Consists of letters, words, or numbers, or their equivalent, set down by handwriting, typewriting, printing, photostating, photographing, magnetic impulse, mechanical or electronic recording, or other form of data compilation.

Y

YEA AND NAY - Yes and no.
YELLOW DOG CONTRACT - A contract by which employer requires employee to sign an instrument promising as condition that he will not join a union during its continuance, and will be discharged if he does join.

Z

ZONING - The division of a city by legislative regulation into districts and the prescription and application in each district of regulations having to do with structural and architectural designs of buildings and of regulations prescribing use to which buildings within designated districts may be put.

ANSWER SHEET

TEST NO. ______________ PART ________ TITLE OF POSITION ______________________________

(AS GIVEN IN EXAMINATION ANNOUNCEMENT - INCLUDE OPTION, IF ANY)

PLACE OF EXAMINATION ______________________________ (CITY OR TOWN) ______________ (STATE) DATE ____________

RATING

USE THE SPECIAL PENCIL. MAKE GLOSSY BLACK MARKS.

1 A B C D E	26 A B C D E	51 A B C D E	76 A B C D E	101 A B C D E
2 A B C D E	27 A B C D E	52 A B C D E	77 A B C D E	102 A B C D E
3 A B C D E	28 A B C D E	53 A B C D E	78 A B C D E	103 A B C D E
4 A B C D E	29 A B C D E	54 A B C D E	79 A B C D E	104 A B C D E
5 A B C D E	30 A B C D E	55 A B C D E	80 A B C D E	105 A B C D E
6 A B C D E	31 A B C D E	56 A B C D E	81 A B C D E	106 A B C D E
7 A B C D E	32 A B C D E	57 A B C D E	82 A B C D E	107 A B C D E
8 A B C D E	33 A B C D E	58 A B C D E	83 A B C D E	108 A B C D E
9 A B C D E	34 A B C D E	59 A B C D E	84 A B C D E	109 A B C D E
10 A B C D E	35 A B C D E	60 A B C D E	85 A B C D E	110 A B C D E

Make only ONE mark for each answer. Additional and stray marks may be counted as mistakes. In making corrections, erase errors COMPLETELY.

11 A B C D E	36 A B C D E	61 A B C D E	86 A B C D E	111 A B C D E
12 A B C D E	37 A B C D E	62 A B C D E	87 A B C D E	112 A B C D E
13 A B C D E	38 A B C D E	63 A B C D E	88 A B C D E	113 A B C D E
14 A B C D E	39 A B C D E	64 A B C D E	89 A B C D E	114 A B C D E
15 A B C D E	40 A B C D E	65 A B C D E	90 A B C D E	115 A B C D E
16 A B C D E	41 A B C D E	66 A B C D E	91 A B C D E	116 A B C D E
17 A B C D E	42 A B C D E	67 A B C D E	92 A B C D E	117 A B C D E
18 A B C D E	43 A B C D E	68 A B C D E	93 A B C D E	118 A B C D E
19 A B C D E	44 A B C D E	69 A B C D E	94 A B C D E	119 A B C D E
20 A B C D E	45 A B C D E	70 A B C D E	95 A B C D E	120 A B C D E
21 A B C D E	46 A B C D E	71 A B C D E	96 A B C D E	121 A B C D E
22 A B C D E	47 A B C D E	72 A B C D E	97 A B C D E	122 A B C D E
23 A B C D E	48 A B C D E	73 A B C D E	98 A B C D E	123 A B C D E
24 A B C D E	49 A B C D E	74 A B C D E	99 A B C D E	124 A B C D E
25 A B C D E	50 A B C D E	75 A B C D E	100 A B C D E	125 A B C D E

ANSWER SHEET

ST NO. ______________ PART ______ TITLE OF POSITION ______________________________
(AS GIVEN IN EXAMINATION ANNOUNCEMENT - INCLUDE OPTION, IF ANY)

ACE OF EXAMINATION ______________________________ ______________ DATE ______________
(CITY OR TOWN) (STATE)

RATING

USE THE SPECIAL PENCIL. MAKE GLOSSY BLACK MARKS.

No.	A B C D E	No.	A B C D E	No.	A B C D E	No.	A B C D E	No.	A B C D E
1	A B C D E	26	A B C D E	51	A B C D E	76	A B C D E	101	A B C D E
2	A B C D E	27	A B C D E	52	A B C D E	77	A B C D E	102	A B C D E
3	A B C D E	28	A B C D E	53	A B C D E	78	A B C D E	103	A B C D E
4	A B C D E	29	A B C D E	54	A B C D E	79	A B C D E	104	A B C D E
5	A B C D E	30	A B C D E	55	A B C D E	80	A B C D E	105	A B C D E
6	A B C D E	31	A B C D E	56	A B C D E	81	A B C D E	106	A B C D E
7	A B C D E	32	A B C D E	57	A B C D E	82	A B C D E	107	A B C D E
8	A B C D E	33	A B C D E	58	A B C D E	83	A B C D E	108	A B C D E
9	A B C D E	34	A B C D E	59	A B C D E	84	A B C D E	109	A B C D E
0	A B C D E	35	A B C D E	60	A B C D E	85	A B C D E	110	A B C D E

Make only ONE mark for each answer. Additional and stray marks may be counted as mistakes. In making corrections, erase errors COMPLETELY.

No.	A B C D E	No.	A B C D E	No.	A B C D E	No.	A B C D E	No.	A B C D E
1	A B C D E	36	A B C D E	61	A B C D E	86	A B C D E	111	A B C D E
2	A B C D E	37	A B C D E	62	A B C D E	87	A B C D E	112	A B C D E
3	A B C D E	38	A B C D E	63	A B C D E	88	A B C D E	113	A B C D E
4	A B C D E	39	A B C D E	64	A B C D E	89	A B C D E	114	A B C D E
5	A B C D E	40	A B C D E	65	A B C D E	90	A B C D E	115	A B C D E
6	A B C D E	41	A B C D E	66	A B C D E	91	A B C D E	116	A B C D E
7	A B C D E	42	A B C D E	67	A B C D E	92	A B C D E	117	A B C D E
8	A B C D E	43	A B C D E	68	A B C D E	93	A B C D E	118	A B C D E
9	A B C D E	44	A B C D E	69	A B C D E	94	A B C D E	119	A B C D E
0	A B C D E	45	A B C D E	70	A B C D E	95	A B C D E	120	A B C D E
1	A B C D E	46	A B C D E	71	A B C D E	96	A B C D E	121	A B C D E
2	A B C D E	47	A B C D E	72	A B C D E	97	A B C D E	122	A B C D E
3	A B C D E	48	A B C D E	73	A B C D E	98	A B C D E	123	A B C D E
4	A B C D E	49	A B C D E	74	A B C D E	99	A B C D E	124	A B C D E
5	A B C D E	50	A B C D E	75	A B C D E	100	A B C D E	125	A B C D E